AGAINST THE TIDE

I want nothing for myself; I want everything for the Lord

Watchman Nee

倪柝聲

Against the Tide

ANGUS KINNEAR

KINGSWAY PUBLICATIONS
EASTBOURNE

ISBN 1 84291 224 0
ISBN 978 1 842912 24 9

01 02 03 04 05 06 07 Printing/Year 10 09 08 07 06

KINGSWAY COMMUNICATIONS LTD
Lottbridge Drove, Eastbourne BN23 6NT, England.
Email: books@kingsway.co.uk
Printed in the USA

Contents

Preface	9
Who's Who	12
1. The Gift	17
2. Honour Your Ancestors	21
3. Revolution	34
4. Choice	47
5. Dedication	56
6. Across the Grain	67
7. The Proof of Faith	79
8. Foreign Fields	90
9. A Fruitful Ministry	100
10. The Old Wineskins	110
11. Fragile Clay	124
12. Disenchantment	138
13. New Horizons	161
14. Count It All Joy	168
15. Rethinking	180
16. Heyday	197
17. Withdrawal	210
18. Return	225
19. Consistent Choice	240
20. The Trap Closes	252
21. Ordeal	264

CONTENTS

22. Last Years   280
23. Unhindered   299

Appendix A: Christianity in China   306
Appendix B: Pinyin Pronunciation   320
Appendix C: Names of Places   323
Appendix D: Chronological Record of Events   326
Appendix E: Further Reading   333

Notes   334

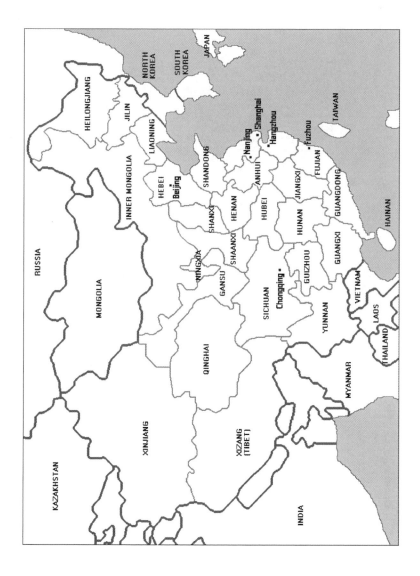

Preface to the Revised Edition

R eaders familiar with *Against the Tide* (first published in 1974) are assured that this revised edition preserves unchanged the essence of Watchman Nee's story, much of it in the original words. However, a quarter century has passed and we now know far more of the China of his last 25 years, of his long imprisonment and of his death. By setting him and the movement he began yet more vividly against the persisting dark backcloth of social and political upheaval in a Marxist state, we can now perhaps bring him within easier reach of a new generation of readers.

This account of the life and ministry of Watchman Nee is presented from the standpoint of an observer at a distance who at no time was involved in the China scene. In 1938, as a young medical missionary about to leave Britain for India, Angus Kinnear had the privilege of spending some weeks with Watchman Nee in London, and his whole outlook on Christian life and service was greatly enriched. From notes taken at that time and the valuable reminiscences of many China-based friends he compiled the 1973 edition. As one might expect, Watchman Nee's message proves to be inextricably woven into his life. By setting the one in the context of the other and making use of his many interpretive anecdotes, we are able to trace God's hand in the course of his pilgrimage through a scene of world-shaking events.

After some 30 years of ministry within China, two brief visits to the West and his return to Shanghai, it was not long (1952) before Watchman Nee was imprisoned with a 20-year sentence, towards the end of which he died.

In the late 1990s Angus Kinnear began this revision of the story to recount more fully the last years of both Watchman Nee and his wife Charity, but he himself died in 2002 at the age of 90. He left, however, copious notes from which the biography has been completed.

The slightly fictional Chapter 1, with its undocumented visit of Watchman's parents to the Fuzhou family home, has been retained.

On advice from Chinese friends, names of places and persons have very largely been changed from the Wade-Giles system of this book's earlier editions to the current Hanyu Pinyin system.

At different periods a great deal of assistance has been given by a large number of people recording their recollections and impressions. In particular there were the gifted versions and translations of the late Miss Elizabeth Fischbacher, who carefully preserved the spirit of the man and of the best of his preaching and writings. Also there has been the mature spiritual wisdom of a friend from boyhood days, Mr Faithful Luke, and later Stephen Kaung.

Our gratitude extends to many others who have contributed, including T. Austin-Sparks, Hubert L. Barlow, Dr Jim Broomhall, David Bentley-Taylor, Joy Betteridge, Lena Clarke, Doris Hinckley, Hilda and Victoria Holms, Witness Lee, Gaylord Leung, Leslie Lyall, James Ma, Shepherd Ma,

Kristeen Macnair, Simon Meek, Carol Stearns, Newman Sze, Mary Wang, K.H. Weigh, Betty Williams, Lucas Wu and Silas Wu.

Lately a group of Chinese believers in Australia have given much help with their advice and by exchanging the Wade-Giles for Pinyin names, and some of them by recalling personal memories of life in China and Shanghai during the relevant years. Two of Watchman Nee's younger close relatives have also contributed. These have all asked that their names should not be given, but their help has been most valuable.

The task of preparing this book has been a rewarding one for all involved, with an awareness of the constant help of God. To his hands, for his use, it is now entrusted.

Angus and Jean Kinnear
London, 2002 and 2005

Who's Who

THE NI FAMILY (or Nga in the Fuzhou dialect)

Watchman's grandfather

The Rev. Ni Yu-cheng (U.C. Nga) of Fuzhou, born *c.*1840. Congregational pastor with the American Mission Board, Fuzhou. Died 1890.

Watchman's parents

Ni Wen-xiu (W.H. Nga) of Fuzhou, born 1877, the fourth of nine boys. Officer in the Imperial Customs Service. Died in Hong Kong, 18 December 1941.
Married 1899: Lin He-ping (Peace Lin) of Fuzhou, born 1880; died in Shantou 1950.

Their nine children

1. Ni Gui-chen, born 1900 (Mrs H.C. Chen).
2. Ni Gui-zhen, born 1902 (Mrs P.C. Lin).
3. **Ni Shu-zu**, or Henry Ni, born in Shantou on 4 November 1903.
   In 1925 he took the name **Ni Tuo-sheng**, or **Watchman Nee**.
   In 1934 he married Zhang Pin-hui (Charity Chang) of Fuzhou.

No children. He died in Anhui Province on 30 May 1972.

4. Ni Huai-zu, or George Ni, research chemist.
5. Ni Xuan-zu, died in school years.
6. Ni De-zhen (Mrs L.H. Wang).
7. Ni De-cheng (Mrs Zhang).
8. Ni Hong-zu, or Paul Ni.
9. Ni Xing-zu, or John Ni.

THE ZHANG FAMILY

Charity's father

Zhang Ru-zhou of Fuzhou, Master of Surgery, sometime President of Ren Ji Hospital, Shanghai.

His children

1. Zhang Pin-tseng, or Beulah Chang (Mrs G.S. Ling).
2. Zhang Pin-fang, or Faith Chang (Mrs K.L. Bao).
3. **Zhang Pin-hui**, or **Charity Chang** (Mrs Watchman Nee), born in Fuzhou; died in Shanghai 7 November 1971.
4. Zhang Yi-lun, or Samuel Chang.

SOME CHRISTIAN ELDERS, WORKERS AND OTHERS associated with the Church Assembly Halls ('Little Flock') Movement:

John K.Y. Chang (Zhang Guang-rong), early Shanghai worker.

James Chen (Chen Ze-xing) of Xiamen, worker in Hong Kong and Bangkok.

Stephen Kaung (Jiang Shou-dao), worker in Chongqing. US editor into English of W. Nee's writings.

Miss Ruth Lee (Li Yuan-ru), worker in charge of Shanghai Gospel Book Room. Editorial assistant to W. Nee.

Witness Lee (Li Chang-shou) of Yantai (Chefoo), worker in Taiwan and San Francisco.

Philip Luan (Luan Fei-li) of Shandong, worker in Hangzhou.

Faithful Luke (Liok, or Lu Zhong-xing) of Gutian, worker in Singapore and Indonesia.

Shepherd Ma (Ma Mu), Christian merchant in Shanghai.

Simon Meek (Miao Shao-xun) of Lian-jiang, worker in Manila.

Daniel Tan (Chen Zhu-yan) of Xiamen, worker in Singapore.

John Wang (Wang Lian-jun), elder in Fuzhou.

Miss Peace Wang (Wang Pei-zhen), worker in Shanghai.

K.H. Weigh (Wei Guang-xi) of Gutian, worker in Hong Kong.

K.S. Wong (Wang Kai-seng), Christian merchant in Singapore.

Lukas Wu (Wu Ren-jie) of Jin-jiang, worker in Manila.

Alan C.L. Yin (Yin Zhu-lan), Christian manager of China Biological and Chemical Company.

Dr C.H. Yu (Yu Cheng-hua) of Zhejiang, ophthalmologist, elder in Shanghai.

Y.A. Wu (Wu You-an), elder in Shanghai.

D.C. Du (Du Zhong-chen) of Shandong, elder in Shanghai.

Zhu Chen of Shanghai, elder in Shanghai.

OTHER CHRISTIAN LEADERS mentioned in the story:

Mary Stone, MD (Shi Mei-yu), first Chinese woman doctor and founder of Bethel Hospital, Shanghai.

John Sung, PhD (Song Shang-jie), revivalist preacher associated with the Bethel Evangelistic Band.

Leland Wang (Wang Zai) of Fuzhou, founded China Overseas Missionary Union.

Wang Ming-dao, conservative evangelical pastor of the Tabernacle, Beijing.

Wilson Wang (Wang Chi) of Fuzhou, brother and colleague of Leland Wang.

Miss Dora Yu (Yu Ci-du), evangelist and Bible teacher used by God in the conversion of Watchman Nee. She died in 1931.

1

The Gift

Spring was well advanced in the Middle Kingdom and the season of Pure Brightness had given way to the season of Corn Rain. The night air was clear, with fleecy clouds drifting across a silvery moon. Ancient Fuzhou had closed its seven gates beneath their fantastic storeyed towers. From the crumbling, crenellated walls obsolete cannon looked out over broad rice fields and spreading suburbs. Foot traffic had ceased on the eight-century-old Bridge of Ten Thousand Ages that linked the town on the north bank with Zhong-Zhou and Nantai Islands. Tonight no mist shrouded the huddled sampans of boat-dwellers on the River Min.

Among the close-packed streets and houses the day's cacophony had long since died. Gone were the rhythmic noises of the streetside craftsmen, the song of bamboo coolies hefting giant loads, the grinding of huge pestles hulling rice, the unending slip-slip of straw sandals, the squeal of trussed pigs borne to market, the cries of hawkers and the whining pleas of beggars. All these had fallen silent and so too, very gradually, had the last home-bound foot-steps through the narrow lanes: a sedan chair with toiling bearers bringing home a late-working scholar official; a chattering band of longshoremen returned from loading a junk to catch the tide; a shuffling addict drawn along by his ceaseless craving for the deadly 'foreign smoke'. Now at last all was still. In the rambling Ni home the large household slept.

Po-po! Po-po! Beside her sleeping husband Lin He-ping stirred uneasily on her mat, aware tonight of the third child secretly within her. She listened. From Gui-chen and from the little one there was only quiet breathing. Po-po! Po-po! Again that staccato sound, and louder. It would be the nightwatchman on his circuit, alert while most men slept, to give the alarm of fire or thief or any danger. Po-po! Po-po! The assuring clapper-note (*tuo-sheng*) of his bamboo rattle was receding now as the voice came back reed-like, calling: 'Past midnight, neighbours. All is well!'

An oil lamp with floating wick bathed the little room in its faint glow. The flame guttered and flared as He-ping lay back, somehow reassured. She closed her eyes once more, but not to sleep. Again, perhaps for the hundredth time, she whispered, 'Let it be a boy!' She recalled with burning resentment today's household gossip, the barbed, mocking words that had made so painful this visit to the home of her in-laws. Chinese society placed a premium on male offspring, and to her gentle Ni Wen-xiu she had already borne two girls. Her Cantonese mother-in-law had been furious. The unfortunate wife of her eldest son could conceive only females – six of them – and Wen-xiu's woman, she affirmed, was just such another. 'Avenge me, O God,' He-ping cried now in bitterness, 'and take this reproach away from me!' Then somehow there came back to her mind the half-hearted promise she had made and as quickly forgotten when a year back her second child was on the way.

'God,' she had prayed then, in words that echoed Hannah's, 'if you will give me a little boy, I will give him back to you to be your servant all his days.'[1] They were good, familiar words. She had known the Samuel story from childhood. But now, all at once they aroused in her heart an impulse she had not felt before. She would not only say them: she would mean what she said. She did not hesitate. 'I'll keep my word, Lord!' she exclaimed. Quiet then came to her at last. Smiling, He-ping drifted back again to sleep.

Long weeks were to pass, and a return journey by sea to their home in Shantou, her husband's workplace. But her pangs came at length, and oh, the inexpressible relief when she heard him cry, 'It's a boy!' Tension was released in tears as joy overwhelmed her. This time therefore, when the red-tinted duck eggs went out to neighbours and friends, it was to announce the longed-for son and heir.

Thus on 4 November 1903 Henry Ni came into the world to be the delight of his quiet father and his strong-willed mother. Chinese names are significant, a child being given or assuming a new one at some fresh turning point in his career. In childhood he was Nga Shu-jeo in the local Fuzhou (Foochow) dialect, and in the northern *bai-hua* speech Ni Shu-zu, 'glorifying the ancestors' merits', with his English name scarcely used. By 1925, however, conscious of a new mission in life, he sought a fresh name expressing his duty as God's under-shepherd to watch for his people, and he tried Jing-fu, 'one who warns or admonishes'. But this seemed harsh, and it was then that his mother proposed Tuo-sheng, a gong-note, reminding him of her prayer in the waking night while the watchman struck through the streets his bamboo gong or rattle (*tuo*) to send out its far-reaching note (*sheng*) with its ill news or good.

So he became Ni Tuo-sheng, or in English, Watchman

Nee, and by this latter, after his childhood, we shall generally know him. He disciplined himself through life to be like
Samuel, alert while others slept, God's priestly bell-ringer
who should warn his people of peril or arouse them to a
new day's dawning.[2]

2

Honour Your Ancestors

Fuzhou is the capital city of Fujian Province and one
of south China's gateways to the Pacific. For genera-
tions it had been home to the Ni (or Nga in the local
dialect) family, whose members went each springtime to a
nearby hillside to tend the graves of their ancestors. In
1839, around the time when our subject's grandfather Ni
Yu-cheng was born, hostilities had broken out between
China and Britain over what those intruding Westerners
found so galling: the Empire's ban on foreign trade. Some
50 years earlier the learned Qing Emperor Qian Long,
knowing perhaps something of British encroachment in
India under Clive and Warren Hastings, had patiently
explained in a letter to King George III of England that his
Empire's self-contained economy had no room for the curi-
ous products of people living far away across a remote sea.
'As your envoy can see for himself, we possess all things. I
set no value on objects strange and ingenious, and have no
use for your country's wares.'

In official circles that view still prevailed. Yet Europe had
lately discovered China as a potential market and source of
raw materials, and the wealthy people of its maritime lands

soon began to demand her porcelain, silk and lacquer goods to adorn their homes. Since by imperial edict barter was denied them, the trouble for English merchants was that they must pay for everything in silver. This acute cash-flow problem was only resolved when they found the Chinese could be induced to buy, illegally, their Indian opium. The principle of exchange could then work out to the foreigner's advantage. To this the Mandarins reacted strongly, hardening their resistance and burning vast quantities of opium. A three-year Opium War with Britain followed, which ended in China's deep humiliation. She was charged a six million dollar indemnity, and was compelled to open diplomatic relations with the West.

By the 1842 Treaty of Nanjing, China ceded Hong Kong to Britain, and Fuzhou, along with four more key southern seaports, was forcibly opened to foreign commercial interests with all their scandals and abuses. While Fuzhou's coastal trade in timber, paper, fruits and textiles continued, alongside it there began to rise a new and unwelcome business settlement of foreign factories and residences on the mid-river islet of Zhong-Zhou and on the further hill-slopes of Nantai Island. Other foreign nations, France, Germany, Portugal, and soon Japan and the United States, were to follow Britain's lead. Imperialist powers who had divided up Africa's territory between themselves would in turn strangle China with an economic 'occupation' of her key seaports and riverside cities, plus a stealthy encroachment on her legal, policing, banking and services infrastructure in the guise of economic aid and financial loans. As early as 1842 the Imperial Customs Service was brought effectively under foreign control. Revenue from it now went into foreign-owned banks operating in China, and out of this were deducted the war indemnities and the interest on foreign loans. It was foreigners too who decided when (and to whom, as surety for good behaviour) the Chinese balances were paid. By 1851 the import of opium became legalised.

The thing that above all else caused trade to soar was Europe's demand for tea. In 1853, when Ni Yu-cheng was aged around 14, the first cargoes of Fuzhou tea, brought from the Wuyi Shan highlands by coolie and sampan and downriver by local junk from Nantai to the deep-sea anchorage, were already being exported to markets in Europe and America. The ocean port itself was at White Tooth Rock, a sharp peak midway down the 22 miles from the Fuzhou bridge to the estuary's mouth. Here the Min River's course makes a right-angle turn northwards to curl round the foot of an island pagoda by its left bank; hence the name Pagoda Anchorage. It was in fact across the fair-way in the deeper outside of the bend that the tall sailing ships dropped a bow anchor and then secured their sterns to a low right-bank cliff. While coolies transferred the tea chests from junk to hold, they took the opportunity here to paint ship and, as sailors will, also to write large in paint their proud ships' names on the nearby cliff face. 'In 1938 one could still read there those of *Thermopylae, Cutty Sark*, and other famous vessels.'[1] Thus year by year, until steamships replaced them, these tea-clippers came, loaded up, and raced back across the world with the new season's first clip of leaf, to make Fuzhou second only to Shanghai in that prosperous traffic.

As an indirect consequence of the Nanjing Treaty and the grasping foreign trade, Protestant Christianity with its quite different message also began to enter China. The vermilion pencil of the Qing Emperor had decreed that the Christian faith be tolerated throughout the Middle Kingdom, but regrettably this too was a decree extracted under military pressure. This threw wide the door for dedicated Western missionaries, with their evangelistic zeal and true humanitarian concern, to move in and stake out new claims for righteousness in Chinese hearts. And come they did, a variety of established Christian missions from Western church denominations, all with the best of intentions. The first to reach Fuzhou in 1847 were Congregationalists of the American Board, to be followed that same year by American Episcopal Methodists and in 1850 by Anglicans of the English Church Missionary Society.

Not surprisingly, the missionaries were quick to protest against the iniquitous opium imports; yet they themselves, as distinctive 'red-haired' aliens, could claim like the traders extra-territorial privileges of residence, so were all too easily linked in native minds with them and their trade. Of the 1842 Treaty and its sequels one contemporary Western writer could say with astonishing complacency, 'The ways of God's dealings with this people began to open, and He entered into judgement with them that He might show them His mercy.'[2] It was perhaps conceit such as that which drew from the Manchu Emperor's brother Prince Kung his oft-quoted advice to Sir Rutherford Alcock: 'Take away your missionaries and your opium, and you English will be welcome!'

The first school offering Western-style education was opened by the American Board in a suburb of the old city in 1853 and it was here that as a boy Watchman Nee's grandfather Ni Yu-cheng learned of the love of God in Jesus Christ and was won to him. Four years later, in 1857, the year in which the first Christian church or fellowship of believers in Fuzhou came into being, he was one of a group of four pupils to declare his faith in Jesus by being baptised in the Min River.[3] He progressed so well and with such zeal and love for his Lord that the missionaries trained him as an evangelist, and soon, for their modest wage, with other young men he was proclaiming the gospel in this city of half a million souls. Ordained eventually as a pastor, and indeed the first Chinese to be so honoured in the three north Fujian missions, he would be remembered long after his death in 1890 for his perceptive gift in expounding the Scriptures.

But it was when as a maturing young man his time had come to marry that his big test came, for few women in Fujian as yet believed in Christ and no suitable Christian bride for him could be found there. Fuzhou folk of those days were extremely conservative and would on no account flout convention to intermarry with those of another province with its alien customs. Yet he must either look further afield or compromise his testimony by marrying an unbeliever. It says much for him that his faith prevailed over tradition. From Guangdong at the mouth of the Pearl River and 450 miles away by coastal boat, he accepted a Christian girl who proved to be God's choice for him and made him a true, if somewhat sharp-tongued, life partner.

They were blessed (in Chinese eyes) with nine boys. Of these Shu-zu's father Ni Wen-xiu was the fourth, being born in 1877. As a pastor's son Wen-xiu was given Christian elementary schooling, and then went on to learn by rote the Confucian classics for the state's competitive examinations by which to attain to the mandarinate or civil service. Fuzhou was a literary centre where twice in every three years several thousand students from the prefecture gathered for the first degree examinations, and again twice in five years from the whole province for those of the second degree. With age-old ceremony, at the appointed time, Wen-xiu and a throng of others entered the vast examination area north-east of the city, by a gateway that bore the characters, 'For the Empire: Pray for Good Men.' Confined there for three days in his own individual cell he adorned his scroll of ruled paper with columns of beautiful characters, pouring out his classical knowledge in a poem and two essays on the theme now set. The papers were judged with strict impartiality, and his success in the second degree gained him, shortly before his marriage, the secure post of a junior officer in the Imperial Customs.

His wife Lin He-ping, born in 1880 and so three years younger than him, was of peasant stock, the last of a big family. Very poor and darkened by superstition, they lived in fear of demons and dragons and fox-fairies. It was a famine year in Fujian, and with so many hungry mouths to feed she stood little chance of survival. Even in normal conditions an infant girl, just because she was one too many, might be exposed or drowned or buried alive by her father. Indeed, a child still living but sickly or pining from hunger might be cast, along with the dead, into the high aperture of Fuzhou's capacious baby-tower, an urn-shaped granite receptacle at the town's edge designed to save the expense of child burials. For just a few girls the Roman Catholic orphanage outside the southern gate offered a home. The inscription over its entry ran, 'When thy father and thy mother forsake thee, the Lord will take thee up.'[4]

In fact He-ping's father did better for her. For the three or four dollars he so desperately needed he sold her, through a go-between, to a better-off family in the city who thought of bringing her up as their slave girl. But she was a lively child, and soon this family was approached, again through an emissary, by a merchant named Lin employed in a foreign firm in Nantai. His concubine was barren and desired to adopt her as a daughter, so again He-ping changed hands.

In the providence of God the merchant too loved children, and here she found a home. Though there were already two boys and a girl in the family the couple took the spirited little newcomer to their hearts and brought her up as their own child.

When she was six, according to almost universal custom, her adoptive mother began binding her feet. By this procedure, the toes were balled under the sole and the as yet unossified heel and tarsus forced together, the bindings being tightened daily to withstand growth and hobble her for life. As a peasant girl He-ping would have escaped this treatment, for the Fuzhou field-women had long resisted the custom. They strode about fiercely adorned with daggers in their hair, and took their place alongside boys and grown men in the rice cultivation. But though she wept copiously each morning from the cruel pain, she never once thought of resisting. She was now a merchant's child, destined for better things. Lily feet were a part of the price she must pay.

But that year Mr Lin sickened with a mystery disease that defied the skills of all the doctors. Now it happened that a business superior of his named Zhang had become a Christian Methodist, and this man suggested that they ask the Methodist pastor to come and pray for him. The Lins could scarcely refuse, and to their surprise prayer was answered. So moved were they by his dramatic recovery that they themselves sought Christian instruction. At length, trusting in the Lord Jesus, they threw out the ugly little idols from their place of honour in the home and Mr Lin and his wife were baptised into the Methodist church near his place of employment.

Because it was closer at hand for them, however, the concubine and her child now attended the Church of

England. To He-ping's joy the painful foot-binding ceased and she could run again freely. As she learned the hymns and Bible stories she found her heart warming to divine things. Her new happiness soon proved infectious. Asked by her primary teacher why she was always singing, she told him the family's story, with the later result that he too with his wife and children joined the church.

A foreign businessman had opened a primary school locally with Christian teachers, where He-ping was sent to study before going on in 1891, aged eleven, to the American-staffed Methodist Mission School for Girls in Fuzhou. Here she did consistently well in class, while through spiritual default and repentance she tasted, she says, something of the mercy of God. Yet her religion remained for the present one of merit-seeking through good conduct.

It was when she was nearing the top of the school that there returned to Fuzhou from training in Philadelphia a young Chinese woman doctor, Wu Jing-en, at that time only the second woman in all China to graduate in medicine. Her arrival in 1895 to work in a mission hospital in the town aroused ambitions in some local girls and set He-ping dreaming. Next year, at the age of 16, she asked her teacher to begin negotiations for her, too, to enter a medical school in the USA. Her secondary school progress was such that, to her joy, the provisional answer was favourable. She therefore prevailed on her father to send her, in company with a school friend, to the Chinese Western Girls' School (McTyeire School for Girls) in Shanghai to improve her English. It was her first venture forth from Fuzhou and the sea voyage, touching at fresh ports backed like her own by hills, was exhilarating. Past the islands the hills ceased with the Yangtze's silt-laden plain and as they entered the Huangpu River Shanghai's great foreign buildings soared high above its levels. In the city, when she reached it, tur-baned Sikh police controlled the busy, prosperous crowds and the many wheeled vehicles that thronged the wide streets of the International Settlement. Beyond, in the wider city, behind the walled houses of the wealthier classes, narrow lanes led to the dwellings of the poor. And still, at that date, the foreign park gates along the Settle-ment Bund bore notices warning, 'No dogs, no Chinamen.'

Among Chinese of a strange staccato speech He-ping was soon homesick, but ambition held her there. She began to excel in her studies and be captivated, too, by the higher liv-ing standards of this semi-foreign city where every man was all for himself. Soon she was diverting the fees sent to her for music lessons and using other devices to raise the dollars with which to dress herself more modishly. 'I learned there', she writes, 'much of the pride of life and some of the sins of the flesh.'

For her, in the plan of God, one particular encounter was to prove significant. A certain Miss Dora Yu (Yu Ci-du), a young woman not so many years older than herself, visited the school one day to address the pupils. Dora was from a cultured background and like many others had encoun-tered Christianity while at a Western-style school. Success-ful in her studies, she had gone to England to train in medicine. After qualifying and visiting home, she had set out once more for postgraduate studies there. Passing Suez, her ship entered the Mediterranean. There God met her, calling her to abandon her career and return to China to preach Christ to her people. She went to the ship's captain into whose care she had been entrusted, and told him what had transpired. Thinking her out of her mind, he became angry; but she stuck so firmly to her request that at last he agreed to tranship her to a liner returning from Marseilles.

Back in Shanghai, her reception by her incredulous family was no less hostile in view of the cost of her education, but her quiet testimony was so convincing that they had to recognise the hand of God upon her. From that day she steadfastly set herself to witness to her Lord through preaching and Bible teaching, and all the more effectively because she received no foreign salary but trusted God alone for her needs.

Hearing Dora's story from her own lips, He-ping was much moved. She called on her in her room to offer her a treasured gold ring, the gift of her own mother, and Dora's obvious reluctance to accept such a present from a young girl went even further to convince He-ping of her genuineness. 'Then', she says, 'I knew she loved God, and not money.'

But to He-ping herself at the age of 18 it seemed to be no call of God that came, but sheer catastrophe that struck. Her adoptive mother had been pining for her and had all along opposed her going to America, so when in Fuzhou the Cantonese widow of Pastor Ni Yu-cheng sent a man seeking a match for their son Wen-xiu, she leaped at the offer. Unknown to He-ping a marriage with Wen-xiu was arranged, and now a letter backed with full parental authority broke the news to her. It devastated her dream of studying medicine, for no Fujian girl had as yet so violated custom as to break such a parental arrangement. He-ping means Peace, but Turmoil would better have described her now. For days she was in agonies of near-despair. The lovely sea voyage home, with the vessel threading its way among the rocky coastal islands, was passed under a dark cloud of depression. In her heart she nursed a growing hatred for the mother to whom she owed her upbringing, for now the residue of that life seemed in ruins.

On her arrival home she was called in and formally given Ni Wen-xiu's photograph and the betrothal gift that clinched the contract. By it she was irrevocably tied to this young man whom she had never seen. As the summer of 1899 dragged by and the marriage arrangements moved forward, her heartache was unabated. 'Only unwanted girls are given as brides,' she told herself. Others could be independent and rise to professional fame. Life, for her, was at an end. 'Marriage: how I hated that word!'[5]

October arrived, and the season of Cold Dew (*Han Lu*). On the nineteenth day they celebrated in Nantai the union of the late Congregational pastor's son Ni Wen-xiu, government officer in the Maritime Customs with a new posting to Shantou, and Lin He-ping, adoptive daughter of the wealthy and generous convert businessman. It was a day of joy and hopefulness. The young couple went for two weeks to reside in the Ni home, where Mrs Ni Senior ruled over seven sons and five daughters-in-law. The brief time there in the uneasy role of a junior wife was, she discovered, more than enough to restore her affection for her own sweet mother. She determined that if she had children her girls should never suffer, as she did then and later, at the hands of that house's contentious women! It was thus a relief when the time came to set out, bag and baggage, for Shantou and the new appointment.

Amid the farewells of both families Ni Wen-xiu took his young bride once more the eleven miles down river by sampan to the ocean anchorage opposite Pagoda Island to board the southbound coastal boat. Like the previous ones, it was crowded with deck passengers, with their bedding and bundles and little pigskin trunks, and with livestock of every kind. But again the congestion and discomforts of the sea voyage were offset by the rugged coastal beauty as the silt-laden river waters gave way abruptly to the clear green of the South China Sea. A cruise of 250 miles past yet more hill-beset southern anchorages brought them at length to Shantou, the little treaty port at the rock-bound mouth of the Han River. Though tiny compared to Fuzhou, it had a rich hinterland and its brisk trade would fully engage Mr Ni in his taxation work. Here in its official quarter the young couple now set up home, while he eagerly learned from his superiors the intricacies of the customs duties, first of the native coastwise business and in due course of the international trade.

That year, 1900, was one of uneasy peace. Away in the northern provinces a peasant rebellion, the Yi-he-quan or Righteous Harmony Fists whom the foreigners knew as the 'Boxers', was spreading across the land, murdering Chinese Christians and Western families and spreading anti-foreign madness. In Beijing the Qing dynasty of Manchurians (a powerful minority people from beyond the Wall ruling as Chinese but treating their Han subjects as inferiors) had after two centuries fallen on ill times and were fading. For some years now the power behind the Dragon Throne had been the Tartar woman Yehonala, 'The Orchid', who in turn as royal concubine and, since widowed in 1861, as Dowager Empress, contrived to rule as co-regent with consecutive Emperors, her minor son and another weak relative. Fickle and unprincipled, she now gave erratic support to the revolutionaries, willing to harness their movement to her own xenophobic ends. 'Let them, if they so wish, destroy all aliens China-wide!' But when a foreign military force rode to the rescue of the Beijing embassies, she fled to the country. New indemnities and oppressive demands were placed on the Chinese people.

Happily at this crisis the southern viceroys, at great

personal cost, had elected to stand by the 'unequal treaties' and ignore her edict. In Fuzhou city at the critical time floods providentially broke the Min River bridge, cutting off the murderers from their desired missionary victims. Here at Shantou also a precarious quiet prevailed.

Into this comparative calm there was born to our young couple a first daughter, Gui-chen, to be greeted with rejoicing as God's undoubted gift. But when a year later Gui-zhen followed, their joy was more qualified. Such was the strength of tradition that a sense of guilt weighed upon both parents. Why should God have to trust them with a second mere girl? Simple Christians as they were, their confidence in him was tested. Happily their anguish brought them to their knees to put their problem to him.

There in Shantou, the third pregnancy reached term, and at length there came the delighted father's cry, 'It's a boy!' In this male child God had given to He-ping the desire of her heart. Weak Christian though she was, she kept her pact with him. Coming with her new baby for his christening in the Anglican tradition, like Hannah she brought her treasure back to her God. 'It was this boy that I prayed for, and the Lord has given me what I asked. Now I lend my Shu-zu to the Lord; for his whole life he is his.'[6]

God would in his time have a watchman for his people.

3

Revolution

During the years following the birth of the first boy to the Ni Wen-xiu family their children increased to nine in all, five boys and four girls. After Gui-chen, Gui-zhen and Henry (Shu-zu, one day to be Tuo-sheng, Watchman) there came George (Huai-zu) and a third son, Xuan-zu, who would survive just to school days. Then with an interval two more girls followed, De-zhen and De-cheng, and lastly two boys, Paul (Hong-zu) and John (Xing-zu). As a junior official in the Maritime Customs Ni Wen-xiu's salary of 35 taels a month was not large, and nearly half of this sum went to his widowed mother. Thus the growing family had to be content at first with life's essentials: food, clothing and a house to dwell in, though with fresh vegetables and seafoods at hand to garnish their rice they grew up fit and healthy. Childhood toys were simple, made locally of pottery, bamboo and paper, and there were kites to fly at Christmas time when the monsoon winds blew strong.

But Lin He-ping was full of drive. To help their finances she enlisted her father's aid to build up in Shantou a personal export business in piece goods of drawn-thread-work and figured cloth. This soon proved very profitable with a steady flow to markets in Malaya, Great Britain and North America. Her husband too came to be valued by his superiors as a careful and exact man, and through conscientious work in the Service he attained steady promotion. Some years of prosperity passed, and then a transfer to Suzhou inland from Shanghai put an abrupt end to the cloth business and threw the family's affairs into disarray. After 12 months there his mother urged him to apply on compassionate grounds for a fresh posting back to Fuzhou, and to his joy he obtained it. There he would in due course be thought of highly by the Customs Service.

While in Shantou the parents themselves had taken care of the children's education, drilling them in propriety and good manners and teaching them to write their first brush-stroke characters. Once back in Fuzhou, however, Ni Wen-xiu engaged as tutor a *xiu cai*, or graduate of the first degree. From this man they learned calligraphy and the literary and moral principles of Confucius contained in the Four Books and the Five Classics that had formed the basis of Chinese moral culture for two millennia. For though in 1905 the old civil examination system had been abolished and the road to official advancement now lay through new schools modelled on those of the West, yet no child might escape study of these ancient philosophies and still claim to be educated. Young Shu-zu proved quick to learn, and usually outdid his elder sisters to win the dollar prize which the tutor would sometimes offer for successful study. The Ni family was also musical, and he instructed them in the ancient Chinese system called the Melodies, while along with their Bible lessons He-ping herself taught them Christian hymns. Later, when her husband could afford to do so, he bought them a piano and he himself copied out sheet music for the children to play.

They had a spacious house, No. 18 Customs House Lane near the Nantai shore and bridge, with outbuildings and a large garden, and here they grew up in comfort and security. By tradition a Chinese father would rule his family with a heavy hand, but this was not in Ni Wen-xiu's nature. Grave like his father, he was disinclined to scold. In the words of a first grandson, 'He was humble, friendly and lovable, so that you had a sense of freedom and could open your heart to him.'[1] Though ever thus approachable he stayed in the background, occupying himself as a Chinese man should with official duties and men friends, so that in the home it was He-ping who wielded the rod. To her, discipline was the household's glory and she ruled her high-spirited children by fear. It was her family principle that domestic tidiness was a duty shared equally by all. Her pleasure was to have the home clean and orderly with everything in its place. If something had fallen to the floor she expected the one nearest to put it back; and none, on the plea 'I didn't drop it!' was excused a duty to act. Shu-zu himself was a troublesome but gifted child, always trying something new and leaving behind him a trail of litter and breakages, so when he was young he was regularly punished. The elder girls at times found this excessive and conspired to shield him by themselves owning up to some of his misdeeds.

They were fortunate in having another Fuzhou family, the Zhangs, living close to them on the Nantai shore overlooking the bridge. Zhang Ru-zhou was a dear Christian friend and a remote connection of their father. His children's ages were near to their own and the two families were always on easy terms together. The two eldest Zhang daughters became special friends of the elder Ni girls, while in their childhood play little Pin-hui, or Charity, much the same age as Shu-zu, became his frequent companion. (Someone likened them to 'a plum blossom and a bamboo horse'.) He was the one with the ideas who took the lead and soon became 'deputy eldest brother' to them all.

From their home it was but a short walk to the busy fish-market whence an ancient granite-piered bridge with worn flagstones led out to the tight-packed islet of Zhong Zhou. From this the much longer Bridge of Ten Thousand Ages completed the Min crossing to its north shore, where began the three-mile road up to the city gate of old Fuzhou. That was too far for the children to venture alone, but on the bridge close at hand they could spend long, fascinating hours. Here they might find traders' stalls and picture shows, a geomancer foreseeing auspicious days for funerals, a dentist extracting teeth before amused onlookers, or maybe even some victim of Manchu justice, restrained round the neck by the heavy wooden cangue that bore his offence inscribed on its planking. Above the islet lay the close-packed sampans of the river-dwellers, ever busy with life. Downstream the cormorant-fishers on tiny rafts worked their patient birds, rewarding each one with a dose of bottled fish-oil for the live catch which it brought back, but with a tight ring around its neck could never swallow.

From the south-bank quay near their father's office the children would watch the coastal junks come up the sweep of the river to the Nantai anchorage, their flared bows painted with great direction-seeking eyes, their stiffened sails brown against the blue of the Gushan hills. They were of as many designs as their far ports of origin and the car-goes they unloaded were even more varied. There was, too, a brisk outgoing trade in farm products, and in tea and tim-ber from the Fujian hills; but the city's own industries for export were minor, stopping with silk and lacquer and such home articles as oil-paper umbrellas and red wooden pillows. In this respect Fuzhou was behind the times. Elsewhere China had entered upon great industrial changes, with textile factories springing up in the coastal towns, railways probing into the interior and foreign engineers keenly exploiting her mineral resources.

It was perhaps in Shu-zu's sixth year that the family had returned to Fuzhou, and he would be nine when a revolution broke upon the country that would soon sweep away the Qing dynasty. We must pause here a moment to view the world in which he was growing up. The present Han Viceroy of Zhejiang and Fujian Provinces, splendid in his princely *yamen* in old Fuzhou, was but a subject in fact of the northern Manchu overlords. Their Tartar general and his indolent bannermen dwelt at ease with their painted womenfolk in another special quarter within the walls. Yet the Manchu regime in Beijing had outlived its day, and since becoming involved in the Boxer episode was wholly discredited. Thus among educated Chinese these were years of mounting unrest, directed against both intruding Manchu rule and grasping Western exploitation. Large numbers of students had gone abroad to benefit from the new learning, and they returned with minds in a turmoil of revolutionary ideas.

Their hero was one who for much of 20 years had laboured in exile for China's renewal. Dr Sun Zhong-shan (or Sun Yat-sen in his Cantonese tongue) was a man of humble Guangdong origin and Protestant Christian faith, but he was to become also the prime ideologist of revolution and an architect of modern China. 'I belong not to the Christianity of the churches but to the Christianity of Jesus, and He was a revolutionary!' he is reported to have said.[2] (There is, as we shall see, an element of truth in that last clause.) Moreover the common people who met him loved him, because to them he was genuine. Here at last was a Chinese leader who would not betray the people. Though his lack of administrative flair was to be his undoing, his Three Principles of nationalism, democracy and socialism (*san-min-zhu-yi*) were destined to capture and hold the popular imagination. He had long been compelled to work overseas, and because foreign powers were shoring up the Manchu rule for their own ends he was practically homeless, hounded from land to land by Chinese and local agents eager for the huge price placed on his head. Once while on the way to church in London he was kidnapped and, with some British connivance, confined by the Chinese for some days in their embassy. Only then did the alertness of two English friends rescue him from illegal shipment to Beijing and a certain death there by torture.

Then in November 1908 the Qing Emperor Guang Xu died. Intelligent but weak, he had been wholly dominated by his mother, the aged and superstitious Empress Dowager. Known to many as 'the old buddha' in ironical recognition of her crafty staying powers, she had proved to be China's evil genius. Self-seeking and reactionary to the last, her own death followed on the next day. Few mourned her going, but alas Guang Xu's nephew and heir to the throne, now proclaimed Emperor under the name Xuan Tong, was aged just three. There followed a spell of uncertainty marked by a growing conviction that the dynasty had forfeited the Mandate of Heaven. Then three years later, on 10 October 1911 ('the Double Tenth'), the accidental discharge of a conspirator's bomb set off revolt in Wuchang, capital of Hubei Province. A train of events began then that would lead to the imperial abdication, the rise and decay of the Republic, the Nationalist dictatorship, and the eventual triumph of the fresh and innovative Communist Party. China would change beyond recognition.

In December Sun Yat-sen returned from overseas and at Nanjing, the 'southern capital', was provisionally elected President of the Republic of China. There he declared a government based on the will of the people. To repudiate Manchu rule his followers cut off their queues, the form of wearing the hair imposed upon the Han men to mark them as subject and inferior to that smaller Chinese race. No longer now would the Fuzhou schoolboys stand in file on the hostel verandah plaiting each others' pigtails. Was not the Tartar general himself suing the Han for mercy while his soldiers ran in terror to the hills? More significant still, after two millennia the Dragon Throne itself, the golden kingpin on which Chinese civilisation turned, had been torn from its place in the state fabric to be succeeded, hopefully, by a democracy.

But Sun and most of the southerners prominent with him in revolution were returned exiles, out of close touch with the mood of their country. Nursing vague dreams of a China reshaped on some Western pattern, they were unaware that for an effective democracy she lacked the essential bases. From afar Sun had looked for help in China from many quarters. For example, he mistakenly gave to the Triad gangs a semblance of patriotism by enlisting their support for his campaign. Home now at last, he was to find them already in seats of regional power and eager for political unrest in pursuit not of democracy but of their own goals. Inevitably, too, an ambitious northerner arose to challenge his leadership. Yuan Shi-kai, a general of the Empire with personal designs on the throne, contrived quickly to displace him as President. Sun's own selflessness and lack of pride were to be his undoing.

Before being forced back into exile in August 1913, Dr Sun was constrained therefore to organise a 'Second Revolution' in the seaport cities of the south. Here, on a local scale, the Ni family too became closely involved in these affairs. Sun's 'Love One's Country' movement was capturing many hearts.

For his work on the Nantai foreshore Ni Wen-xiu was now highly thought of in the Customs Service; yet just at this point he is described as 'a retiring man who could not utter a word in public'. Needing, however, to educate his family with a salary from one of the notably foreign-dominated sources, he may well have been wise to maintain a quietly low profile. Certainly his wife was just the opposite: eloquent, forceful, ready enough to assert a new-found release from customary female subservience. Careless of the fighting and bloodshed around her she set out on a tour of lectures, having first publicly donated to the cause her own gold bangles and jewellery in a gesture that many men and women were moved to follow. By energetic letter-writing she formed a Women's Patriotic Society backed by prominent local leaders, and served it herself as General Secretary. When in July 1913 Sun Yat-sen arrived in person in Fuzhou,[3] He-ping was given an official role in the presidential reception. It turned out that Dr Sun's private secretary, Miss Song, had been her own Shanghai classmate, so in that lady's company she attended every feast and function of the four-day tour.

Shu-zu was now ten years old, and able to listen with a boy's inquisitive ears to the political talk. The revolution had surely brought new hope to his country. At first, too, an upsurge of pro-foreign feeling hinted at the rapid expansion of Christian missionary enterprise, and who could tell what doors for overseas study might, as a consequence, open to

him one day? But a year later the European War broke out
to awaken in China fresh disillusion with the West. At
home, too, the revolution seemed stillborn, with the land
dismembered by rival warlords and by Japanese encroach-
ments under the guise of aid to Britain and France. Their
ally Japan presented to China on 18 January 1915 her grim
Twenty-One Demands. Starting with claims upon Shandong Province, and including among many other specified
details the virtual surrender to Japan of all harbour works
at Fuzhou, it would go on to make of the Middle Kingdom
a puppet state. And that same year, as though to crown all
in the President of China's new democracy, Yuan Shi-kai
announced his delighted reversal of all Dr Sun's hopes by
proclaiming his own ascent of the Dragon Throne. Needless
to say, he ended his days in shame.

In 1916 at the age of 13, impressionable, ambitious and
buoyed with hope, Ni Shu-zu entered the Church Missionary Society vernacular Middle School in Fuzhou to begin
his Western-style education. In due course he would go on
to the English medium High School of St Mark's. This was
part of an Anglican complex in Nantai comprising primary,
middle, normal, high and divinity schools, together known
then as Trinity College, Foochow, with nearly 400 on the
roll. The missionary staff were mainly Irish from Trinity
College, Dublin.[4]

As he passed up through the school Shu-zu did well
enough in his class work, overcoming rare setbacks of
minor illness for which friends blamed He-ping's mother,
who now lived with them in Customs House Lane and who
shamelessly spoiled him. Often he came out top in his class.
He tells us how, like any schoolboy, he enjoyed stamping in
ink 'Ni Shu-zu' on his books, papers and whatever lay to
hand, using the homemade version of a junior clerk's

'chop'. The characters incised in reverse on its square base would, after pressing on an ink pad, produce the proud name in white on a scarlet background. He was thinking of course of a senior official's treasured ivory stamp or seal of office that one day might conceivably become his. In more serious matters, we are told, he was frank and straight-forward, albeit a shade priggish with his keen sense of justice; for once, when a street hawker visiting the school complained that one of his wares was missing, Watchman aroused popular resentment by indicating the boy who had taken it. At sport he showed little enthusiasm for the team games of basketball, volleyball or football which the others played, seeming to lack the stamina for them, but he was growing fast now into a lean, lanky lad, a head taller than most of his fellows.

He was soon at ease in the unfamiliar northern dialect known to Westerners as Mandarin, which was now claiming priority as the national language. (Written Chinese ideograms are the same everywhere and legible to readers throughout the land. In the many regional dialects it is only their sounds that differ.) Moreover, with this change there came also another literary shift. All of Shu-zu's early reading had been of books in the classic literary style, which scholars had a vested interest in preserving because, though learned by rote and barely understood, they were still required by the fossilised state schooling system. But China was in a process of cultural change. For a new medium of expression and in response to popular demand, younger authors like Lu-Xun and many others were turning to the vernacular argot hitherto left to the cheap gutter-press novelists whose writings Shu-zu and his schoolmates concealed under their desk-tops and read by stealth. Soon they would find themselves in line with current fashion, for by 1922 the Ministry of Education itself would give sanction to this development, ordering school textbooks to be rewritten in the freer colloquial style, or *bai-hua*, of the people. It was a change destined to have tremendous effect on the spread of ideas through literature in the years ahead, and not least also on the popular dissemination of easily readable Christian thought.

Just now, however, religion had fallen into disfavour among students. Indeed, in 1918 an Anti-Religious Movement had been promoted through the Beijing magazine *New Youth* by Chen Du-xiu, Dean of the Peking School of Letters and a strong influence on educated thought. His movement was to blossom in the Great Federation of Anti-Religionists of 1922 and in the emotional outbursts against Christianity that followed.[5] Chen himself was later to become Secretary General of the Chinese Communist Party. Another political event of even greater influence that must claim our attention here is the May Fourth Movement. With victory in World War I and the Versailles Treaty of 1919 China expected the return to her of the German concessions in Shandong, instead of which they were awarded by Britain and France to their other ally, Japan. Indignation among young Chinese on the discovery of what they felt was a sell-out to imperialists by their own incompetent government led on 4 May 1919 to a massive spontaneous protest by Beijing students,[6] prominent among whom was a young man of 23 named Zhou En-lai (Chou En-lai). There followed student-led strikes in Shanghai and Fuzhou and a proliferation of new Marxist ideas, helped forward by the Soviet government's offer in 1920 to renounce altogether Russia's own large extra-territorial rights. The May Fourth Movement would prove highly significant in paving the way for Chinese Communism.

Meanwhile, nearer at hand, sporadic fighting dragged on in the Province between warlords and the Kuomintang (the National People's Party), whose fragmented armies, whenever pay was short, turned readily from soldiering to banditry (if that distinction matters). Schoolfriends returning from rural areas brought tragic stories of civil chaos and mounting peasant distress. Shu-zu was now in his sixteenth year and susceptible enough to student moods and outbursts of feeling. He had also just completed Middle School, and the stimulus of his move to St Mark's with its new phase of studies may have done something to counter in him the disillusion affecting those around him. His rebelliousness extended little further than a frequent breaking of school rules, while on the other hand he continued to come top in most class examinations. The challenge now would be success in essay writing, and his efforts at this were often posted up on the bulletin board for others to emulate. He liked to read novels and attend movies. He wrote articles for newspapers and with the payment for these he bought lottery tickets.

He was developing, too, a strong aversion to the church. He despised preachers, considering them as dogs, fawning always on the missionaries. When told by his father that he, Shu-zu, had been promised to God to be a preacher he could not have disagreed more. 'Not so,' was his firm response. He was planning his own future in a far different direction. 'I trusted my judgement implicitly,' he said later, 'and had my youthful dreams and plans for my career. If I worked hard enough I believed I could attain any level I wished.' He vowed he would never become a preacher!

In his home there was in fact much also to disenchant a growing boy. His mother's involvement with the Party had begun to lose its glamour for them all. Earlier, in recognition of her political zeal, the Fujian governor Sun Dao-ren had nominated her for an award, and in due course Beijing had responded by promoting her to the Order of the Second Class for Patriotism. Once this honour was hers, however, her zeal lapsed. Love of country gave way, she says, to enjoyment of status and praise for its own sake. Social and cultural entertainment took the place of church-going, and 'from contact with unbelieving revolutionaries I became almost an unbeliever myself'. Daily the society ladies came to her home to play cards and *mahjong*, and when the Methodist pastor called to ask for a subscription He-ping would say mockingly, 'Sit down here and let's see what my winnings amount to. If I win plenty I'll give God some!' and he, poor man, complied. 'Even the outward mask of a Christian', she admits with shame, 'had gone.'

4

Choice

He-ping's discipline of the children, generally fair and impartial, seemed now to be prejudiced and unjust. One day in January 1920 at the end of the winter holiday a valuable vase in the house was found smashed. Settling in her mind where the fault lay, He-ping decided that Watchman, as the obvious culprit, should confess. When he declined to do so she subjected him, a 16-year-old, once more to the indignity of a thrashing. When on later inquiry she discovered that after all he was innocent she was not without remorse, but she left him nevertheless to nurse his grievance. Thus he went back to his second term at High School sore and embittered.

That same month some unexpected news reached her. Dora Yu, the woman who years earlier in Shanghai had so impressed her, was coming to Fuzhou at the Chinese New Year to conduct a fortnight of revival meetings in the Methodist Tian-an Chapel (Heavenly Peace Hall). They would run from 15 to 29 February, Sunday to Sunday. Miss Yu had become known as a gifted evangelist and had travelled widely among missions in northern China and Korea, as well as establishing her own Bible seminary in Shanghai. He-ping had not seen her since that day in 1898 when she had been moved to offer her a gift. Now at the start of the Fuzhou meetings she invited her to an evening meal with a group of her gambling friends. She spoke warmly to them of the visitor, and at the end announced, 'Tomorrow Miss Yu will preach at the Heavenly Peace Hall. Please all be there.' Someone asked, 'And you?' 'Of course I shall go,' she replied.

Thus 15 February came, and the first meeting. He-ping was on time with the others, sitting well forward. The preacher, her bound feet encased in tiny brocaded shoes, stood stiffly up to announce as her text God's words to Eve: 'Neither shall you touch it, lest you die.'[1] From these words she preached that day and the next with great power on spiritual death as separation from God. But the subject bored He-ping. She had known all this from childhood and she decided two meetings were enough. Her friends fretted at the loss of gambling time.

So on the third day amid cries of rejoicing, and again on the fourth, out clattered once more the white and red *mahjong* tiles on the hard-topped table – but not without a pang of conscience in He-ping's heart. 'I sat there playing', she recalls, 'as one already dead. I knew God's Holy Spirit was dealing with me.' After two uneasy days she could stand it no longer. 'I am a Christian,' she exclaimed suddenly to the others. 'Miss Yu has come a long distance to preach here. Not to attend is a breach of propriety. Say what you like, I shall not play tomorrow!'

Next day Dora Yu saw her arrive and came at once to greet her. 'Where have you been?' she asked innocently. 'I was not well,' He-ping lied. Miss Yu looked at her kindly. 'May God himself shine on you and heal you,' she said, and the words struck home. How far removed was sickness from *mahjong*! In stark reality she saw her deceitfulness for what it was. All through the address she shifted guiltily in her seat as the preacher's telling phrases found her out. Forty years old and a public figure, she could not conceive that anyone should so expose her! This now would certainly be her last meeting. Yet when Dora asked, 'Will you be here tomorrow?' how could she excuse herself? And when tomorrow came, though God accused her still, his servant now recounted afresh the sufferings of Jesus on the cross for sinners. 'Her every utterance was just for me,' He-ping says. 'Thank God, each day a strength beyond mine brought me back for more.' The climax came when she confessed to him her need and thanked him for his mercy. His grace had won her.

Her husband, who had attended some of the meetings, was mystified. 'You neither sleep nor eat,' he protested. 'Instead you do nothing but shed tears. Others are happy when they are converted! If this is its effect on you, give it up and stay away!' 'But you don't know my inward state,' she exclaimed. 'I have lied to you; I have diverted so much of our family money to games of chance,' and she went on to recount the ways in which she had defrauded him. Then came his turn to confess his faults to her and soon they were both in tears. The 'Peace' that her name implies had come to her at last. She never touched the playing cards and *mahjong* sparrow tiles again.

The High School boys were free to attend Miss Yu's meetings and a number were doing so. With her new-found joy He-ping had assumed the role of interpreter, and was turning Dora's *bai-hua* into the Fuzhou dialect for their sake. Watchman had until now absented himself. Susceptible as he already was to the agnostic mood of his friends, he had been more than ever disillusioned by Christianity's failure as a vital force in his own home. Though his mother had invited him to attend he could be as stubborn as she was, and had declined. How could she expect otherwise? So now came the moment of truth. She knew she should confess her injustice to her eldest son, but her pride rebelled against such humiliation. It would be without precedent. Did not Confucius himself teach that parents were never in the wrong?

Something else, however, she could put right, and this she was determined to do. With three dollars in her hand she set out to buy a Bible and hymnbook with which to recommence family worship. Next day she began to play and sing the first hymn – but the Spirit of God arrested her. If she would worship God publicly she must first, she knew, confess her faults. 'But how can I, a mother, confess to my son?' she protested. Quite distinctly God spoke in her heart: 'You must do precisely that. It is the only way.'

To the utter surprise of her husband and the entire family she quickly stood up, walked over to her son and threw her arms around him. 'For the Lord Jesus' sake,' she cried, 'I confess to beating you unjustly and in anger.' 'You did so, honourable Mother,' was his matter-of-fact reply, 'and I hated you for it.' Looking him in the eyes, 'Please forgive me!' she appealed, but he turned away without answering. Family prayers went on.

That night God took hold of Shu-zu. He had been touched deeply by He-ping's confession. Never had he heard of a Han parent accepting such loss of face. If his own mother could be thus transformed, then there must be something powerful in this visitor's preaching. Christianity must be more than just a creed. This lady preacher deserved a hearing. He would go and see for himself. Next morning he arose early. 'I am ready now', he told his mother, 'to go and hear Yu Ci-du.'

He went, and from that day attended the remainder of Dora Yu's meetings; but they were days of agony and turmoil for him. For most people the prominent feature of their being won to God is an act of deep repentance for sin leading to the joy of his forgiveness. For Shu-zu the question was an infinitely larger one. More than merely accepting salvation and becoming a disciple of Jesus, was he further prepared to become his lifelong servant? That, he knew, was the real issue. Did it not say of his disciples that they left all and followed him?[2] And was that not too costly? Later he told a close friend that during those few days of Ci-du's preaching he weighed the matter carefully, knowing the choice must, for him, be all or nothing.

And after all, why not? We know rather little of Shu-zu's cultural tastes, though clearly the family had some artistic sense. Moving freely about Fuzhou, he must have come across a tasteful creative task in progress in the old city's lacquer street, one which also a Western traveller had just now come upon and described. In one of the shops an anonymous craftsman had already spent six years on three hardwood leaves of a four-leaf screen, carving reliefs of flowers in the natural wood, a lovely pale tone against a black lacquered surface. For this he was paid 80 cents a day, 'rain, shine, holidays or revolution' (as the shop-owner put it), plus his rice and vegetables and a plank to sleep on. Having once acquired creative skill for this work, he might make only two such screens before eyes and nerves failed and he was flung out with the beggars.[3] If human creative gift could be thus squandered for an avaricious employer, was anything too good to give back to a God who had not withheld his own Son but had given him up for us all?

Much later he told a group of colleagues, 'I was 17 years of age. On the evening of the 29th I was alone in my room,

struggling to decide whether or not to believe in the Lord. I
was still reluctant, but as I tried to pray to him I growingly
saw the magnitude of my sins and both the reality and the
efficacy of the Lord Jesus as Saviour. I pictured his hands
stretched out on the cross, and all at once they seemed to be
welcoming me. "I am here to receive you," he was saying.'
Realising the effectiveness of Christ's blood in cleansing his
sins and being overwhelmed by such love, he accepted the
Saviour then and there. Previously he had laughed at
people who accepted Jesus, but that evening to him the
experience became real and he wept and confessed his
many wrongdoings, seeking the Lord's forgiveness. 'As
I made my first prayer I knew joy and peace such as I
had never known before. Light seemed to flood the room
and I said to Jesus, "Lord, you have indeed been gracious
to me."'[4]

In Jesus Christ Shu-zu had found a living Saviour and
Friend, but in doing so he had also met with a sovereign
Lord who needed and expected his service. 'Following my
being saved,' he continues, 'all the past ten years of planning became meaningless and there were to be many
changes. My cherished ambitions were discarded. With the
undoubted assurance of God's calling I knew from that day
what my life's career was to be. I understood that God had
brought me to himself both for my own salvation and for
his glory. He had called me to be his fellow worker. Formerly I had despised preachers and their preaching because
in those days most were employees of European or American missionaries, having to be servile to them and earn
from them payment of eight or nine silver dollars a month.
I had never imagined for a moment that I would become a
preacher, a profession which I saw as trifling and base.'

Now, however, his eyes were turned elsewhere. Soon

they lighted on the apostle Paul's words, 'Present yourselves to God as men who have been brought from death to
life, and your members as his instruments of righteousness.'[5] This was clear enough. 'God required of me', he
explains, 'that I now regard all my faculties as belonging to
Another. I dared not squander an hour of my time or a few
cash of my money, nor yet any of my mental or physical
powers, for they were no longer mine but his. It was a great
thing when I made that discovery. Real Christian life began
for me that day.'

Thus in an act of youthful committal he pledged himself
to serve God wholly and utterly, and for all his failings he
never went back on his word. God in turn had responded
with a new birth in his spirit that would progressively
heighten his love for his Lord and utterly revolutionise his
life. On that night years ago when the local nightwatchman
beat his drum, God had heard his mother's prayer and was
keeping his side of the compact. Following his mother's
promise to God, Shu-zu himself must now keep his.

At once there were wrongs to be righted. First of all, in
one school subject, the burdensome Scripture Knowledge,
he had till now preserved an absence of interest that
ensured him consistently low marks. Affected till now by
other boys' coolness towards religion, yet as the scion of a
Christian family, he disliked the loss of face this entailed in
a Mission High School. He had therefore resolved to help
himself in examinations by writing selected facts on his
palms and concealing them in his fashionably long-flowing
sleeves. This was enough to win him 70 per cent marks,
which, since it more nearly approached his standard in
other subjects, aroused no suspicion in his teachers.

Now, being born anew by the Spirit of God, he at once
abandoned his cheating. 'After my being saved,' he tells us,

'while others brought novels to read in class, I brought a Bible.' But of course by now he lacked the basic ground-work, and try as he would, in Scripture Knowledge he failed even to attain pass marks. God, he realised, could not help him in this problem while his sin remained un-confessed.

But he had reason to hesitate. The Principal had warned the school that any boy found cheating would be summar-ily expelled, and expulsion would destroy all hope of a uni-versity scholarship and eventual study abroad. (At that time the final two years at Trinity were equivalent to the first year at St John's University, Shanghai.) So on such a prac-tical issue it was for him a real struggle to decide that Jesus Christ was in fact more precious to him than a career. He went to the Principal and told him frankly what he had done and why he must confess it – and to his joy and relief he was not dismissed. In this experience he found with God a new peace.

Can we recognise God's hand, too, in the timing of these events? Here was a determined young man who was set significantly on a new way of life that consciously gave a supreme place to our Creator God and who, being tested, at once showed himself ready to pay the price of doing so. Ni Shu-zu saw it as his calling from God to continue in that path of integrity wherever it might lead him.

As we have already seen, other powerful ideologies were competing too for the allegiance of thinking Chinese, and other radical conversions were in the air. In these very months a man ten years Watchman's senior was devouring classical Marxist writings, some only now available in his language, and through them arriving at profound inward convictions. Born in 1893 to a Hunan peasant family, Mao Ze-dong (Mao Tse-tung), sometime assistant librarian at

Beijing University and lately a political agitator in Changsha, had arrived in Shanghai in the spring of 1920. His purpose was to visit Chen Du-xiu, the original Secretary of the Chinese Communist Party. They discussed Marx's works together at length, and it was through Chen's confession of political faith that Mao now committed himself to become and to remain lifelong a convinced and ardent Communist.[6]

From such cosmic earth movements as these, seeking minds in China were experiencing the slow early rise of a century-long planetary tide. Like some freakish mountainous tsunami, it would sweep inexorably across the populous lands, eventually to disintegrate in thundering breakers. Against this strange menace and caught by an alternative living stream, the younger man's opposite course was now, under God, being straightly set.

5

Dedication

It was not until 1925, in his twenty-second year, that with parental approval Ni Shu-zu opted to change from his childhood name and become Ni Tuo-sheng, or Watchman Nee as he is now known worldwide. (We will use that English name for him, and for the convenience of many readers we will also generally use the English names of the better known among his co-workers.)

Three months after his conversion Miss Dora Yu, on her way back northwards from Xiamen (Amoy), paid a return visit to Fuzhou to address the girls at the Church Missionary Society High School, and according to its Year 1920 Report the movement of God continued and 'many lives were transformed'.[1] Watchman will have met her once again and affirmed to her his new-found faith. At this period the region was militarily disturbed, with sporadic fighting in the countryside and the city swinging pendulum-like between northern and southern spheres of influence. Around 9 May the High School boys were involved in anti-Japanese demonstrations, for each year on this National Day of Shame China remembered Japan's Twenty-One Demands of 1915. The unrest continued and for a second year running the school curriculum was much disorganised.

Seeing this, and feeling the need to adjust himself to a whole new direction in life, Watchman quietly disappeared. His classmates had no idea where he had gone, and his family kept the secret until his return some months later. He had in fact taken ship to Shanghai, a city where the New Tide Movement in education, fostered by the recent visits of John Dewey, Bertrand Russell and Rabindranath Tagore, was making a big impression on student minds. No longer, however, on his. He had gone there to join Miss Yu's Bible School for a year's training in the Scriptures that till now he had found so difficult. He put his heart into the work and he could not have had a better teacher. From her he learned above all the secret of trusting God alone for his needs, as she had done through life. She taught him, too, to let God's Word speak to his own heart and not merely – essential though that was – to store his mind with its text.

However, after a shorter time and without explaining why, Miss Yu told him it was not convenient for him to stay on, and he returned home. 'I understood later', he says, 'that the problem was in me – in my gourmet appetite, dilettante dress and tardy rising in the mornings. My desire to serve the Lord had been dealt a serious blow. There remained many more things to be changed.'

On his return to Fuzhou, his mother said to him firmly, 'Go back now to Trinity and finish your college course.' He did so, and since the entire class's curriculum had suffered he had little difficulty in catching up. But he was a changed student, and now he did not waste a moment. He plunged into his studies with a will, but he also took every opportunity to speak about Jesus to his fellow pupils and was ready to talk earnestly with anyone about God's way of salvation through Jesus Christ.

'When I was newly saved I did not know how to lead people to Christ. I thought that the more words I spoke to them the better; but I was a total failure, no one got saved and I felt powerless. Later I met a lady missionary, Miss Groves, who asked me how many souls I had won. I replied that I had preached the gospel to my fellow students but they would not listen, so the fault lay with them. She suggested, however, that the fault probably lay with me. Was there anything, hidden and unconfessed, standing between me and God? I had to acknowledge that there were such things. Yes, I was willing to deal with them immediately.

'She further inquired how I witnessed to people. I had no plan: I simply said what I felt like saying without regard to their listening or not. "You are wrong," she said. "Speak first to God, and then to men. Ask God for whom he wants you to pray. Write their names in a notebook and then pray for them daily. Then when opportunities arise, preach the gospel to them." I accepted her advice. That very day I dealt with many sins and unrighteous matters. I asked the Lord for forgiveness and for cleansing with his blood. From that day onward I prayed for those whose names were accumulating in my notebook. Eventually they would number over 70. Even in class I prayed secretly for them.'

But after some months Watchman was still just everyone's laughing stock. Because he carried the Bible with him everywhere, 'Here comes the Bible Depot!' they would exclaim, and determine not to listen to his talk. But he constantly read it, and having in a short period gone completely through it several times he knew what it held. His photographic mind retained much and his grasp of biblical truth increased. Slowly his changed life and evident sincerity began to compel their attention.

A young Fuzhou student at the Guangdong Naval School, Wang Chi (Wilson Wang), had transferred from nautical training to enrol in Watchman's class in the sixth year at Trinity, and he was one of the first to join him in informal student prayer in the college chapel. It was more than a year before solid fruits from this began to be seen, but slowly, as a result of talks in Watchman's room, several boys came under conviction, and one by one discovered in Christ the new joy they had been seeking. Chief among these were Miao Shao-xun (Simon Meek) from Lieng Chieng district near the coast, and Lu (or Liok) Zhong-xing (Faithful Luke) and Wei Guang-xi (K.H. Weigh), who were both from Gutian (Kutien) further up the river.

Not content with witnessing in the school, a handful of these High School boys began to carry the gospel out into the town, making use of Sundays and festivals and the frequent student strikes as occasions for this. They procured a loud and resonant gong, and with it went singing through the streets, proclaiming to all who would pause and listen the good news of a living Saviour. There was already incessant noise in the town, of drums and firecrackers and squealing pigs, the cries of traders and vociferating coolies, and the cacophonous bands that attended funerals. No one minded a little more. They handed out leaflets and carried big character placards and posters plainly stating the way of salvation. These last they pasted up on public walls to compete with the gaudy red cockerels advertising cigarettes, the chromos depicting the merits of kerosene lamps, and the lurid wall paintings of the man-eating blue tiger, terror of hill-dwellers in the Fuqing jungles to the south. The Chinese language, being written vertically, lends itself to 'sandwich-board' publicity, and soon a fresh idea inspired them. They made themselves white cotton singlets which they adorned with red appliqué characters bearing such messages as 'God loved the world of sinners' and 'Jesus Christ is a living Saviour'. The suburbs on both sides of the river became aware of a spiritual awakening among the Christians.

At Mawei (Pagoda Anchorage) Watchman early discovered a kindred spirit who was to become a valued friend. When disembarking there on his return from Shanghai he had, at Dora Yu's suggestion, called on Miss M.E. Barber, a former Anglican missionary now working independently. Born at Peasenhall in Suffolk, Margaret Barber had sailed for Fuzhou with the Church Missionary Society in 1899 and for seven years had taught in the girls' Middle School. The Mission records reveal her as a zealous and devoted worker and a very radiant personality. When on furlough in England in 1909, however, she had felt God challenge her about baptism as a believer, and had gone for this to D.M. Panton, minister of Surrey Chapel, Norwich. Understandably her bishop wrote advising her not to come back to Fujian, notwithstanding which she returned at the age of 42, trusting God for her supplies and backed by the prayers of the Surrey Chapel congregation.

She was joined by an independent Chinese preacher, Li Ai-ming, and to avoid embarrassing her former colleagues at Nantai she found at low rental the bungalow of a retiring missionary of the American Board at White Teeth Rock (Bai Ya Tan) by Mawei, across the river from the Luo-xing Island pagoda. Here, joined from home by Miss M.L.S. Ballord, 20 years her junior, she based her future operations.

For ten years the two of them laboured patiently among local women and, where possible, men. Periodically they paid visits to Fuzhou to distribute tracts in the city's markets, feeling, as single women missionaries do, the limitations placed upon their sex and the anomaly of their situation on the doorstep of a vast and spiritually dark province. Back in her first year in Fuzhou, Margaret Barber had witnessed the baptism as a Christian of the second priest from the nearby Boiling Spring hill-temple, once famous for its Buddha's tooth. Such things did not happen now. The winning of rural China for Christ seemed a far-off dream – unless, they told themselves, God himself should choose and call for the task young men and women from all over the land. Yet why should he not do so? They began to make this their constant prayer.

One day early in 1921 a warship of the Republic dropped anchor off White Teeth Rock and a young naval officer came ashore. Walking past the Customs station, he was arrested by the sound of hymn-singing coming from a mission building, and he went in and introduced himself. This was Wang Zai (Leland Wang), a native of Fuzhou and the elder brother of Watchman's classmate Wilson Wang. After passing out from Yantai (Chefoo) Naval College, he had been posted to a ship stationed at Nanjing, and while there he had been wonderfully converted to Jesus Christ. He was now 23 and had already determined to relinquish his commission and become a full-time preacher of the gospel. Here on their doorstep was a token that God was answering the two women's prayers.

The Wangs' home was in the Qishan (Chien Shan) suburb on the Nantai side of the river, on the hill slope a little above that of the Nees, so Wang Zai (Wang Tsai) was soon brought into touch with Watchman and his friends. Once his discharge from the Service was through he returned there to make it his headquarters as an evangelist, a ministry in which he proved to have a real gift. Being slightly older and more experienced than them all, he was warmly welcomed and looked up to by the student group.

The Ni home too, with the transformation God had wrought in He-ping's life, became now a centre of action and movement of a fresh kind. It took people a little while to adjust to the idea of the worldly political speaker turned Christian witness, but soon, with her forthright testimony and her sensitive use of Scripture, Mrs Ni came into demand as a Methodist preacher in meetings for women and girls throughout north Fujian. As, with a friend's help, she attained more facility in the *bai-hua*, these engagements would take her even further afield. She walked very close to God and sought his will in everything, keeping short accounts and making swift amends for her mistakes, and it seems that God signally honoured her witness.

Though again often away from home, she was sensible nevertheless of the needs of her large family. One hot season, after speaking at a fortnight's meetings for the Fuzhou YWCA, she declined the invitation to stay on for a much needed rest, feeling God had warned her of something impending at home. Back there that evening, as she strolled with her husband at the waterside before the house and watched the ceaseless coming and going of the river craft, she was moved to remark, 'It is so dry tonight, I fear there may be a fire.' In the early hours cries in fact awakened them to the fierce crackle of flames from bamboo and thatch house roofs along the street. They prayed, and she received from God a strong assurance that their own home would not be touched and that she need not even wake the smaller children. Sure enough, the wind changed quarter and blew from the south, and the fire that had destroyed a dozen houses stopped short just three doors from their own.

Ni Wen-xiu was much moved by this evidence of God's care, but he was not pleased when only seven days later, as again they walked to and fro in the hot evening, his wife spoke apprehensively of another fire. The uproar that this time aroused them at 4 a.m. was even more terrifying than the previous one. A strong rain-laden wind was helping the flames, which were leaping northwards from the market area near the bridge. 'As you see it,' her husband asked, 'will our house be burned this time?' She lifted her heart to the Lord, and could only reply, 'It may be.' So they roused the older children first, and then the stampede began of packing and evacuating essentials. In the midst of this, suddenly Genesis 18 came to mind, and Abraham's (as she felt) premature conclusion of his prayer for Sodom.² God seemed to rebuke her with the question, 'Why don't you pray?'

So she abandoned her activities and knelt once more. 'O God,' she prayed, 'in this quarter of Fuzhou my family is the only one that believes in you. Give me some answer to these unbelievers so that they cannot say, "Where is now your God?"' At once came the assurance, 'Though a thousand fall at your side and ten thousand at your right hand, this calamity shall not come near you.'³ Accepting this as from God, she told her husband. But the flames were fast approaching before a driving wind, and he berated her sternly for her inaction. Then the incredible happened. The city fire brigade, baulked by the holocaust around the bridgehead, arrived instead by water at their very doorstep to make their home the headquarters for fire-fighting. Their skilled efforts, combined with a fresh change of wind and some rainfall, stopped the conflagration short two doors away. The two fires in one week had left an island of five riverside houses miraculously untouched amid the devastation. How could such mercy fail to strengthen the family's faith in God?

One day a little later, on her return from a preaching engagement, He-ping learned that the two ladies from White Teeth Rock had called seeking her. She had not so far met Margaret Barber and her colleague, though she knew that Watchman and his school fellows sometimes went to Pagoda for Bible instruction. She had in fact avoided contact since hearing that Dora Yu had stopped off there on her way home to Shanghai and had been baptised by them in the river. This, He-ping felt, had undone much of the good achieved by her revival meetings and she had not hesitated to speak out openly against it.

But now, a few days before Easter, Watchman came to her. 'Honoured Mother,' he said, 'tomorrow I have three days holiday from school. I want to go to He Shou-en (their name for Miss Barber) for Bible study. Would you care to go with me?' 'Wait until I have asked the Lord,' she replied, and went upstairs. Kneeling, she prayed, then sat combing her hair. As she did so she felt God say to her, 'Go, and be baptised!' As quite a small child she had been baptised as a Christian along with her mother. Now God was asking her to do publicly the thing she had spoken against so strongly as being unnecessary: to make a fresh adult affirmation of her faith. Clearly it was *He* and no other who was pressing her to this act of obedience. She remembered God's word to Jesus at his own baptism: 'Thou art my beloved Son; with thee I am well pleased.'[4] After some thought she went downstairs and called Watchman. 'I have decided to go with you to Miss He,' she said, 'and moreover I want to be baptised.' 'I, too,' he replied at once, 'am going for that purpose.'

For him it had been no less a matter of obedience, of giving to God 'the answer of a good conscience'. He had read in the New Testament Paul's words linking baptism with the death of Christ and Peter's linking it with his reign. He had glimpsed the fact of two mutually hostile worlds and the impossibility of serving their two masters, the prince of this world and the Prince of life. He knew now he must express in this public way his complete break with the one and committal to the other. 'I go out,' he was saying, 'I make an exit from the Satan-governed system. I belong no more to this pattern of things. I set my heart instead on that upon which God's heart is set. I take as my goal his eternal purpose in Christ, and I step into that and am delivered from this.'[5]

Hearing of their plan, Watchman's brother George expressed too the desire for baptism, and thus it came about that next morning the three of them set out by river boat for Mawei. Miss Barber greeted He-ping delightedly: 'Have you eaten your rice? What good tidings bring you to us?' and was amazed to hear from her own lips how, without human intermediary, God had spoken to her of baptism. Since learning through Dora Yu of God's dealings with her, they had not ceased to pray for her. Now they all knelt and thanked God together.

It was late March 1921 and they went out to the riverside at White Teeth Rock. The tide was slack and shipping in the anchorage was quiet, but the day was dull and the sky overcast with a light rain falling to dampen their spirits. That morning one of He-ping's occasional bouts of tachycardia had assailed her and Miss Barber had offered to postpone the event. But she was insistent. 'I would rather die in the will of God', she said, 'than live any longer in my own will.' She tells how, as the aged evangelist Li Ai-ming waded with her out into the shelving Min, she asked God for a sign of his good pleasure. Li immersed her, and just as her eyes broke water the Easter sun burst through the clouds. As Watchman and George followed it bathed them all in its golden light.

By this act Watchman had declared where he stood. 'Lord, I leave my world behind. Your cross separates me from it for ever; and I have entered into another. I stand where you have placed me in Christ!' They returned to the meeting hall with a song in their hearts.

6

Across the Grain

Leland Wang and Watchman Nee now grew very close, sharing as they did a common zeal for the spread of the gospel among young men and women in the town and in the local schools and colleges. The street preaching went on and was carried into neighbouring villages. The long New Year holiday was used partly for this and partly for a convention for the scattered believers, to guide them in their spiritual growth. In this latter work Watchman's diligent study of the Bible began to bear fruit, for very quickly he displayed a gift and clarity of exposition that was to prove most helpful to his hearers.

In Leland Wang's home there was a room large enough for meetings, and a few would gather there for prayer and Bible study. One Sunday evening in 1922 a small group of just three persons, Leland and his wife and Watchman, remembered the Lord together in the bread and the wine.[1] They found such joy and release in thus worshipping him without the intervention of priest or minister that they began frequently to do this. After a few weeks they were joined by others, including Simon Meek, Wilson Wang, Faithful Luke, Watchman's mother and a second ex-naval officer called John Wang, unrelated to the other Wangs.[2]

Near that year's end another woman of character who has a major place in this story visited Fuzhou to conduct a gospel mission. Ruth Lee (Li Yuan-ru), small but full of fire, was a native of Tianjin employed now in a Nanjing school. Once a convinced atheist and an avid reader of Chen Du-xiu's *New Youth*, she had gone to Nanjing first as principal in a government normal school, arriving there with the boast, 'Though the whole world turn to Christianity, I will never believe!' Learning that there was already some religious interest among the girls, she searched for and publicly burned the New Testaments that several of them were reading. Two pupils, joined by a part-time teacher in the school named Christiana Cai (Tsai), set themselves therefore to pray for her conversion. One term an epidemic of plague closed the school and Ruth had to accompany some of the students back home by river to their villages. That quiet trip through the fields of spring wheat somehow brought her face to face with God as Creator. A new hunger awoke in her heart which now her secret reading of the Bible began to satisfy, until at length she found Jesus Christ as her Lord and Saviour. She then resigned her government post to find mission employment as a full-time Christian worker.[3]

Because Leland Wang had met her at the time of his own conversion in Nanjing, he invited Ruth Lee to stay on and conduct a further four days of open meetings in his home. They were remarkable meetings, crowded with men and women, old folk and young, and it was a time of great blessing. To at least one student, Faithful Luke, they were a spiritual landmark. He had attended all Dora Yu's meetings with a heart hungry for God and had eagerly participated in the two years of activities that followed; yet to him the full assurance of salvation only came through Ruth Lee's fiery preaching. Others too found the Saviour at this time and it became necessary to prolong the meetings after she had left. So night by night, while young men went out and gathered people in, Leland Wang, Watchman Nee and John Wang in turn preached Christ to mounting numbers.

That winter was exceptionally cold with the hill-tops white with snow, a thing rare on the Fujian coast. People went about hugging to themselves their little baskets of glowing charcoal as though they contained their very own spark of life. Simon Meek had gone 30 miles downriver to the narrows and across the coastal range for a brief holiday at his home town of Lianjiang. He was there for scarcely a week when a postcard arrived from Watchman. 'Most urgent,' it read. 'God is doing a big work among us and we need your help. Please return quickly.' Though the weather was appalling, and though rival armies were active in and near the city, Simon at once made the hazardous journey back over the hills to Fuzhou.

What he found amazed him. God's Spirit was at work, and the student boys and girls who had repented of their sins and believed on the Lord Jesus were quite transformed. Moved himself by the spirit of joy and humble thanksgiving manifest among them, he too dedicated himself afresh to follow the Lord in singleness of heart. 'On earth as it is in heaven,' are the words he uses to describe the days they had entered upon.

The meetings continued in strength each evening and over the weekends, and when term restarted they just went on after school. Bands of young men with gospel shirts and banners proclaiming 'Jesus is Coming' and 'Believe in the Lord Jesus Christ' went out with music, gathering people in to services that quickly filled with attentive listeners. As the days passed and enthusiasm increased, it became clear that more space was needed. Watchman went ahead and rented a house in Qishan and the Lord provided the 27 dollars that they needed for the first three months' rent. Together they made rough plank benches for seating. Simon and Watchman went into residence, to be available when not in class to serve the needs of inquirers. Each evening a band of boys came from school, washed their clothes and ate, and then went out preaching. The spiritual awakening that followed in Fuzhou is remembered as the Qishan Revival.

More ambitious outgoings for village witness occupied such public holidays as the Dragon Boat Festival. Once freed from their studies the band of young men would set out, 60 or 80 strong. They passed along by one or other of the granite-paved roads through the rice and sugar cane, where peasants clad in the same blue cotton as themselves trod endlessly the squeaking wooden water-lifts or waded deep in mud behind buffalo ploughs. Anyone literate whom they encountered on the road or at the rest houses was given a gospel tract. Men of all classes, from scholar officials to coolies and soldiers, were readily engaged in conversation, for these 'educated' boys could anywhere command a hearing. Reaching their chosen village they camped out in a borrowed church building, setting apart a room for 'prayer without ceasing' where they took turns to maintain a 24-hour watch. In the evening when the labourers were home from the fields they set out again in orderly groups, going from house to house inviting the villagers to their gospel preaching.

Simon Meek affirms that Watchman was the planner and ringleader of these ventures. As he strode out smiling and cheerful with the singing bands or guided the less experienced in their personal contacts and witness he was always looking ahead, concerned for the future of these dedicated lives and excited by the potential they offered to God. For this reason he insisted that the time not spent in evangelism be given to Bible instruction designed to unfold to them God's wonderful purpose and the high standards of discipleship set for them by Jesus himself.

For his own spiritual renewal Watchman would sometimes take the launch to Pagoda, where often up to two dozen young men and women attended the Bible classes run by the English ladies at White Teeth Rock. Margaret Barber did most of the teaching that from now on was to prove increasingly fruitful. Watchman found himself valuing more and more her counsel and friendship. Invited one day to join her in prayer, he found her in the throes of a controversy with God. God wanted something of her and she knew it, and in her heart she wanted it too. Yet it was costly and she could not bring herself to face it and give in. He listened as she pleaded with him nevertheless not to reduce his demands. All she asked for was time. 'Lord, I confess I don't like it, but do not give in to me! Please just wait, Lord, and I will give in to you!' She was so evidently sincere that he began to see in her one to whom he could safely bring his own problems, which were many.

Relations among the brothers were not always free from strain. With all his zeal and devotion to God, Watchman, as we have seen, was impatient of injustice. 'In my early days,' he recalls, 'I set myself to avoid all that was evil and to do what was good, and I seemed to make splendid progress. At that time I had a fellow worker five years my senior, and we two were always disagreeing. Moreover our disagreements were about public matters, so our disputes were public too. I would say to myself: if he insists on doing things that way I must protest, for it is not right. But protest as I would, he never gave in. I had one line of argument: right and wrong. He also had one line of argument: his seniority. He justified his every action by reasoning that he was five years older than I, a fact I could not refute, so he always won the day. I resented his unreasonableness and inwardly I never gave in, but in practice he gained his point every time.'

One day Watchman took his grievance to Miss Barber and appealed to her to arbitrate. Was that other brother right or was he? But she, knowing God, and hating pride and jealousy in herself, ignored the rights and wrongs of the situation and quietly answered, 'You had better do as he says.' Watchman was thoroughly dissatisfied. 'If I'm right,' he protested, 'why not acknowledge it? Or if I'm wrong, say so! Why tell me to do what he says?' 'Because', she replied, 'in the Lord, the younger should submit to the older.' Watchman was still a High School student and, knowing little of self-discipline, gave vent to his annoyance. 'In the Lord,' he retorted, 'if the younger is right and the older is wrong, must the younger still submit?' But she simply smiled and said once more, 'You had better do as he says.'

The trouble was that this cast a shadow over their brightest days. That spring of 1923 a first group of those newly born again had asked to be baptised. To the brothers this was a most significant time. 'Anyone who has seen men turn to Christ in a pagan land', Watchman points out, 'knows what tremendous issues are raised by baptism.' But the solemn expectancy with which they faced the occasion was somewhat marred for him by this tension in the background. Three of them were to bear responsibility together, Watchman, the brother five years older, and one seven years older than he. What, he now wondered, would happen when they discussed arrangements? Would he who always bossed his junior by five years submit in turn to his senior by seven? They met, and the unyielding brother remained unyielding, dismissing every suggestion put forward by his senior. Finally he sent them both away with the remark, 'You two can leave things to me; I shall manage them quite well.' 'What kind of logic is this?' thought Watchman, disgusted.

The day itself was in fact a highlight in their history, with 18 young men, mainly students, bearing joyful public testimony in the river to their union with Christ in death and resurrection. To the watching crowd the gospel was plainly preached. Afterwards he once more sought out Miss Barber with his problem. 'What annoys me', he protested, 'is that that brother has no place for right and wrong.' But she, always strict with herself, could therefore be most candid with others. Rising to her feet, she looked him frankly in the eyes. 'Have you,' she asked, 'right up to this moment, never seen what the life of Christ is? Do you not know the meaning of the cross? These past few months you keep asserting that you are right and your brother is wrong. But do you', she went on, 'think it right to talk as you have been talking? Do you think it right for you to come and report these matters to me? Your judgement of right and wrong may be perfectly sound, but what about your inner sense? Does the life within you not protest against your own resentful behaviour?'

By meeting him thus on his own ground she had touched him on the raw. Dumbfounded, he had to admit to himself that even when by human logic he was right, the Holy Spirit within pronounced his attitude as quite wrong.[4]

Margaret Barber often scolded Watchman in this way, yet to Faithful Luke she one day observed, 'He will become a great preacher,' and in later years he repeatedly acknowledged her influence upon the course of his life. 'I always thought of her', he says, 'as a "lighted" Christian. If I but walked into her room I was brought immediately to a sense of God. In those days I was very young and had lots of plans, lots of schemes for the Lord to sanction, a hundred and one things which I thought would be marvellous if brought to fruition. With all these I came to her to try and persuade her; to tell her that this or that was the thing to do. But before I could open my mouth she would say a few quite ordinary words – and light dawned. It simply put me to shame. My scheming was all so natural, so full of man, whereas here was one who lived for God alone. I had to cry to him, "Lord, teach me to walk that way."'

At about this time she gave him to read the life of Jeanne de la Motte Guyon (1648–1717), the French mystic imprisoned by King Louis XIV in the Bastille for her faith. In Madame Guyon's writings the note of acquiescence in the will of God greatly moved him and was to have a strong influence on his future thinking. This book somehow deepened his awareness of the things in the unseen that are eternal. Another fruit of his access to Miss Barber's bookshelves, and to the writing of G.H. Pember, Robert Govett and D.M. Panton, was a quickened sense of God's future dominion. The near return of the Lord Jesus became to him a real prospect, to be looked forward to and prepared for with a feeling of urgency. Faithful Luke recalls how at this time he expounded the books of Daniel and Revelation with enthusiasm and great effect, firing his hearers with a readiness to pay any price that would make ready the way for the coming of the Son of Man.

But not everything was going smoothly for him. At about this time, he tells us, God showed him that during the college vacation he was to go and preach the gospel on an island known to be infested with pirates. It was, he says, quite a struggle for him to be willing to do so, but he took the call seriously. What might not God do if he obeyed?

After much prayer he paid a visit to the island, which was far out in the Min Estuary. To his joy he found the people willing to receive him, and with some difficulty he rented a house, got it repaired and had everything ready. The project had caught the imagination of the brothers and 100 of them were praying for him and had contributed towards the expenses. All this time his parents raised no objection. Then, five days before he was due to set out and when all was ready packed up, they suddenly stepped in and forbade him to go! The house was prepared, the money was spent, the will of God was burning in his heart: what was he to do? His parents said 'No', and God had said, 'Honour thy father and mother.' In deep distress he sought light from God. What God told him amounted to this: 'Yes, it is my will that you go. On the other hand, it is no joy to me when you force that will through to its fulfilment. What I want you to do is to be subject to your parents; so you will just have to wait and let me work out my will in some other way.' The trouble now was that Watchman found he had no liberty to explain to others the reason for his change of plan, namely that it was his parents who had stopped him. 'All misunderstood me, therefore,' he says, 'and the one whose opinion I valued most said, "It will be difficult to trust you in future."'

He pondered this problem long and bitterly, until one day he came on Jesus' words in Matthew's Gospel about the Jerusalem temple tax: 'The sons are free: however, not to give offence to them, take the required money and give it to them, for me and for yourself.'[5] All at once he felt the weight of that 'however' – and he understood. Even Jesus could accommodate himself to those who would be offended by the liberty that was his. Years later Watchman could interpret the experience objectively in the light of the crucifixion. The will of God may be clear and unmistakable, but for us his way to it may sometimes be indirect. 'Our self-esteem is fed and nourished because we say, "I am doing the will of God!" and it leads us to think that nothing on earth should stand in the way of that. Then one day God allows something to fall across our path in order to counter that attitude. Like the cross of Christ it cuts across, not just our selfish will but – of all things! – our zeal and love for the Lord. That setback is most difficult for us to take.' At the time indeed he could not take it. All he could feel was resentment at his parents' attitude, which he largely blamed on his mother. It would take him a while to get over this.

He asked Miss Barber if she could not lend him something to read on the subject of the cross of Christ in the believer's experience. Yes, she said, she had two books, but she would not give them to him at present; she would rather wait until he was mature enough to read them. 'I could not understand the reason for this,' he says, 'and I wanted those two books very much, so I obtained them by guile. I inquired from her the titles and author without her realising what I was doing, and I wrote off to Mrs Penn-Lewis in England, who sent them to me as a gift and wrote me a nice letter as well! One was *The Word of the Cross* and the other *The Cross of Calvary and its Message*.[6] Well, I read them most carefully, but though I received help of a kind, to my disappointment they didn't settle my biggest question. To give us quick answers is not, I find, God's way.'

For the last month of the summer term of 1923 a strike closed the school, and Faithful Luke with four others took this opportunity to testify in baptism to their break with the world and their union with their Lord. Luke's experience was typical. An influential uncle hurried from Gutian in hot anger that, having been brought up an Anglican, his nephew might by his action have forfeited his prospects of a grant to enter St John's University. He urged him to repent of the step, but Luke quietly replied, 'My repentance is towards God and for my sins. I am at peace.' Even his principal had thought him out of his mind when he made his intention known. Trinity College was a doorway to state or mission employment and boys went on from there to positions often of great influence. 'Do you mean, then, that you will not go on to further study?' he asked. 'No,' was the impetuous answer, 'I am going to preach the gospel.' The missionary was sincerely troubled. Watchman, he feared, was becoming a disruptive influence in the student community. 'Go and pray,' he said, 'and come back to me after three nights.' But on his return Luke's mind was unchanged. 'I have decided', he said, 'to serve the Lord Jesus only,' and through life he never went back on this decision.

The two boys who completed the year with Faithful Luke continued training for the Department of Customs (the Mandarin route was by now no longer used), whereas he himself went to Pagoda. The English ladies were understandably full of praise for the flood of answers in recent months to their long praying, and Miss Barber invited him now to act as host for the young men coming to her for instruction, while her colleague took care of the women. He would serve God there for six years.

Now it was Watchman and Wilson who were in their final year at Trinity in a somewhat larger class. In the college through the winter months the evangelical fervour burned steadily on, and there were three daily prayer meetings among the boys, one in the early morning and two at night. In the city too the gospel witness flourished as Leland Wang and John Wang preached night by night in the little rented hall. Sunday worship there with the breaking of bread was now a regular thing. Meanwhile, Watchman gave what time he could to the spiritual growth of the converts and young workers, and even published for them a few issues of a mimeographed paper, *Revival*, embodying some of his Bible studies. The first issue of 1,400 copies was published in January 1923. The New Year conference took place again in February and with the spring vacation the gospel bands went out once more into the villages. The summer term was disturbed by severe floods that put a heavy strain on the low arches of the ancient bridge and brought cholera and plague to the riverside homes, but the boys were able to complete their college year. In the final examinations Wilson Wang came out top with Watchman Nee a close second; in fact, it was virtually a dead heat.

Watchman was now 21 years old. For graduation he wore a new ten-dollar gown bought for him by his paternal grandmother, the Guangdong lady with the caustic tongue, now happily reconciled to her daughter-in-law. But to him far the most gratifying thing of all was the fact that within the past twelve months God had won to himself scores more new converts in the Fuzhou colleges and city and in the countryside around. For this the students now met at term-end to give thanks together.

7

The Proof of Faith

From time to time during these years the Zhang family made rare home visits to Fuzhou from Shanghai, where Dr Zhang (Zhang Ru-zhou) was employed as senior surgeon in that city's largest medical institution, the Ren Ji Hospital. They and Watchman's parents had remained firm friends, and the general relaxing of strict customs of the past meant that the growing children could still meet socially. Such encounters had awakened in Watchman an interest in his one-time playmate Charity, who was both intelligent and now a very charming young lady.

But when Watchman found Jesus as his Saviour and Lord he had undergone, as we have seen, a total revolution in his outlook on life. Since then, with his school graduation, he had, like Faithful Luke before him, made another radical choice. He would not proceed to St John's University, nor pursue further his formal education as his parents had hoped. Instead, from now on he would direct his life to the task of preaching Jesus Christ to his countrymen. The decision, made from personal conviction alone, would be far-reaching. It was not long after this that he realised how much Charity Zhang had, in her absence, occupied his thoughts. There had been no hint of a match, yet at some stage the idea had certainly found lodging in his mind. He had quietly followed her progress and knew she was doing extremely well at school. However, their next encounter after a longer interval brought him to a dilemma. From their brief conversation what he already feared was all too evident. Her worldly tastes and her passion for stylish clothes seemed to him the mark of something deeper. Though a Christian in name, she in no way shared his compelling love for the Lord with its new scale of values, but had other goals of her own, ambitions for success in the world's eyes that he himself could no longer entertain. The directions in which they each were heading clearly diverged.

For a while he shelved the problem, until one day he opened his Bible at Psalm 73. In verse 25 he read, 'There is none on earth, O God, that I desire beside Thee' – and abruptly the Spirit of God arrested him. 'You have, do you not? a consuming desire upon earth: your attachment for Miss Zhang. What qualifications has she to be a preacher's wife?' His response was an attempt to bargain. 'Lord, I will do anything for you. If you want me to carry your good news to the unreached tribes I am willing to go; but this thing only I cannot do.' With himself just coming up to 21, how could he detach his mind from one who for long had so pleasurably engaged it?

He threw himself into the work of the gospel yet further. There were many doors open to him, and after participating acceptably in the New Year conference in Fuzhou he gave himself to village work and especially to the instruction of new believers. Here he soon learned new lessons. 'For a year after my conversion,' he tells us, 'I had had a lust to preach. It was impossible for me to stay silent. Something was moving within me that drove me forward and I had to keep going. Preaching had become my very life.' He had had a good education and was by now well versed in the Scriptures, so naturally he considered himself thoroughly capable of instructing village folk, of whom the women in particular were mostly illiterate. But now, after several visits to one group to help confirm them in their faith, his self-esteem was sorely deflated. Despite their illiteracy these women had come, he discovered, to an intimate knowledge of the Lord Jesus. 'I knew', he says, 'the Book they haltingly read; they knew the One of whom the Book spoke. The Spirit of God was himself instructing them.' Watchman was learning humility. There was no flagging of his zeal, but he was encountering a divine principle of fruit-bearing, that 'apart from me you can do nothing'.[1]

At this time also, with his college grant ended and no paid employment in prospect, he began to face what it was going to mean to trust God for his material needs. From among books borrowed from the English ladies' bookshelves he was greatly influenced by accounts of the faith of George Müller of Bristol and Hudson Taylor of the China Inland Mission.[2] These men had shown their confidence in the unseen by putting to proof God's sufficiency for the seen and tangible needs of his work, as well as for their own lives. Nearer at hand Margaret Barber herself was to him a living example of this. She had started from Britain with no guaranteed backing beyond the assurance of a faithful Hebrew Christian: 'If it is God who sends you, he will be responsible.' Often, Watchman knew, she had been down to her last dollar, but God had never yet failed her. In 1923 she had spoken to the brothers of her prayer for a ten-room hostel for expansion of her work at Customs Point, with no idea whatever of how this might be provided. Watchman was astounded when a little later a neighbouring industrial school ceased operation and God caused its 20 rooms to become available to her at a paltry rental.

Such faith was infectious. He was there one weekend when a friend of his with $2 in his pocket was in urgent need of $150 by the Monday morning, and the mail boat did not run on Saturdays or Sundays. After committing the matter to God, this brother went out preaching and met a man who reminded him of a $1 debt, which he paid at once. The other coin still in his pocket now assumed a new value, and when he met a beggar he thought of changing it into brass cash before making a gift; but God checked him and he gave the whole coin to the beggar. As that dollar went out, God came in. He returned home and slept peacefully, and on the Monday morning by telegram he received a wholly unforeseen gift of $150.

To Watchman this divine principle of 'give, and it will be given to you' was to become a rule of life. If we would concern ourselves solely with the needs of others, then God, he believed, would make all our concerns his own. But he went further. We should never, he held, divulge to others our own financial needs, even when such secrecy might lead our friends to misread our poverty as wealth. Moreover, aside from brief hospitality, we should 'take nothing from the Gentiles' for God's work, and thus avoid placing him under obligation to unbelievers.[3]

He was soon to put these principles to the test. A classmate of his, Wei Guang-xi (K.H. Weigh), had earlier left Trinity to go on to Nanjing University, and just now was at home in Jianou (Kienning), where his father was a doctor in the English Church Mission Hospital. Some 150 miles upriver from Fuzhou, Jianou is situated deep in the mountains at the confluence of several streams, and is a centre of the paper industry and an emporium of inland trade. In the spring of 1924 Watchman received an invitation from the Mission to address a series of evangelistic meetings there. He felt sure his expenses would be met, and after prayer he wired in reply that he would set out on the Friday.

The problem was how to get there. He had only some $30 in hand and the fare by motorboat would cost $80 at the very least. What was worse, he became aware that here in Fuzhou another brother in Christ was in at least as much financial need as himself. When, that Thursday, God reminded him of this he knew he must act, and with much trepidation therefore Watchman sent him a gift of $20 by the hand of Leland Wang.

Next morning no one gave Watchman anything before he left, and as he crossed by ferry to the anchorage with a mere $10 in his pocket he prayed in desperation, 'Lord, I am not asking you for money; only to be taken to Jianou!' Upon arrival at the landing stage he was accosted by the owner of a small steam-launch, who asked him, 'Are you going to Nanping or Jianou?' 'To Jianou,' he replied. 'Come with me, then. I can take you.' 'For how much?' 'Only seven dollars.' Amazed, while eagerly lifting his baggage aboard he asked the reason. The boat, he learned, was under county charter, but the owner was free to earn a little extra by letting a seat to one passenger if the hirers did not need it. Thus he made the long journey unmolested by brigands and free of endless delays from *likin* tax collectors at Shuikou, Nanping and other stopping points.

It was a scenically beautiful trip, the first section through a fertile half-hilly country where here and there the slopes were clothed with groves of *longiens, lychees* and *pomelos*, and of the green and golden oranges that Watchman had loved from childhood. He was expressing a widely held view when he used to say with pride, 'I think there are no oranges in the world to equal those of Fujian.'[4] Further upriver the pine-clad mountains drew in close and there were jagged rocks and floating timber to negotiate in the swirling waters as beneath frowning cliffs the boat chugged its slow way to their destination.

At Jianou Watchman preached throughout the two weeks with much liberty in the Word. His messages were well received, and his friend K.H. Weigh was one who entered into a new blessing there and dedicated himself afresh to God. At the end there was a farewell meal at which Archdeacon Hugh Phillips took the young preacher aside. He was a man of long experience and the survivor of incredible hardships undergone for the gospel's sake. 'We have been much helped by your preaching,' he said. 'Please may I share in your expenses?' Impetuously Watchman replied, 'There is no need. All is fully provided.' Truth to tell, he was uneasy about accepting missionary help. God, he felt sure, would work in his own way. But next day, with a balance of $1.20 in his pocket, on the road to the river with many new friends coming to see him off, he found himself praying, 'Lord, you can't just bring me here and not take me home again!' Halfway to the boat a messenger overtook him with a note from the missionary: 'Although you have someone to pay your fare, please by accepting the enclosed let this aged brother play a small part.' Recognising God's hand in this, he accepted the token of fellowship. It proved to go far beyond his expenses, for the same chartered boat was there ready to return, with the same seat vacant at the same cut price. On the exhilarating run down the Min rapids his heart was at peace. Back once more in Fuzhou, he discovered too that his own gift to the fellow worker before starting out had met a really desperate need.

It was an experience he would not forget. As he put it later, the way of God is not 'save and you shall grow rich', but 'give, and it shall be given to you, good measure, pressed down, shaken together, running over'.[5]

However, there was another area where Watchman saw there was need and this was in the matter of self-preparation. He seems already to have glimpsed the fact that the preacher matters to God at least as much as the message he delivers. God, he saw, needed first to work out in his life what he would proclaim through him. He continued to edit *Revival*, the small devotional paper which he had begun to publish as early as January 1923. It consisted almost entirely of his Bible expositions, reproduced as spoken, supplemented by translated extracts chosen from a few Western spiritual writers. *Revival* appeared at irregular intervals as God sent him the money in small gifts of a few dollars and cents, and it was distributed without subscription to all who asked for it. With its helpful messages setting forth God's redemptive purpose in Christ, the little magazine soon found its way further afield and this led to fresh invitations for his preaching and personal testimony.

In Nantai, however, a subtle change had come about in Watchman's relationship with his colleagues operating from the rented hall. It is by no means clear in detail what led the two older brothers, Leland Wang and John Wang with the support of a few more, to put him out of their fellowship. True, he had disappointed them over the pirate island venture. Yet not this, but one single issue of principle is quoted by those involved at the time, and it seems a surprising one to have arisen in so young a group.

In his search for new avenues of outreach and for a fresh breakthrough in the work of the gospel, Watchman had sought to return to first things. God, he saw, is the Originator of any work truly to be called his, and God too must be its goal. But what of the task between? Was he not also, in a sense, its Agent – the One who must empower it all? Here, he felt, was something Christians generally overlooked. He put it this way: 'When we see a man of keen intellect, eloquent, energetic and with administrative flair, we say, "What an asset that man would be to the cause of Christ!" But this is like saying that while the beginning must be of God and the end for him, the middle is within man's power to accomplish.' Notwithstanding the evangelical zeal with which Watchman drove himself so unstintingly, he was haunted by the statement of Jesus that 'the Son can do nothing of himself, but what he sees the Father doing', and by God's no less explicit words to Paul: 'My strength is made perfect in weakness.'[6] The latter he saw not just as a re-assurance to believers, but as a principle of Christian life. An element of divine miracle seemed to him the mainspring of all true achievement for God.

During the previous New Year's holiday Watchman had tried, in a series of addresses long to be remembered, to express this view in some talks to the believers. Expounding a passage of Old Testament history, he had drawn an analogy between the testimony of God as expressed in Israel's ark of the covenant borne before them through the wilderness and the witness of his people today. (Nee would later become known for his sometimes helpful excursions into allegory.) He reminded his hearers that at Jericho the ark, symbolising the Lord's own presence, had accomplished that city's downfall. Later on in a sorry day of defeat, whereas the priestly ritual might still linger on at Shiloh, it was that same ark in exile that God stood by, to the acute discomfiture of its Philistine captors.[7] Like the eventual temple of King Solomon, city churches are by definition local (and so much missionary enterprise, he well knew, led to structures and institutions that were by their nature static). Something more flexible, more mobile, seemed needed. The question Watchman asked was, 'How might God today have a work with mobile workers to which, as he did the ark, he could equally commit himself?' In his own mind he was pondering already how God might more widely win to himself the people of China.

Developing this thought further, he pointed next to an item in the ark's contents, namely Aaron's rod that had once budded. It had been set there as a memorial of a historic occasion: a dark night and a resurrection morning.[8] He believed this hinted at God's one sure way of fruitfulness for every servant of his. We do not accomplish God's work merely by yielding to the appeal of open doors and great opportunities. There is sometimes also a darkness to be endured with patience for the sake of a new dawn. When that dawn breaks God will disclose buds and flowers beyond man's power to produce. In the case of our Lord Jesus that resurrection life blossomed and fruited in its fullest sense when he pleased his Father by assenting to endure, with heaven closed above him, the darkness and death of the cross. 'The Son of Man must suffer,' he had said. While in such experiences the disciple follows his Master only at a distance, yet 'the servant is in no way greater than his Lord'.[9]

Those New Year studies had appeared in print in the occasional magazine he edited, one issue of which had been paid for with Archdeacon Phillips' gift at Jianou.[10] What to the others may have seemed a too quietistic approach to active Christian service perhaps provoked their disapproval.[11] But aside from differences of outlook among them, there were also external pressures. With the

Anti-Christian Movement at high pitch in the cities, some in mission circles would certainly have preferred the student witness to take less uncompromising forms. Few could deny the stature of Leland Wang and John Wang, both strikingly converted ex-naval officers. Hopefully men such as these might be 'contained' within some part of the foreign missions establishment. Indeed, Leland Wang had lately chosen this course by receiving in Shanghai formal ordination as a priest at missionary hands, thereby making easier in their circles his wide acceptance as an evangelist. Fair enough, but Watchman did not seek this and, by contrast, may have seemed less pliant and thus a potential source of division, just at a time when any appearance of disarray in the Christian cause would be better covered up. Attempts were now being made by some of the mission-staffed colleges to forbid students from attending the revival meetings, and one missionary at least had categorised Watchman Nee outright as 'a devil and a deceiver of many'. Was this becoming a more widely held view?

For one or more of these reasons Watchman was asked by the Wangs to discontinue worshipping with the group. Many very soon regretted the step taken and by most the decision was later reversed. 'We did a very foolish thing,' one of them observes, 'but maybe we were moved also by envy, for our brother in Christ was so much more gifted than the rest of us.' Yet for a while reservations about his preaching remained, and to his great sorrow the breach with a few of the brothers was never completely healed.

Watchman admits that his excommunication shook him from his rest in Christ and plunged him deep into discouragement. In this state he took the ferry across to Customs Point to seek out his friend and counsellor. 'It has come to this!' he exclaimed, and outlined to her what had happened.

Miss Barber said very little in reply, indicating by her silence how much she felt for him in his sorrow. Nevertheless, he went from her with his spirit lifted and his courage renewed. Next he found Faithful Luke who, while remaining loyal to the older brothers in Fuzhou, had been deeply grieved by their break with his friend. Together they sought God in prayer. Watchman was realistic enough to value criticism from any source and he humbly put to God his question: notwithstanding the many real conversions they had witnessed this very year, had he in some way displeased him? Had he given the brothers just ground for their attitude? As they prayed together, the answer came clearly in their hearts: 'Leave your problem with me. Go now and preach the good news!'

8

Foreign Fields

In 1924 Watchman went to Zhejiang Province to speak at meetings in Hangzhou City, and thence overland to Nanjing, capital of Jiangsu Province and a main centre too of missionary enterprise. To gain experience in publishing he worked there for some months with the Spiritual Light Publishing Society of the Presbyterian Mission, where his friend Ruth Lee was now on the editorial staff. He valued the technical training the missionaries offered and was glad to serve with them as a brother in Christ. Returning by way of Shanghai, he heard news of Charity. It was long now since they had met, but he could not yet rid his mind of her. At college in Tianjin she was, he learned, doing brilliantly and hoped in due course to proceed to Beijing and a place in Yanjing University. Of her social interests, however, what he discovered merely deepened the conviction that if he would follow the Lord utterly he must abandon thoughts of her. Sorrowfully, therefore, he set himself to eliminate her from his thinking. He went to his room, knelt and committed the matter firmly and finally to God, and then wrote his poem 'Boundless Love'.

What length, breadth, height and depth!
What greatness is His love!
How else could I, a sinner vile,
Be in such grace and bliss?
My Lord has paid the price
That I might ransomed be;
So, willingly I'll bear the cross,
And follow faithfully.
The dearest things of earth,
I gladly leave behind;
Nor life, nor death can hold me back–
'Tis Christ my soul would find.
Jesus my gracious Lord,
My true comfort to be;
Whom have I on earth or in heav'n
To love, save only Thee?[1]

One morning, while passing through Shanghai, Watchman's Bible reading brought him to the words of Jesus: 'I must preach the good news of the kingdom of God to other cities also; for I was sent for this purpose.'[2] Shortly afterwards there came a telegram from his mother: 'I have been invited to preach the gospel in Malaya. Are you free to accompany me?'

A month or so earlier at a friend's birthday feast Ni He-ping had met a visitor from Malaya named Chen, a man ethically much confused and in evident spiritual need. She felt the Lord say to her, 'I preached to the woman of Samaria. Now you tell to him the words of life!' He had, it appeared, heard of the wonderful conversion of the Ni mother and son, and when she testified to him he responded eagerly to the claims of God upon him. Now from Perak State he wrote appealing to her on behalf of his home church in Sitiawan, few of whose members, he explained, knew the salvation in Christ that he himself had found. Would she come and preach the gospel to them also? He would pay all travel expenses and they would be the guests of his sister and brother-in-law, Mr and Mrs Ling Ti-kang, both sincere Christians. He-ping laid the matter before the Lord, and he gave her confirmation in the same words from Luke's Gospel: 'I must preach the good news to other cities also.' With this assurance she had cabled Watchman, who now joined her from Shanghai.

They set out in November 1924 for what would become a fruitful six-month journey. Travelling via Singapore and Ipoh, they reached Sitiawan to find a warm welcome in the Ling home. Their reception at the Methodist church, however, was cooler. 'A month ago,' the pastor observed, 'two Americans held revival meetings here for which we put forth much effort to gather in church members. The first day there were over 300 present, the second 60, the third only 12. Now the situation is much worse, for all are out tapping the rubber trees and we have no free time except on Sundays.'

When they arrived next evening at the church, the door was locked. They sought out the pastor and found him calculating the day's yield of latex. He had, he explained, forgotten the meeting time. Showing no displeasure they took the key and opened up, setting to work to clean out the building with a borrowed broom, while an Indian believer stood in the street inviting folk in. The numbers at first were discouraging, until Watchman in his personal testimony alluded to the words in Luke, 'I must preach the good news to other cities also.' Then He-ping realised how God had used the identical Scripture to call them each forth on this venture. Greatly encouraged, she proclaimed the Word now with increased liberty and fire. Many repented with tears, confessing their sins, and there was much setting right of wrongs. Now the numbers rose steadily to a capacity 300 and beyond, with overflow crowds standing listening at the windows. Only the pastor was cautious of so much emotion, and after 16 days felt it right to terminate the meetings. Even then, at the Lings' invitation, they continued in homes a while longer with Bible studies designed to establish the new believers in the Word. Before leaving Sitiawan, Watchman cabled Faithful Luke to come and follow up this work, but it was some years before the latter felt the call to make Malaysia and Indonesia his own field of service.

During these weeks Mrs Ni had found herself very much at ease in the Ling home, and was particularly taken with their eldest daughter, Ai-qian, a promising young Christian. In her she thought she saw the perfect match for her son. She spoke to the girl's parents about this and communicated with her docile husband, but with little reference to Watchman. Other preaching invitations held them in Malaya for a while longer and thus the families met again. Impetuously He-ping pressed the matter, forgetting her own bitter experience as a girl, while filial obedience demanded that Watchman suppress his doubts. In due course a formal exchange of cards and a small feast proclaimed a betrothal that was almost at once to prove a source of great unrest of heart to him. For while he and his mother were still in Singapore awaiting a northbound ship, a schoolteacher with designs of his own on Miss Ling came to Watchman with a false but plausible story defaming her character. Watchman was most reluctant to believe it, yet the effect on him was to heighten his own sense of uncertainty. In a matter so deeply affecting God's purpose for his life, he was desperate to take no false step. He spent agonising days in prayer, weighing before God what he should do, and eventually, on reaching Shanghai, he told his mother that God was giving him no liberty to go on with the arrangement. He prevailed upon her to return the tokens of betrothal, while he himself wrote to the Lings as courteously as he could explaining his position.

His mother found this difficult to accept, for she already loved Ai-qian as a daughter. There was thus some coolness between them as, at the invitation of Dr Mary Stone (Shi Mei-yu), they next ministered the Word at her Bethel Hospital in Shanghai. But then an invitation to He-ping to give her testimony at the Western Girls' School (McTyeire School for Girls) brought things into perspective by recalling to her her own unwelcome betrothal while a student there, and she began to see things Watchman's way. On the coastwise boat home to Fuzhou, she was ready to admit that she could have been mistaken.

On these ventures the appeal of Watchman's own preaching lay first of all in his gift of making so plain the way to God that at the outset relies solely upon Christ's finished work. All too many Christians, having been given wrong priorities, were striving after a salvation based on merit earned by their own good works, a way that is little removed in principle from Buddhism. It is presumptuous, they were told, to say with assurance that you are saved. Thus it was that the preaching of new life as God's free gift amazed them by its novelty. Of course Watchman did not stop there, for a walk on earth 'alive to God' and pleasing him flows from that transforming miracle. He himself was finding now much personal help from the writings of Andrew Murray and F.B. Meyer on the practical life of holiness and deliverance from sin. He read, too, all he could of Charles G. Finney on Christian revival, and of Evan Roberts and the Welsh spiritual awakening of 1904–5. He delved into Otto Stockmayer and Jessie Penn-Lewis on the questions of soul and spirit and of triumph over Satanic power. His own New Testament study supported the view that here were great issues of Christian experience that must somehow be brought in simple terms to his fellow believers.

As such themes began to appear in his addresses, and over the years were reproduced in the magazine, they met with a warm response from readers throughout Fujian Province and far beyond. No doubt much that he proclaimed was but the fruit of diligent study by an acute mind, and needed still to be worked out in his own experience. Yet with the enthusiasm of youth he was soon turning over in his mind the idea of writing in the Chinese vernacular a compendium of the spiritual life of the Christian. So much of what he had read and rejoiced in found no mention at all in the mission churches around him. He would be called as speaker to a convention and would tell his hearers that to receive forgiveness of sins and the assurance of salvation was but the beginning. A man must learn to know the risen Saviour as his very life, for only so might he hope to display conduct giving pleasure to his God.

They would listen eagerly. These were fresh ideas to folk who thought of the gospel as designed only for sinners – a promise of heaven which, once trusted in, had no more to offer them in the present than comfort in adversity. So the theory had been, 'Receive the Saviour and then turn to a human philosophy of life.' This went some way to explain how the ideas of Confucius and Mencius contrived still to carry nearly equal weight with the Bible in many nominally Christian homes.

How infinitely far removed was this from the fruits of the new birth! It gave no place at all to the indwelling Spirit of

God. Watchman was coming more and more to lean upon
the Holy Spirit who, in one of his roles, is the teacher of the
unlearned. He had discovered one day a humble tailor
named Chen who, months before, had picked up and read
the detached last page of the Gospel of Mark. Lacking any
Christian teacher or scholar to counsel him (or perhaps
warn him of the dubious attribution of these verses to Mark
himself!), this man had selected from verse 18 what he concluded was the least of the signs listed there, namely that of
healing. Trusting God, he set off down the village street to
put the Scriptures to the proof. Then, convinced by a neighbour's dramatic recovery from illness, he simply went back
to his tailoring to witness there faithfully for Christ.

Experiences such as this helped to resolve one difficulty
that had troubled Watchman. He tells us that in his early
days he was much afraid of meeting an atheist or a modern
'higher critic', lest such a man should demonstrate to him
that the Bible was untrustworthy, and thus undermine his
faith. But as, both personally and in the lives of others, he
came face to face with the living Christ, he knew he had the
answer. To all their arguments he could safely reply, 'Yes,
there is reason in what you say; but I know my God. That is
enough.'

In another village a newly believing farmer and his friend
had faced a crisis. Their strips of rice field lay close to an irrigation stream on the terraced hillside from which they daily
drew water for their paddy. But one night as they slept a
neighbour with land beneath them on the slope defrauded
them of their essential and laboriously pumped supply by
breaching the clay of their retaining bank and running it off
on to his own land. Next morning they saw what had happened but, controlling themselves, said nothing. Again they
raised their water, and again next night it was all drained

off. Still they uttered no word of protest when at dawn they discovered the mean trick the man had played on them. This went on for seven successive days, and they were justly irritated. Were they not Christians, and should not Christians be patient? The Scriptures speak of loving your enemies, rejoicing in sufferings, and counting it pure joy when you meet various trials,[3] and their restraint seemed irreproachable. In desperation they went to some older believers for advice. 'It is unjust!' they exclaimed. 'How is it that, having suffered all this wrong for a full week and kept faith with God, we are still unhappy? Tell us in this situation what we should rightly do next.'

One of those senior brothers had some experience. First they all knelt together in prayer; then he replied, 'If we do the right thing and no more, then surely we are unprofitable servants. We ourselves should go beyond what is merely right. Maybe you are not yet happy because you have not gone the full distance. Let me suggest that you try going the second mile.[4] First yourselves irrigate that farmer's paddy field, and after that irrigate your own. Go back and test it out, and see whether or not your hearts find rest.'

They agreed to try, and next morning were early afoot. Carrying forth their wooden trough with its 'dragon's backbone' water-lift[5] and going to work once more on its treadmill, they made it their first task to irrigate the field of their enemy who had so persistently robbed their own field of its water. And now this amazing thing happened: the more they laboured in the day's intense heat watering their persecutor's land, the happier they became. By the time, in late afternoon, they had finished lifting sufficient also for their own paddy field, their hearts were at perfect rest.

When the brothers had repeated this for two or three

days the man came with his friends, dumbfounded, to apologise. With every show of sincerity he asked for the explanation. 'If this is Christianity,' he said, 'then we want to hear more about it,' and soon he too was drinking in the Word of life.

In telling this episode Watchman was distinguishing between the principle of right and wrong and the principle of life. 'Those two had been most patient,' he explains. 'They had laboured to irrigate their paddy, and without a word of complaint had suffered others to steal their water. Was that not very good? They had done all that man could require of them, but God was not yet satisfied. They lacked peace of heart because they had not met the demands of his life. When however they conformed to his standards, joy and peace welled up in their hearts.

'What is the Sermon on the Mount?' he continues. 'What does Jesus teach in Matthew chapters 5 to 7? Is it not this, that we dare not be satisfied with less than what meets the demands of the new life God has put within us? It does not teach that provided we do what is right, then all is well. No, we overlook the inner life whereby his Holy Spirit moves us to further action. Many say that Matthew 5 to 7 is too difficult. It is beyond us. I admit that it is. It is sheer impossibility. But here is the point. You have an inner life, a Person close at hand, and in a given situation that new life tells you that unless you do as the Sermon on the Mount requires (and "love" is a key word) you will lack rest. The whole question lies here: are you walking in the way of good and evil, or in the way of life?'[6]

It was devotion to God and his Word of the kind displayed by those simple villagers that in the ensuing years Watchman felt called to foster and serve. Here were people who took the Bible seriously. Here was a true fellowship of newborn souls. In it he began to see both the essence of God's church on earth and the spearhead of his Holy Spirit's witness to paganism. Every least child of God should be such a testimony to the gospel's transforming power. Every small, fragile group of his own should become a centre of worship and witness where the will of God is discovered and sincerely pursued, and where Christ is encountered in his living presence.

9

A Fruitful Ministry

Watchman went down to Ma-shan, a small village on the north shore of the Min between Pagoda Island and Mawei, and there he rented a tiny hut with a window looking across to the deep-water anchorage with its splendid scenery and its constant movement of river craft and ocean-going vessels. Upriver lay the Mawei shipyard and nautical training school. Just downstream on Luo-xing (Falling Star) Island in the elbow of the river stood the 90 foot high pagoda that gave the anchorage its name. Here, where the two arms of the Min reunited that for eight miles had encompassed Nantai Island, the scour of the river's waters had produced depth enough for big freighters to lie in midstream. Above rose the hills, some cultivated in terraces almost to the summit, others so steep as to admit only a stunted growth of firs. About the shipping sampans and lighters bustled, their decks echoing to the gulls' cries and the rhythmic 'Woo-ho, woo-ho, woo-ho!' of perspiring coolies.

Here at Ma-shan, living very simply, Watchman made his base from his twenty-second to his twenty-fourth year for what was to be a period of transition and spiritual growth in his life. For some of this time Watchman was in indifferent health, afflicted with a cough, and when this was so he gave himself to studying and meditating on the Word, and to wide reading of borrowed books that ranged from Alford and Westcott on the Scriptures to the lives of Luther, Knox, Jonathan Edwards, George Whitefield and David Brainerd. When again he was fit he divided his attention between preaching tours and more serious work on the magazine he had tentatively issued.

He began to set himself goals. While at school he had tried to ride a bicycle by fixing his eyes on its handlebars with the idea that if these were steady he would ride straight, whereas all that happened in the narrow streets was that he constantly ran against walls and grazed his knuckles. Then a friend who could ride showed him where the fault lay. 'Look off at the road,' he said. 'Keep your eyes fixed on the way ahead.' He now sought to apply this principle to his work for God.

Ma-shan now became the base for his preaching tours. One or two young brothers stayed with him for fellowship, and Faithful Luke was not far away at White Teeth Rock across the water. About this time the doctor in charge of a CMS hospital downriver, a Miss Li, approached Watchman. She had adopted and brought up a boy whom she had named Guo-qing, but he had turned out to be a disappointment. At the age of 16 he was expelled from school, and in desperation she brought him to Ma-shan and appealed to Watchman for help. So he took him in and gave time to teaching him the Bible, and before long the lad trusted his life to Jesus. To his mother's delight and that of her whole family his conduct bore convincing witness to the change.

With January 1926 the Lunar New Year approached and

with it the usual holiday convention in Fuzhou, drawing together, as before, believers from in and around the city. But this year, with the break in fellowship with the brothers there, Watchman decided to use the time for gospel outreach. Watchman says he rarely spoke publicly of the incident that follows, so deeply had it moved him, but it is recorded once in his gospel preaching some three years later. It was told to assure would-be atheists that there is, after all, a living God who answers prayer (and he mentions too where six eyewitnesses might then be found). He also told it in some detail in the author's hearing in 1938, and ten years later one of those six, Faithful Luke, kindly added some details.[1]

It happened that Faithful Luke's adoptive mother was working just then as a midwife in a fishing community of some 2,000 families on an island named Mei-hua, 'mayflower village', in the north part of the Min estuary where it opens out east into the Pacific. A place of pagan darkness, its people were wholly ignorant of the gospel of Jesus Christ. Faithful Luke and Watchman with four others resolved now to spend part of the New Year holiday preaching Christ to the villagers there. At the last minute the newly converted Li Guo-qing came along too, making up a team of seven. Watchman wrote ahead to a former Trinity student, now head teacher of the island school, but when coming off the steamship they proved to be preachers he refused them use of the empty school premises as a base for their witness. They then searched until dark for a place to stay and eventually bedded down on planks and straw in an attic, above the shop of a kindly herbalist.

Next day, the seventh of the First Month,[2] they ventured out for the first time to preach. During the holiday the island population of fishers and farmers, freed from their normal tasks, occupied themselves variously in social entertaining, ancestor worship, payment of annual debts, gambling, displays of fireworks, disbursement of charity, preparing celebrations, and honouring with gifts of food their household gods. Even so, between such scattered concerns some at least should be free to listen and talk.

'But,' says Watchman, 'an unusual atmosphere seemed to pervade the entire village. The people were most courteous, but after hearing a little they would stop us and walk away mumbling something. When we asked them why, nobody would give a reason. We were much perplexed, for we found all seven of us had had the same experience. We inquired of the herbalist who was generally frank with us, but even he would not discuss the matter. On the following days we tried again to preach and sell Gospels across the island, but it was hard going.

'When by the ninth day there was still no response to our approaches, young Li Guo-qing committed a serious blunder. Impatient with our prolonged silent treatment he seized on a villager and demanded an explanation. "Don't you see," blurted the man, "we have enough gods already and have no need of another. Moreover we serve here one wholly dependable Lord, Da-wang (the Great King), honouring him each New Year with a splendid procession through the streets on a perfect sunny day. You have come at the wrong time since this year his choice, disclosed by augury, is the 11th, two days hence. We know that will be a day of sunshine since for 286 years past there has never been rain on the day Da-wang chooses. We are all too occupied with him now to heed talk of your Jesus."

'So exasperated by this was Li, our headstrong teenager, that impetuously he cried, "Then I promise you that our God, the true God, will this year bring rain here on the 11th day!"

At once many younger villagers seized on the challenge. "Say no more. If it rains on the 11th then your Jesus is indeed God. We will be ready to hear him." Borne thus by them the news spread like wildfire through the little town: "A group of preachers has just promised that rain would fall on Da-wang's festal day!" Within two hours all knew of it; and among the youth speculative talk went: "With rain once more absent Da-wang will be confirmed as god; but if conceivably it should rain, is then this Jesus . . . ?" – and they hesitated.

'I had been preaching elsewhere in Mei-hua, and when we others returned to the herbalist's house and learned of the affair I was horrified. The Lord's honour seemed rashly put to hazard. "How could you have made such a declaration?" I protested to the young Li. "*You* have no control over heaven!" Shamefaced: "Well, let us go and pray," he whispered contritely. "Indeed we may pray," I said, "but will God answer our prayer? Is this according to his will?"

'Nevertheless, we all began praying. Though supper was prepared, we had no heart to eat it. All seven of us must, I knew, share responsibility for this. Here we had lightly committed God to something he might be unwilling to support. Yet were he not to support it, what future could his gospel have in the islands? Had we in our pride sinned irrevocably? Should we leave now and let this "Great King" reign? In deep humility we sought the Lord, ready to receive his rebuke.

'We continued thus addressing God until all felt at peace and free of anxiety. To assure me personally there had come the words of Elisha when recrossing the Jordan after losing his master: "Where is the Lord, the God of Elijah?" The river that had divided before the two of them had opened also to him alone.[3] Would not heaven open to us? But I did not at once share this with the others, for every one of us seemed to be quite sure of God's answer. Only then did we eat our supper.

'As we did so we told the herbalist, "We all know now that it will rain for Da-wang's procession on the 11th." "In my opinion," he replied, "it will not rain; and I advise you not carelessly to assert otherwise. For one thing, among the 2,000 families living in Mei-hua almost all the men live by the sea. Would they fail to know the weather? They regularly forecast it some days ahead. But secondly, please consider my little shop. I live by keeping this shop; so kindly do not implicate me in this affair. Da-wang", our host went on, "is a true guardian of peace and tranquillity, protecting his worshippers from sickness, their fields from pestilence and their women in childbirth.[4] On his festal day he can be counted on to reward their zeal with cloudless skies."'

With this, some of the party were sorely tempted to ask God for rain then and there, but Watchman could now reassure them with the words from Elisha's story he had earlier received from God. So clear now was their assurance that next morning they went out and themselves broadcast the challenge widely. Then, so as not to waste time, they left the scene and crossed to a nearby island – in fact the pirate island of Watchman's earlier disappointment – where at once three families turned to Christ, confessing him and publicly burning their idols. They returned late that night, tired but rejoicing.

'Next morning,' continues Watchman, 'we all slept in later than usual. As I lay by a small window, the light of the sun's direct rays shone in my eyes. "This is not rain!" I thought. "What shall we do?" It was already past seven o'clock. So I knelt down and started to pray, and as one by one the brothers awoke they knelt and joined me. "O God, this is the day to show forth your glory. Please send the rain to prove that you are indeed God." We all began praying most earnestly – but then once again the words rang in my ears, "Where is the Lord, the God of Elijah?" I saw our weakness. Why pray thus when God had already answered? Humbled, I led them downstairs in silence.

'We sat down to our breakfast, the seven of us and our host, all very quiet. There was not a cloud in the sky, yet we knew God was committed. As team leader I tried to boost their spirits by telling the one responsible that he need prepare no picnic lunch, since it would rain today and we would not be going out. We said grace before eating, and suddenly one brother continued to request God to keep his faith with us. "Yes," I said, "I think the time is indeed up. Rain must come now. We can bring it to the Lord's remembrance."

'Quietly we did so and once more the assurance came, now with no hint of rebuke: "Where is the Lord, the God of Elijah?" As we finished our rice *congee* we heard a few drops on the tiles. Looking at each other, we knew what it meant. As we went for a second bowl I asked the others whether we ought to pray. "Ask God", one said, "to send a downpour and prove it is no mere chance: he sends it on purpose!" While we prayed the sky began to turn pitch dark and there came a steady shower which grew heavier and heavier. By the time we had returned to and finished our second bowl, heaven had opened and the rain was coming down, as they say, in bucketfuls. The street outside was already deep in water and the three shallow steps at the herbalist's house door were soon covered.

'And what of the villagers? After breakfast we stood at

the door of the little shop watching for Da-wang. His public procession had been announced for 9.00 in the morning, but rain poured down without stopping from 9 to 11 o'clock. Already a few younger ones, we learned afterwards, had begun to say openly, "There is God; there is no more Da-wang, for rain keeps him indoors!" But his priest and worshippers were not to be put off. Since by tradition the event must not be postponed more than an hour, the bearers lifted shoulder-high his image in its sedan chair, ready to carry him out through the streets. Surely he would dispose of the first mere shower! Then began the downpour. They emerged from his temple, and the rain did not stop. After only a few steps the bearers stumbled. One fell into the water which was already three times ankle depth; and down, too, went Da-wang, fracturing three fingers, his left arm and his jaw, and badly twisting his head. Still determined, they picked up the image, adjusted the head, reseated him and marched on. A few young people following shouted, "Woe is Da-wang this year! Woe is Da-wang!" Yet somehow, slipping and stumbling, they dragged or carried him back and forth through half the streets of Mei-hua before the floods defeated them. Some village elders, old men of 60 to 80 years, bareheaded and without umbrellas as their faith in Da-wang's weather required, had fallen and were in serious difficulties. The procession had to be halted, and the image was carried into the family shrine of the Chens.

'There that noontime fresh divination was made. "Da-wang had never intended to come forth at all today," came the answer. "His correct day this year is the 14th, with the procession at 6 o'clock in the evening." The old people accepted the verdict, but many youngsters protested. To us this news came with the immediate assurance from God that he would act again. The afternoon was now free, and at lunchtime we asked him to clear up the sky so that we might go out and preach. Since we must leave on the morning of the 15th, "Lord," we asked, "please send rain at 6.00 on the evening of the 14th and give us meanwhile fine days of sunshine until then." The sky cleared at once, and now we had a good audience and quickly sold all the Gospels we carried.' (And knowing Watchman, who would never have children himself, one can imagine him buying two of the New Year loose-skinned *kek* oranges for young Li, as a gesture of reconciliation!)

'In the three short days remaining God gave us over 30 real converts in Mei-hua and we made many friends. At last the 14th came, another perfect day, and we could feel the people's rising tension and expectancy; yet still we had a good hearing. We now decided to hold that evening a gospel meeting in the herbalist's shop – for by now he too had believed in Jesus (and remains till the present a good brother in the Lord). At the temple, worshippers marshalled their gongs and cymbals, fireworks and paper lanterns. As dusk approached we once again climbed to the attic and sought our God. Some of the town were present in the shop below when, not a minute late, his answer came as before with torrential rains and even heavier floods. Satan's power manifested through that idol was annulled and no more in Mei-hua could Da-wang be acclaimed a consistently effective god.'

The team's time was up, their New Year venture over. Already before dawn on the 15th they had embarked and left for home. The mission whose field included these islands would by comity assume care of the new converts, but those who had shared in this experience would never forget its spiritual lessons. Just now, for Watchman himself and those closest to him, it was the episode's perfect timing that so convinced and reassured them. Keep close to God and press on humbly with the work he gives you, and he himself will take care of the consequences.

10

The Old Wineskins

From Trinity College chapel, with its surpliced choir, its ordered services and its elegant liturgy, it was but ten miles to Watchman's thatched riverside hut where two or three young believers met informally to pray and worship God with him. Yet in that short land-surface distance Watchman had already travelled a long way in his thinking. Here, too, as at Nantai, the extremes of East and West forced themselves upon him. A settlement of comfortable foreign holiday bungalows clothed the hillside behind, while across the water the coastal liners and world freighters from Japan and the West lay at moorings in the fairway or slipped out on the tide. Criss-crossing between them and bobbing and lurching in their wash were the tiny sampans and slipper-boats of the local longshore and fisher folk, worshippers of the goddess Ma-zu. Here on the shore around him their simple dwellings were huddled amid the sounds and smells of the native bazaar. It was a mixed-up world. How, he continually asked himself, could his Christian vision find fulfilment in so complex a setting?

In Nantai it was the dominant Anglican 'stone church' or its North American red-brick counterpart that symbolised the Christian faith. There once a week, as a contemporary describes it, the 'community' of consuls, port officials and merchants condescended to join with the missionaries in a brief hour of religious exercise formally conducted by the port chaplain. That completed they went back, the representatives of Jardine Matheson or Gillman & Sassoon, to their traditional after-church task of fixing the week's price of tea, the rest to the British Club and their Sunday relaxations.

Of course the smaller town and district congregations built up with such devotion over many years were more nearly Chinese in membership and ministry, and God had many who were truly his own among them. Yet even they partook of a structure and ethos that was essentially Western. Their laity was largely passive, dependants of a cumbersome ecclesiastical organisation with at its apex a dedicated foreign bishop. Poor man, weigh he heavy or weigh he light, he must always rank four bearers to his palanquin! And, too, there was a chronic shortage of ordained clergy. The proportion of pastors qualified to administer the sacraments was often considerably less than one man to seven congregations. The Methodists in Fuzhou only offered Communion quarterly. As another Fujian missionary describes it to us later, 'The inevitable result followed. A sacramental system that is exalted but practically unusable falls into contempt. The indigenous sects spread their influence.' In Watchman's early youth it had been the True Jesus Church, *Zhen Ye-su Jiao*, founded by Barnabas Tong, that had drawn away many Fujian pastors and church members into its fellowship. 'If your own Church cannot provide you with an effective ministry and frequent sacraments, and is not organised in such a way that you feel you are a member of a spiritual fellowship, you will, if you mean business, more often than not join some other which can provide these blessings.'[1] So speaks an Anglican missionary by hindsight 25 years after these events.

Let us hear Watchman himself, also some years after them, tell an incident from his own experience on the same theme of the sacraments. 'I know one man who hated another. The other had deeply sinned against him and so great was the injury that to have killed him would have seemed scant revenge. Then the one sinned against met the Lord and was saved, and for a few years saw nothing of the other man. Later he paid a visit to a certain city and on Sunday went to the local church assembly hall for the Communion service. Just after he was introduced by name he suddenly saw there his former enemy. "He is here!" he said to himself. "I did not know he was saved. What shall I do? What folly to have let myself be introduced!" During the next prayer he quietly got up, went out and began to walk away, and as he walked he thought on the one hand of his salvation and on the other of his grievance against the man. The further away he got the worse he felt at having thus left the meeting, and on the other hand the more incensed against his enemy. He thought back ten years to the time when he was saved and how the Lord had blotted out all his past: yet all the same he felt that he could not forgive his foe. Then at length the Holy Spirit brought to his mind the word, "By this shall all men know that you are my disciples, if you love one another."[2] Now he broke down and gave in. "Lord, I forgive him," he exclaimed, and turned and went back to the meeting with tears streaming down his face. When now he entered they had ceased praying and were about to break the bread. He got up, asked permission to speak, and confessed the whole affair, telling how God had brought him to the point of forgiving the other man.'

Such a movement of the Spirit of God in his gathered people was what Watchman looked for, and he believed it could rarely happen in the narrow context of a sectarian group. So we find him again, a little later, telling a congregation, 'If, as we gather around the Lord's Table today, our horizon is bounded by our own company we are not qualified to break bread, for the possession of Christ's life has brought us into relationship with the whole church, not merely a section of it. Oh, we need to be enlarged so that our hearts embrace all the children of God; otherwise we shall eat this bread unworthily. We proclaim here that all the children of God are brothers and sisters; therefore we refuse to harbour divisive thoughts. Let us remember that the same Holy Spirit who has come upon us has also come upon them.'

Here, in developing form, was his attempt at an answer to the problem of imported foreign denominations whose past history and values were, he felt, nearly impossible for a new convert to appreciate. By afflicting the potential church in China with sectarian differences the missions were tending only to fragment it. Among young Christians at this time Watchman was not alone in asking himself whether some return to a simple New Testament obedience might effectively reaffirm that organic unity of believers for the creation of which Jesus had prayed and then laid down his life.

He well knew that for any move away from the established churches the danger lay in its tendency to become nationalistic and anti-missionary and to end in denouncing all other Christian bodies as false. But among the Westerners whose writings he was now enjoying there were some, such as J.N. Darby, Govett and Panton, who for conscience's sake had resigned their Anglican orders and whom God had evidently honoured in their search for a more primitive pattern of worship and ministry. Such obedience to God's voice in Scripture should be a sufficient safeguard. His stand, above all, should be for spiritual quality of life. He could not forget the little respect commanded by the pastor who used to visit his parents' home. 'Apart from coming to ask for money, well knowing it was often gambler's winnings,' he recalled, 'he never showed his face among us.' 'In God's work,' he says elsewhere, 'everything depends upon the kind of worker sent out and the kind of convert produced.' If always he made quality his goal, there would be no need for any crusade against the missionary establishment. He dare not confuse his own spiritual pilgrimage with the current mood of nationalism.

These four years from 1925 to 1928 were witnessing a fresh wave of nationalistic feeling among students. Their teachers had long been telling them that they were their nation's hope, destined some day to be its saviours. Yet with the passing of the ancient system of civil service entry, their postgraduate prospects seemed not more but less secure. Moreover, being young they were idealists, impatient with the old and clamouring for the new, ready enough to assume the role of leaders of any hopeful mass action. One event was to bring this home with tragic force to the Ni parents. Their third son, Xuan-zu, brought up under the influence of his indulgent grandmother, had taken early to politics. A source of constant anxiety to them, he was seldom out of trouble. Ostensibly 'to save the nation', but in fact to evade study, he had joined first the Iron and Blood Volunteers and then the Dare to Die Corps, two revolutionary societies. At length the family's sorrow was complete when one day word came that in a revolutionary rally he had lost his life.

Already at the New Year of 1925, an anti-missionary riot had broken out in Fuzhou's old city in which the Roman Catholic sisters and some Church Missionary Society ladies were roughly handled and narrowly escaped with their lives. On 12 March that year the death in Beijing of Dr Sun Yat-sen left a power vacuum that was not at once filled; and on 30 May there occurred the historic Nanjing Road Incident in which the foreign-employed municipal police of Shanghai's International Settlement opened fire on a student demonstration. This aroused a surge of anti-British feeling and led to further violence in the cities of the south. The Fuzhou missionaries in their summer hill-retreat swiftly resigned their remaining administrative posts in favour of Chinese staff in the hope of reopening Trinity College for the autumn term. The revival of ancient superstitions about the pale-eyed foreign devils was placing severe pressure on Chinese nationals in mission service, and among these long-suspect 'running dogs of the foreigner' there were some examples of extreme loyalty and immense courage for Christ's sake. So widespread indeed were the disturbances promoted by the Anti-Christian Alliance of the following year that by the spring of 1927 all up-country missionaries were evacuated temporarily to the coast. That summer the junior school was burnt down, while January 1928 saw the destruction by fire of the splendid dormitory building of the high school at the hands of a Marxist enthusiast. The honeymoon period of Protestant missions seemed to be ending.

Yet Watchman himself must continue to honour as servants of God those missionaries to whom historically he owed so much, many of whom of course shared his living knowledge of the Saviour. Early in 1926 he was invited by some of them to Xiamen in southern Fujian to address students of the Talmage College and Seminary of the American Presbyterian Mission. Here in the graduate class he met two keen Christians, Daniel Chen and a pastor's son called James Chen, who in later years were to become close colleagues in his work. In the second half of the year Watchman made another tour for further meetings in Xiamen, Zhangzhou, Tongan and Gulangyu Island and several local assemblies were begun. But while there in south Fujian he became ill. He had developed an exhausting cough, and a doctor warned him that he should rest; it might be serious.

He had been invited meanwhile back to Nanjing to help edit a Bible study course, and in this he saw the possibility of both paying his way and getting a time of quiet. The journey by way of Shanghai proved valuable in making new friendships. Many readers of his magazine *The Christian*, which during 1925 had succeeded *Revival*, lived there and in the north or up the Yangtze, and he saw afresh Shanghai's potential as a base of operation for the country as a whole. With its atmosphere of cut-throat competition and political intrigue it was a stimulating, if dangerous, city. Someone had condemned its morals with the remark that 'if God spares Shanghai he owes an apology to Sodom and Gomorrah!'³ But it was well established as the main commercial, industrial and financial centre of China. By contrast Pagoda Anchorage, remote and linguistically provincial, gave small room for manoeuvre; and since the dispersal of the original Fuzhou band of brothers it now offered less prospect of fellow workers on his own age level. Should he, he asked himself, move his base to Shanghai?

In Nanjing in the autumn of 1926 he set to work at once on correcting the Bible course. He was persuaded too to address some students at Jing-Ling University and was used to lead several to Christ. But it was the renewed fellowship with Ruth Lee that was especially valuable to him. She was ten years his senior and of greater spiritual experience than himself, and he felt the need of such an 'older sister'. He shared with her something of his vision for reaching China with the Word of life and found in her a wise counsellor and kindred spirit. She confirmed his feeling that the present unrest was awakening a new spiritual hunger among young Chinese turning to Christ but dissatisfied with established Christianity as they found it. Could he not minister to this need? She gave support also to his view that Shanghai was the strategic place from which to work and said she felt called to resign her Nanjing post and join him there, especially to set forward his written ministry.

He had completed very little of his editorial assignment when his illness struck again. The cough, which had never really left him, became worse. In the evenings he felt chilled and at night he perspired freely. He found himself longing for his warmer home climate and after prayer he knew certainly that he must return. He set out again downriver, spiritually refreshed but downcast in mind and weakened in body. On his way south he sought medical advice.

The Shanghai physician who examined him ordered an immediate chest X-ray. It showed, we are told, heavy tuberculous invasion of the whole of one side and part of the other. While the doctor viewed the wet film and Watchman awaited the result he overheard him say to the staff nurse in English, 'Poor fellow: just look at that! Do you remember the last case we had with a picture like his? He was dead in six months.' Watchman was called in. 'You have extensive TB in both your lungs,' he was told. 'Go home and rest and eat nourishing food. That's all you can do. You may recover.' On the ship home Watchman was in an agony of mind. He had been so full of plans, so hopeful of great things. Now God had said 'No' to them all. He began to examine himself, his actions, his motives, his ambitions. One desire was uppermost with him now: to be pure before God. He confessed his sins, seeking where he might have given God ground for displeasure. The question that still troubled his conscience concerned the girl Ling Ai-qian of Sitiawan. He had long ago discovered how his informant had deceived him. Had he himself sinned therefore in not showing filial obedience right from the start? Had he wounded her and her family in giving ear to lying tales? Had he misread God's guidance in the whole affair? He was willing to remain unmarried all his days for the work's sake. There seemed nothing else he could do to make amends.

It was on a day late in 1926 that the coastal steamer came up on the tide through the Min narrows and dropped him off at Pagoda Anchorage. His hut at Ma-shan when he reached it seemed a bleak place to return to. His whole way of life there suddenly seemed so fruitless. He wanted to cry out in protest to God. He wanted to question everything.

He tried to settle down to work. From a box in the hut he took out the outline of the book it had earlier been his plan to write. As much as three years ago he had sketched a first draft of two and a half chapters on the subject of the man of God, his spirit, soul and body. He had then shelved the project as too theoretical, for at so many points it lacked the proof of experience. But much had happened meanwhile. In his own Christian life he had tasted new realities and he had seen many other souls liberated from the power of darkness. If God was soon to take him to himself, Watchman felt he must somehow set down for them in writing the precious things God had given him. He sat looking out over the river, and took up ink and brush.

But even as he did so, the fever took him: he could not

write, he could not even compose his thoughts. So he gathered up his Bible and the manuscript pages. He knew now he could not get through alone. Shutting up the house once more, he went down to the wharf at Luo-xing Ta and took a sampan across the mile of river to Customs Point. At the hostel door his beloved Faithful Luke welcomed him and gave him a room in the men's quarters. There he lay down on the little cot and let himself fall into the hands of God. It was some comfort to him that the hostel was still there. His father had earlier warned him that the industrial school whose premises it occupied and of which he was a director was about to reopen with new engineering staff from the United States. Yet wholly at rest in God, Miss Barber had set out for the hot summer weeks to Guling Mountain above Fuzhou, there to receive news that the school's finances had been suddenly liquidated and it would not after all be opening. The accommodation was still hers to use.

On their return the ladies now supplied him with milk and good food and such palliative medicines as were available and the brothers waited on him. The dark days dragged on into weeks as he continued to lose weight and feel his strength ebbing from him. 'He was so humble,' Luke recalls, 'so desirous to be healed. He asked me every day to anoint him in the Lord's name and pray.' When he was too exhausted to read, his memory of Scripture came to the rescue: 'Humble yourself under the mighty hand of God . . . ' But he dared not yet complete that very telling sentence.[4] 'For two months,' he observed, 'I lived daily in the very jaws of Satan.'

Miss Barber came regularly to visit him with the message, 'Christ is Victor.' Yet while he knew the value of the precious blood for sins and believed he could claim healing over sickness from One who has borne our infirmities,[5] he truly felt he was at fault and had given Satan ground to withstand Christ in his life. She had, however, Scriptures that brought home to him the all-embracing effectiveness of Jesus' resurrection, until at length he himself was able to assent in faith, *'Christ is Victor!'* Then slowly, in answer to their united prayers, God took a hand and the diet and rest began to work a change. With the access of a little strength he was soon asking again for paper and ink. Now, for as long as God might permit, he set his whole being to the task he felt so urgent. Like some reporter hounded to a newspaper deadline and doing his best work in the last desperate hour, he poured out his heart in a detailed setting forth of the Christian's spiritual life and the strategy of the heavenly warfare.

Eventually, after months, the first volume comprising four parts of *The Spiritual Man* was ready. It was very analytical and set out the believer's salvation, spirit, soul and body, in exhaustive detail. In his preface he described it as a work of biblical psychology, but warned his readers that to use it merely as a tool for self-analysis would only hinder them from losing themselves in Christ. As a fruit of suffering it was rich in insights, but it lacked something. It was also short on those illustrative lighter touches that so enlivened his preaching. It owed much to his extensive reading, more to the keenness of his mind, but most to his profound knowledge of the Scriptures and his transparent openness to the impact of their message.

By the month of May 1927, though still very weak, he began preparing to leave for Shanghai with his precious manuscript. Ruth Lee had already moved there from Nanjing where pro-Communist riots had caused some missionary deaths. She had volunteered, with her excellent literary Chinese, to tidy up the final draft and prepare the book for press.

Nanjing was shortly to become headquarters of the new regime of Chiang Kai-shek, who at the age of 40 had emerged from the welter of events following Dr Sun's death. In 1926–27, in a league of convenience, he had led Kuomintang and Communist forces together northwards by the central route from Guangdong (Canton) to capture first Changsha in Hunan and then Hankou in Hubei. From there he turned east, seeking total control of Shanghai. Here one Zhou En-lai, his handsome and brilliant 29-year-old former military colleague, organised for him on 12 April 1927 a rousing city welcome. That day masses of workers took to the streets, seized power and hoisted banners proclaiming, 'Hail the Revolution! Hail Chiang Kai-shek!' But Chiang himself was in a drive to win personal power as generalissimo, and now he secretly turned on his allies. Holding back his combined forces, he gave instead a prepared signal for a ruthless coup, a veritable 'feast of heads'. Marshalled in four city districts by a corrupt chief of police and watched by Chiang's own armies, the city's own worst criminal gangs, armed with machine guns and broadswords, were let loose on the mass of Shanghai's unarmed workers with orders to wipe them out in unlimited numbers. Zhou En-lai himself barely escaped the vast massacre; other leaders were less fortunate.

Peace, of a sort, had settled on the city by the time Watchman's boat reached the Huangpu in early June. It was while he was there in Shanghai putting finishing touches to his book that he made a personal discovery in the Scriptures, there in the first letter of the apostle Paul to the Corinthian church. Familiar words came to him as a flash of truth from God that would profoundly affect his own assurance and would freshly inform his future exposition of other well-known passages on the theme of deliverance from human sin. A passage that he knew well and had often spoken from, in another letter of Paul, this time to the Romans, took on now a new reality. He 'saw' the priority of divine fact over the personal experience that flows from faith. Let him tell it in his own words.

'For years after my conversion I had been taught that the way of deliverance was to reckon myself dead to sin and alive to God (Romans 6:11). I reckoned from 1920 to 1927, and the trouble was that the more I did so the more alive to sin I clearly was. I simply could not believe myself *dead*, and I could not produce death. Sin was still defeating me, and I saw that something was fundamentally wrong. So I asked God to show me what was the meaning of the expression, "I have been crucified with Christ." It had become clear to me that when speaking of this subject God nowhere says "You must be", but always "You have been". Yet in view of my constant failure this just did not seem possible, unless I was to be dishonest with myself. I almost turned to the conclusion that only dishonest people could make such statements. Yet whenever I sought help from others I was sent back to Romans 6:11. I appreciated its teaching, but I could not make out why nothing resulted from it. No one, you see, had pointed out to me that *knowing* (verse 6) must precede *reckoning* (verse 11). For months I was troubled and prayed earnestly, reading the Scriptures and seeking light. I said to the Lord, "If I cannot be brought to see this which is so fundamental I will preach no more. I want first to get clear on this issue."

'I remember one morning – how can I ever forget it! – I was sitting upstairs reading Romans and I came to the words: "Knowing this, that our old man was crucified with him, that the body of sin might be done away, that so we should no longer be in bondage to sin." Knowing this! How might I know it? So I prayed, "Lord, open my eyes!" and then, in a flash, I saw. I had earlier been reading in 1 Corinthians 1:30 where Paul affirms: "You are in Christ Jesus." I turned up the passage and looked again. "Of God you are in Christ Jesus" (KJV). That is to say: "That you are in Christ Jesus is God's doing!" I was amazed. I was there by his act! Then if Christ died – and that is history – and if God had placed me in him, then I too must have died with him. All at once I saw my oneness with Christ: that I was in him and that when he died I died. My death to sin was a matter of the past and not of the future. Of course there is more to this, but what had just dawned on me was divine fact. Carried away with joy I jumped from my chair and ran downstairs to the young man working in the kitchen. "Brother," I said, seizing him by the hands, "do you know that I have died?" I must admit he looked puzzled. "What do you mean?" he exclaimed, so I went on: "Do you not know that Christ has died? Do you not know that I died with him? Do you not know that my death is no less truly a fact than his?" Oh it was so real to me! I felt like shouting my discovery through the streets of Shanghai. From that day to this I have never for one moment doubted the finality of that word: "I have been crucified with Christ; it is no longer I who live, but Christ who lives in me."[6]

11

Fragile Clay

Watchman felt strong enough now to continue in lodgings in Shanghai and work on the further sections of the book that he was sure God wanted him to complete. Slowly, under Ruth Lee's literary tutelage, the truths he had learned through so much suffering and failure found written expression. He was well pleased too to take a quiet look at the missionary scene. Here for the first time he came into close contact with the great interdenominational China Inland Mission (CIM), founded by Dr James Hudson Taylor, which for 60 years and more had extended its biblical Christian witness far into the country's interior. Its testimony to God's faithfulness was given fresh point by his friendship now with a missionary in its accounts department, Charles H. Judd, a man of long experience in the field to whom he quickly warmed in spirit. Watchman went often to his home, where they would share their common interest in the Scriptures. To him Watchman disclosed his own hopes of reaching across China with the gospel of Christ, and when his own strength allowed they would sometimes go together with a few young men preaching in the city's lanes and suburbs.

Ruth Lee now introduced to him a dear friend, Peace Wang (Wang Pei-zhen), daughter of a wealthy magistrate, who had been one of her pupils and whose faith Ruth, as a determined atheist, had once sought to destroy. When as a young girl Peace had found the Saviour her parents had tried every means to make her renounce him, first bribing her with jewels, then urging her to suicide, and finally driving her from home. After graduating from the Nanjing seminary she had worked as an independent evangelist and was in special demand in schools, where her striking testimony was used to bring many to Christ. Now, years later, she had had the joy of leading her own mother to him.

It was in Peace Wang's home that one Sunday late in 1927 four of them, Watchman Nee, Charles Judd, Ruth Lee and Peace herself, met first to worship God together in the breaking of bread. They continued meeting thus for some weeks, but Watchman already felt he must take a step of faith and rent suitable premises for Bible teaching and witness. 'Start from a little' was the local saying, and it matched well with the prophet's question, 'Who has despised the day of small things?'[1] At length, in January 1928, he found a property on Wen De Li, a lane turning east off Hardoon Road in the International Settlement. It lay above flood-level to the north of Bubbling Well Road and some three miles west of the Bund. Several others had by now joined them and they moved in, meeting upstairs until the shop space below could be cleared as a preaching hall. Early each Sunday Judd cycled right across the city from the CIM centre at Wusong Road to be with them at the Lord's Table before returning to his own responsibility at the mission's Free Christian Church. But the association was to be short-lived, for scarcely a year later the man in whom Watchman had such confidence was called back to Canada. In the light of subsequent history one may perhaps regret that so potentially valuable a link between this new work and the missionaries was thus abruptly removed.

In June 1928, the month in which Chiang Kai-shek's armies occupied Beijing, the remaining six sections of Watchman's *The Spiritual Man* were ready for press.[2] He had completed the book under the same sense of compulsion with which he began it. It was the first and last book he ever sat down and wrote, the rest of his publications all being transcriptions of his preaching and teaching. It contained a chapter on 'Sickness', and though like the rest this came out of experience, as so often happens to God's servants he soon found himself plunged into a fresh testing of what he had written. For this reason in later years he often stated that he felt *The Spiritual Man* was too complete, too absolute. It gave the illusion of providing all the answers. 'It will not be reprinted,' he said in 1941.[3] 'It is not that what I wrote was wrong, for as I read it now I can endorse it all. It was a very full setting forth of the truth, but just there lies its weakness. When a man has read it he ought not to have any questions left. But God, I have discovered, does not do things that way, and much less does he allow us to do them. For the danger of systematising divine facts is that a man can grasp them, can "understand", without the help of the Holy Spirit. It is only the immature Christian who demands always to have intellectually satisfying conclusions. The Word of God itself has this fundamental character, that it speaks always and essentially to our spirit and to our life.' It must be clear from this that *The Spiritual Man* is to be read today not as a textbook but as a staging post in the author's pilgrimage. He was, after all, not yet 25 when he wrote it.

The Wen De Li meeting room could harbour just 100 persons, but in February 1928 there took place here the small but significant first Shanghai Conference, calling in believers from the city and beyond for a time of exposition of the Word. Watchman's messages on the eternal purpose of God in Christ met with a warm response; but once again the mere effort of preaching, coupled with the demands of counselling the many who came to him, sapped his strength. The cough and the wasting returned, and right through that long year he spent most days on his back in an effort to regain strength. At length, early in 1929, some family affairs claimed his attention and he seized the opportunity to sail away south to Fuzhou for what would prove to be his last meeting with Margaret Barber.

With some hesitation Miss Barber had earlier lent him a few expository writings of the deceased C.A. Coates and J.N. Darby. Finding them to his taste, he had written off to a London publisher for more of these, and as a result had enjoyed for a year or so some happy correspondence with a Mr George Ware in England who belonged to this strictly Darbyite persuasion of the London Brethren. His own search for a more primitive pattern of Christian worship, free of the accumulated debris of tradition, had, he now discovered, led him to follow lines rather similar to theirs. The central act of every Sunday's worship was the evening meeting around the Lord's Table, at which anyone present was free to express spontaneous adoration and thanksgiving to God, before all partook together of the bread and wine.[4] Other main features of the church's life were the baptism of believers, the exposition of the Word among them, their mutual care for one another and for the work of God, and their constant public witness to his saving acts in Christ. But also, like the Brethren, Watchman had begun to apply most rigorously the apostle Paul's restrictions upon women, advising them not to preach publicly in the presence of men and urging upon them the wearing of head coverings in church meetings.[5] Since no Chinese woman normally wore veil or hat, these had to be specially designed and took the form of a standard cap of black crocheted work. The Chinese sisters readily acquiesced in these regulations, although later there was some relaxation of this custom. Except in meetings for women, Ruth Lee and Peace Wang gave up their widely acceptable preaching for the counselling of individuals.

But when, back at Pagoda, he harangued Margaret Barber on the wrongfulness of her taking Bible classes for young men, she listened politely but kept her counsel. In fact she had misgivings about the doctrinaire position of these London Brethren, which she had divulged to Faithful Luke before Luke himself moved on to start a pioneer work down the coast near Putien (Hinghwa). They were, she felt, just one of several mutually exclusive such groups of meetings, each claiming purity of doctrine and practice over a century past and on that ground each refusing communion to all other Christians. To Watchman she said little. Incidentally, however, she introduced to him some publications of another current English preacher and expositor in London, Theodore Austin-Sparks, whose messages on the cross of Christ, owing something to Jessie Penn-Lewis, had in the past year or so brought blessing to her.

The brief visit to her, their respected He Shou-en, enriched him, but in his uncertain health he could not again impose upon her hospitality. He took the river launch to Nantai, but on the two-hour journey his fever returned, and with it the devil to assail him by using the depressive effect of the tuberculosis to draw out his inner questionings. 'You had a bright future, full of possibilities, and you gave it up to serve God. That was splendid. But then you had a promising ministry where with your gifts you were assured of a large reception, only to throw that away as well. For what? You relinquished so much: what have you gained? Sometimes God hears your prayers; often enough he is silent. Compare yourself with that other man thriving out there now in the generous evangelical system. He too had a bright future, and he has never let it go. He is spiritually prosperous and God honours his ministry. He gets souls saved and they go on with God. And moreover, he looks like a Christian; so happy, so assured, so fulfilled. Do you? Just take a look at yourself!'

Disembarking, he went to his parents' home on the waterfront to pay them his respects and to attend to the business that had brought him there. Making light of his own indisposition, he asked after their welfare. In his heart he was ready to say or do anything God required, if only he might recover his health. Next day he ventured out into the town, sorrowfully avoiding the two separate meeting places of the now long-divided local church. Below the bridge the cormorant fishers were at work and he paused to watch them as he used to do as a child, marvelling at the patience of the captive birds. He walked slowly, leaning on a stick.

All at once, there on the street, whom should he encounter but one of his former Trinity College professors. He greeted him with a bow, and the man took him into a teashop where they sat down. After a few sharp inquiries he stopped and looked Watchman up and down, taking in his pinched face, his worn gown and sandals. 'What is this?' he exclaimed with evident dismay. 'We thought a lot of you at High School and had hopes that you would achieve something great. Do you mean to say you are still like *this*?'

Traditionally the Chinese student holds his teacher in high regard, returning to him formal thanks for each scholastic success, so the very pointed question struck cruelly home. Here was one whom Watchman instinctively honoured and who saw him merely as an educational dropout. He quailed now before the man's penetrating gaze, for it was true: his health was broken, his prospects gone; what had he to show? And here was his old teacher of Chinese law asking, 'Are you still not an inch further forward? No progress, no career, *nothing?*' In that moment Ni Shu-zu, grown man as he was, came close to tears.

And the very next instant (as he tells us), 'I really knew what it meant to have the Spirit of glory resting upon me. I could look up and say, "Lord, I praise you that I have chosen the best, the right way." To my professor it was a total waste to serve the Lord Jesus; but that is the goal of the gospel: to give all without reserve to God.'

He remained at home for a while, glad of the renewed contact with his parents and happy to share news of the other members of the family, most now married. He-ping was still her energetic self, out wherever doors were opened for prayer and witness. She had had the joy of leading her aged father, the merchant, late in life to a living knowledge of the Saviour. At his death her brother arranged a Taoist funeral, from which she absented herself by sending to follow the hired bands and white-clad professional mourners a curtained sedan chair, empty save for a huge stone. When her mother learned of this she threatened to hang herself, but eventually she too, who had been self-occupied all her years, responded to her daughter's pleadings and found the Lord.

He-ping tells us that at this time she feared Watchman had not long to live. She worried over him, but because she tended at the same time to assert her disapproval of much that he did, he resented her ministrations – and said so. He rested, however, and prayed over and over again for strength for the work to which he felt so certainly called. At length God seemed to say to him, 'This is my affair. You trust me, and drop it!' Yet so insistent was he that God's will should be safeguarded that, try as he would, he could not relax and let the matter go to him. He still found himself pursuing it obsessively in penitence and prayer.

One day he was out walking on the beach meditating on his predicament. Abruptly he came to a halt. Driving his stick obliquely clean in under the sand, he stood upon it and proclaimed, 'Lord, I trust in you. I have dropped the matter of my healing here!' – and walked away. But scarcely had he gone any distance before the old anxiety welled up again and brought him out in a cold sweat. Involuntarily he began to pray once more, arguing with God that his healing was a desperate need. Then all at once he stopped short in his tracks, aware of what he had done. This temptation was from the enemy of souls and to pray now thus was to yield to him. He turned and walked back to the place where he had driven in the stick. Pointing to it as a witness, he declared, 'Lord God, I dropped the matter of my healing here. It is yours! I refuse to take it up again!'

His business completed, he set out again for Shanghai. At Wen De Li once more, nursing his strength, he preached the gospel each Sunday morning, urging on his hearers separation from the world and total dedication to Christ, while in the evening he met with the believers at the Table of the Lord. Several devoted brothers had joined the group, two of whom, John Zhang and a hospital ophthalmologist called Dr Yu Cheng-hua, were now able to take care of things in his absence. Soon an adjacent property became available, 15 foot by 30 foot like the first, making, when opened up, a larger meeting place where sisters sat one side and brothers the other of a line of pillars. With more space also upstairs the publishing work went ahead fast. *The Christian* continued to be published until in January 1928 *Revival* was resumed with its focus on deeper spiritual revelation.[6] The magazine grew rapidly in circulation and continued to play an important part in the outreach of the work.

A growingly effective adjunct to the gospel witness was the steady flow of splendid booklets and tracts edited from Watchman's own gospel preaching. Clearly set forth in simple but convincing terms and with winning appeal, they presented the goodness of God to the man in the street, and they won many to him. Also, to meet another need that was increasingly felt, Watchman translated hymns for their use in worship, some by Miss Barber, others from an English Brethren hymnbook, and not a few original ones of his own. His health was now improving. Doctors confirmed a change for the better in his lung condition and they now advised a spell of rest in the healthier climate of Guling Mountain.

Guling lies in Jiangxi Province, 600 miles up the Yangtze and just south of the river port of Jiujiang. But the province has, first, another place in our story. Fleeing the April 1927 bloodbath in Shanghai, Zhou En-lai and the surviving Communist leaders, preserving their Russian links, quickly set up a new base in the remote towns of Yudu and Ruijin further south in Jiangxi, some 200 miles west of Fuzhou. There, by 1932, they would feel able to designate themselves 'The Soviet Republic of China'. But of course Chiang Kai-shek, having secured Beijing and established himself as China's outright ruler, marshalled his forces afresh and, with German military advisers, embarked on a series of five remorseless annihilation campaigns to surround and eliminate his foe. In the course of time he would seem to be nearing success.

Back meanwhile in the province's northerly Lushan Range, Watchman faced his own hillside retreat. The sides of Guling Mountain's habited valley were studded with Western-style bungalows where the foreign staffs of Shanghai and Hankou business houses sat out the hot summer season, and where weary missionary families took turns to recuperate. Tall lilies bloomed in shaded gardens, and enticing trails led out to vantage points among the rocky hills. Lower down, outside the wooden barriers that bounded the ceded territory, there huddled the Chinese market town of the Gap, itself 3,500 feet above sea-level.

Advised not to attempt the hill stairway, Watchman was compelled to submit to a sedan chair. Nor, at ten taels a day, could he afford treatment in the well-equipped Mission Sanatorium, so a lady from Nanjing had arranged sleeping accommodation in her unoccupied house, No. 103 at the Gap, and he found mealtime hospitality in a neighbouring home with a local tradesman and his wife. Even here in Guling Mountain friends sought him out for conversations in the mornings, but he gave out that in the afternoons he was otherwise occupied. He was flat on his back!

He had been asked also while there to visit a young man from Xiamen, C.L. Yin, lately returned from engineering studies in Boston, Massachusetts, who was spending his US dollars on treatment of a sudden chest infection. His mother was concerned for his spiritual welfare, but when Watchman called on him in the Sanatorium ward Yin did all the talking, enumerating at length his intellectual objections to his mother's faith. Rebuffed, his visitor could only smile and ask as he rose to leave, 'Are these questions genuinely yours, or have you borrowed them to build a fence against your soul's salvation?' The question clung. Back in Xiamen, unable to shake it off, Yin sought out another Fujian man,

John Sung, himself lately back from Ohio with a doctorate, and this man of God led him to the Saviour.

Watchman now became very friendly with his mealtime hosts, Mr and Mrs Yu, but for two weeks, apart from silently asking a blessing before food, he said nothing to them about the gospel. Yu was an electrician but with very little schooling. Then one day in answer to a question he told them what the Lord Jesus had done for him. They listened eagerly, for their hearts were hungry, and soon came to the Saviour in simple faith for the forgiveness of their sins. With their new birth a fresh light and joy entered their lives. Watchman now read the Bible with them and explained how God's Holy Spirit indwelling them would henceforth open the Scriptures to them. 'I will put my laws into their minds,' God had said, 'and on their heart I will write them' (Hebrews 8:10).

For many weeks he recuperated in Guling, taking occasional walks to a viewpoint from which he could see far below him the brown Yangtze, dotted with motionless sails, winding its way across the patchwork plain. He was re-thinking his Christianity and discovering where lay his real rest of heart. 'When first I came to the Lord,' he says, 'I had my own conception of what a Christian is, and I tried my utmost to be that. A true Christian should smile from morning to night, I thought, and if at any time he shed a tear he had ceased to be victorious. I thought, too, that a Christian must be unfailingly courageous. If under any crisis he showed the least sign of fear he had fallen short of my standard.' But his serial reading of the New Testament had brought him back again and again to Paul's autobiographical letter, 2 Corinthians. There he read 'as sorrowful . . .' and the words arrested him. A great Christian who shed 'many tears', who could be 'perplexed', and who could even 'despair of life itself', must be very human.[7] Is it possible, he asked, that the apostle Paul despaired? This was just where he himself had been! 'Here I discovered', he says, 'that Paul was a man, and the very sort of man I knew.' There began to dawn on him the secret of Christianity that is summarised in the words, 'We have this treasure in earthen vessels, to show that the transcendent power belongs to God and not to us.'[8] Now, as he learned to trust God hourly for his very life, he moved on to a new, steadier place of rest in him.

But the season was changing and the weather turning colder. The day arrived when he must bid farewell to his new friends and return to Shanghai. This time, taking it slowly, he walked down the long stone stairway beside the headlong torrent framed in its jungle gorge. At the mountain's foot the road with its hire vehicles brought him again to Jiujiang and the river steamers.

One day some months later word was brought to him at Wen De Li that a caller was downstairs asking to see him. It proved to be his host from Guling Gap. He was in Shanghai on business and had come to recount an experience he had had. During the winter months he had been in the habit of drinking wine with his meals, often to excess. With the return of the cold weather the wine appeared on the table again, but that day when he bowed his head to return thanks for the meal no words would come. After one or two vain attempts he turned to his wife. 'What is wrong?' he asked. 'Why can't we pray today? Fetch the Bible and see what it says about wine drinking.' But she turned the pages in vain seeking for light on the subject; and of course it might be months before they could consult Watchman, who was many miles away. 'Just drink your wine,' said the wife. 'We'll refer the matter to brother Nee at the first opportunity.' But still the man found he just could not return thanks to the Lord for that wine. 'Take it away!' he said at length; and when she had done so, together they asked a blessing on their meal.

The man told Watchman his story, and then exclaimed in wonder, 'Brother Nee, Resident Boss wouldn't let me have that drink!' 'Very good, brother,' Watchman replied. 'You always listen to Resident Boss!'

One day in May 1930 Watchman received a cable from Pagoda Anchorage: 'Margaret Barber passed to her rest, gloriously carried through by the Lord.' Serene Loland, the Norwegian nursing superintendent at Gutian Hospital, had hurried downriver to nurse her through what was to be her last illness. She was 64. Of the old team of seven brothers only John Wang was present at the end, but Faithful Luke and Simon Meek hurried back to join him in giving her a suitable burial on the hillside above the river. She had died nearly penniless.

As he thought back over her life, Watchman could only give thanks to God. He had often been troubled at her isolation there at White Teeth Rock, concerned that with her living knowledge of the Book and of its Author she was not used more widely. Yet subsequent years were to prove what was already becoming apparent, that many young men and women of promise in evangelical work traced their spiritual wealth to her instruction. In particular Leland Wang, now in Hong Kong, was moving widely as an evangelist among mission churches and in due course was to found in Indonesia the China Overseas Missionary Union. And Watchman was to observe later, 'In those days when I was associated with Miss Barber she was used by the Lord to us all in a very real way.' He recalled now one of her songs[9] that he had grown to love:

If the path I travel lead me to a cross,
If the way Thou choosest lead to pain and loss,
Let the compensation daily, hourly be
Shadowless communion, blessed Lord, with Thee.

Her care was always to see that from her side there were
no shadows. When there arrived from Fuzhou the much
thumbed Bible she had willed to him, he found in it the
prayer, 'O God, grant me a complete and unrestrained revelation of my own self.'

And on the flyleaf she had long ago written words he
would henceforth make his own: '*I want nothing for myself, I
want everything for the Lord.*'

12

Disenchantment

For ten days in December 1930 Watchman Nee and John Zhang enjoyed some happy Christian fellowship and interchange with a visitor from England. Mr Charles R. Barlow of Peterborough was a believer associated with the 'London Group' of Christian Brethren, and his travels for a British engineering firm had brought him to Shanghai. After talks with them and others he observed in letters home, 'Some of these dear brethren are very sincere and thirsting for truth. Watchman Nee is undoubtedly the outstanding man among them. He is far beyond all the rest. He is only 28 but has had a good education and is possessed of marked ability. He is a hard worker and reads much. He is, too, a student of J.N. Darby and has evidently been much helped by his writings.' For Watchman this visitor met briefly a need he had felt since the departure of C.H. Judd, that of a mature and wise Westerner – and this one was not a missionary but merely 'a beloved fellow Christian' in secular employment – in whom he could confide as a friend. He speaks warmly of the help he received from him. Very soon Mr Barlow was invited to address about 40 believers, including a sprinkling of university students, at their usual meeting time of 4 p.m. daily. On Sunday afternoon the numbers rose to 80 or 90. The report he carried back to his fellow believers in England was warmly encouraging.

What most impressed this visitor was Watchman's knowledge of the biblical text. When remarking that he had not noticed a certain expression anywhere in the New Testament he casually added, 'and I reckon to get through the New Testament once a month.' We have no details of Watchman's plan of Old Testament reading, but a like impression is preserved by Faithful Luke. In Shanghai with his wife Eunice some months later, he tells how Watchman called on them late at night with Bible in hand. 'Where are you going to preach at this late hour?' Luke asked. 'Nowhere,' was the reply, 'but for today I still have some chapters to complete.' It is certain too that the diligence of these first ten years was preserved far into those ahead. Long afterwards Witness Lee could say of him, 'I have never met a man so well versed in the Scriptures as he.'

Early in 1931 trouble erupted in the city. The Japanese occupation of the Three Eastern Provinces of Manzhouli (Manchuria) had aroused Chinese anger, which now found expression in a country-wide boycott of Japanese goods. In Shanghai the Japanese demanded action by the municipal authorities to counter this, and then, to protect their nationals, they landed marines who did much damage. Hostilities ceased in May, but it was a brief foretaste of things to come.

In October 1931 in the enlarged Wen De Li premises on Hardoon Road they held their second Shanghai conference. A China Inland Mission observer reports of these 'young Christians carrying on a great work apart from the missions' that this conference lasted twelve days and that they spent up to four hours daily in prayer. He-ping, on a brief visit to

Hardoon Road at about this time, writes, 'What my son preached was too deep and I could not understand it. I was too proud to ask questions and so could receive little from the time; but beholding their life I was bowed to the ground in respect.' Watchman had also written or translated a number of hymns. For this occasion the hymns that till now had appeared only in pamphlet form were collected and published as *Xiao-qun Shi-ge* ('Little Flock Hymns').[1] Many of its 134 translations and original songs, sung maybe discordantly but always with enthusiasm, were to find wide acceptance in homes and churches and to carry their biblical ideas to distant places. But this publication was to have an unwanted side effect.

Watchman had a horror of denominational labels (usually given them by others) such as Anglican, Lutheran, Baptist, with their national, personal or procedural connotations, and tried very hard to limit himself to the simplest biblical terms. The Christian life he spoke of as *The Way* and believers in Jesus as *Christians*, the local meeting place was a *Church Assembly Hall*, the periodical was *The Christian*, the literature office was *The Gospel Publishing House*. For the translation of some biblical hymns Watchman's source had been a London Brethren book called *Hymns for the Little Flock*.[2] This title had appealed to him as biblical, memorable, unpretentious and effective in Chinese. It caught on, however, all too well, and within a year or so the Hardoon Road congregation was to be nicknamed by mission adherents *Xiao-qun*, 'the Little Flock'. Although the book's title was quickly changed simply to *Hymns*, the harm was done; the label stuck. As Watchman's work spread across China all associated local groups of believers were thereafter dubbed by outside observers with a name their members deplored and never themselves used, 'the Little Flock Churches'.

Miraculously Watchman's health was at last improving. God had lifted his hand, and he was free not only to teach the Word but to travel more widely. These were years of devastating floods in the Yangtze basin and much loss of life, but in many small riverside towns work was increasing, as well as in the national capital of Nanjing and in Hankou further up the river. All of these were included in his tours. On another occasion he visited Beijing and there had his first friendly touch with the courageous conservative evangelical pastor Wang Ming-dao.

At Qingdao (Tsingtao) on the Shandong coast he encountered the so-called Spiritual Gifts (Ling En) Movement which was very active in that province. He viewed with caution some of its ill-controlled and extravagant methods of emotional arousal, and in the summer of 1932 published in his *Revival* magazine a series of articles distinguishing between the divinely given baptism of the Spirit and the external signs demanded as essential by some of its exponents.[3] He quotes with approval Miss Barber's observation, 'There is no need for people to feel the power which comes from the Holy Spirit. It is not given for that purpose. Man's duty is to obey God.' At the Shandong resort of Yantai (Chefoo) he met also for the first time Witness Lee (Li Chang-shou). A native of that city, Lee came of Christian parents and had been converted in 1925 at the age of 20 and baptised in 1930. Since 1927 he had received Watchman's magazine and was himself developing fast a gift of preaching and Bible exposition. Future circumstances were to bring the two men very close together at a critical period.

The effect of this new freedom of movement was to bring fresh people in touch with the editor of the widely read little paper. While the Hardoon Road meetings were viewed cautiously by some as sectarian, others in fresh circles were soon to discover Watchman's striking gifts of presenting Christ. At Jinan, the Shandong provincial capital on the Yellow River, some of the staff of Qilu (Cheloo) University were accustomed to invite an evangelist or Bible teacher each year for special meetings. Qilu was a Union University that drew its students from many provinces and was noted for its advanced thinking and Western liberal theology. For several years, however, a small group of evangelical staff had met weekly in the home of Dr Thornton Stearns and his wife Carol to pray for spiritual revival. At holiday seasons they would take groups of students on a retreat in the hills, to which they would invite as speakers the best Chinese Christian leaders and evangelists available. Dr Stearns of the American Presbyterian Mission, Professor of Ortho-paedics in the Medical School and a most humble man, took the lead in these arrangements.

In December 1931 Dr John Sung of Xinghua chanced to pass through Jinan during a preaching tour, and after a meeting in the Stearns' home at which he spoke, some 40 or 50 students found Christ within a few days.[4] God's Spirit began to work among the student body in conviction of sin and the Stearns, to whom they came for counselling, were greatly exercised about whom to invite for the forthcoming spring retreat. The unanimous first choice was Leland Wang, but due to engagements in Java he proved unavailable. Then a student from Fuzhou suggested the name of Watchman Nee as a man with a satisfying message. This little-known Shanghai preacher did not make bookings and was said to be difficult to pin down, but after prayer Dr Stearns wrote inviting him, and he felt free to accept.

He came at the end of March 1932, and God was with him as, over a weekend in the Medical School auditorium, he proclaimed the way of life to exceptionally crowded meetings. The longed-for revival spread as more and more of the students found the Saviour. Among many of them the experience was to become a legend, for heaven itself seemed to open to their hearts. Afterwards a group of more than 100 students gathered at a mountain beauty spot in the Tai-shan range above Taian city, traditional site of Confucius' grave. They studied the Bible and prayed, and before the end a large group of them were baptised in the cold pool of a mountain torrent, publicly confessing Jesus as Lord.

Meanwhile the enthusiasm felt by Mr Charles Barlow on his visit to Shanghai had been conveyed back to the circle of meetings with which he was associated in the English-speaking world. His account created a sensation. It was felt among them that here in China was an original work of the Spirit of God, in its beginnings surely, yet parallel with their own. The fellowship in which it found expression seemed based on the truth as they saw it and to reflect principles which they had inherited from their own fresh beginnings a century before. Accordingly they resolved to send a deputation to Shanghai to meet the Chinese brothers, and from May 1932 exchanged letters with Watchman Nee and his colleagues to prepare the way for such a visit in the autumn of that year.

The Chinese responded warmly and arrangements were made to receive the visitors at Hardoon Road for meetings in November. The eight foreign guests, six men and the wives of two of them, arrived in Shanghai on 23 October and were accommodated in a suitable hotel in the Concession. Mr Charles Barlow and a Californian who joined him in Vancouver carried the good will of believers in Britain and on the Pacific Coast, and besides another British couple there were also four delegates from Australia.[5] They were much moved by the warm Chinese hospitality that greeted them and responded to it with sincere affection. Watchman himself was indisposed on their arrival, but was soon able to take part in the two weeks of friendly talks. The first week the visitors asked to be excused from breaking bread with the Chinese on the Lord's Day, while they prayed and debated, weighing carefully what they had seen and learned in conversations, lest there should be some flaw. How could they associate their friends at home with something God might not approve? But there was so much to reassure them: the attitude of worship and of obedience to the Scriptures, the prayers, the evident authority of the brothers and – no less important to them – the meekness and silence of the women and their seemly head-coverings.

It had been planned that a week's conference should follow on from the Sunday gatherings on 6 November, and to this some 40 representative brothers from distant places were converging to join the Shanghai workers. In addition there were to be some public meetings. Watchman had written earlier to his father asking him to purchase and ship from Fuzhou 200 wooden chairs at $3 each to supplement the existing backless benches. He had earlier, with his return to health, felt moved to write and apologise to his mother for his coolness towards her when he was so ill and she had responded with a stern letter enumerating his crimes, forgetting, she admits, her own failures as a mother. Now she resolved to make amends. The purchase of chairs being somewhat outside Ni Wen-xiu's field, she had placed the order herself and had entrusted them when ready to a shipper. At this point they were nearly lost when a rapacious customs examiner tried both to have the chairs impounded and to embezzle a $50 fee. Her husband got them released, and to save handling time John Wang persuaded the ship's captain to carry them as deck cargo. Then on the morning of the 5th, in the Steep Island passage off the Yangtze mouth, the ship was becalmed in fog and she despaired of delivering them on time. But joined by two friends He-ping prayed publicly to God for the fog's dispersal, visualising, she says, the chairs all set in position at Hardoon Road. The fog lifted within minutes, causing quite a buzz of conversation among the other passengers. They assumed that their first-class tickets included the chairs, but as they were nearing the shore the captain now imposed a charge of $1 per chair. She brought this matter also to the Lord in prayer, and the next morning the captain made an offer of a much more affordable charge, which they readily accepted. But then on the ship's arrival in the Huangpu River, customs once more blocked their unloading at the Bund and late at night the brothers had to retrieve them from the Pudong shore. Yet next morning they were all in place when the meeting opened, and He-ping herself had a hand in dusting and arranging them!

By now the visitors felt sure before God that nothing debarred their home assemblies from identifying with these in China and had cabled their view to agreed links in Vancouver and Brisbane, 'two neighbouring meetings'. Being assured in reply of their fellowship with them in so doing, they now on Sunday evening 6 November joined with the Chinese in partaking at the Table of the Lord. It was a time of unspeakable joy.

Next morning the special conference meetings got under way amid mutual felicitations. The principal speakers were Charles Barlow and W.J. House, with Nee himself as interpreter. Faithful Luke was present with others from the south and there were a number from up the Yangtze and from further north, including two brothers Ji (Gih) from Jiangbei, known to missionaries as 'the Moodies of north

Jiangsu'. 'Some of these brothers from other parts', the visitors observed, 'are men of worth, real gold. The work is spreading and they have much to encourage and much to exercise them.' Several Jiangsu brothers now invited them to visit those church groups, but this northern area had lately been much disturbed and their guests' capture by bandits was felt by all to be too great a risk to take. Two of the party, however, W.J. House and C.R. Barlow, had expressed a wish to visit the scene of the work's beginnings. While therefore they took ship to Xiamen for a gathering of the several groups in that area, Faithful Luke went to meet John Wang and prepare for them a welcome to Fuzhou. It was in the teeth of a monsoon gale that the two visitors at length reached that city, to be entertained by He-ping and her husband in their riverside home. The Fuzhou meetings were large, numbering 250 souls, and they returned to Shanghai much stirred and with their sense of divine history enriched.

The story they all took home was so favourable that in the spring of 1933, invitations came to Watchman to visit Britain and America that summer, bringing with him Dr Yu or Faithful Luke. Yu was sick with tuberculosis at the time and Luke was by now far away, and Watchman did not trouble them with the invitation. Had he, as God's watchman for his people, some presentiment of problems ahead? After prayer with those near him, he resolved to go alone. The sea passage to Europe made possible a stop at Singapore, where he broke his journey long enough to visit Sitiawan and pay his respects to the Ling parents,[6] an action that set its seal on the peace God had newly planted in his heart.

The long sea journey meant time for rest and study and he reached England late in June much refreshed. He was met by Charles Barlow, who took him to his Peterborough home. He visited meetings as widely scattered as Ventnor and Islington, Croydon and Scotland, and tasted the warmth of love expressed within the group. He was shown great hospitality everywhere, for his coming was such a novelty to believers in this very strict and circumscribed group of the Brethren who themselves lacked a missionary outreach.[7] He was invited to tell of the work and was of course welcomed to participate at the Lord's Table and sometimes to minister the Word, though in this last his English may still have limited him. He also had long talks with senior men among them. The Chinese believers were regarded by his hosts as very immature Christians needing a lot of tutoring. Moreover he himself, though 30 years of age, had the youthful looks of a mere student, and with his native respect for wisdom and seniority was ready enough to listen to advice. He astonished them, however, with the kind of practical questions he and his brothers in Shanghai had regularly to face, such as, 'I want to be baptised, and so do my two wives!'

To younger friends he spoke light-heartedly of the simple Chinese rule for meetings, 'No Bible, no breakfast!' or regaled them with stories of the Fujian 'scissor-demons' who cut holes in your oiled-paper umbrella to let the rain in. But mostly when not involved in discussions he quietly listened and observed. He never ceased to respect the wealth of biblical insight to be found within this group, whose written ministry he had devoured. But at the same time he was much disturbed by the complacency that allowed them more than once in his hearing to say things like, 'Is there anything in the field of spiritual revelation that we Brethren do not have? To read what other Christians write is to waste time, for what do any have that we don't?'[8] Their deep spiritual wisdom seemed frozen. Once at a conference at Park Street, Islington, when invited to add his comment to a long discussion of doctrine to which he had listened, he gave vent to mounting impatience. Rising to his full six feet and stretching his arms wide, 'My dear brothers,' he said, 'your understanding of the truth is vast,' and then, bringing finger and thumb together, 'but in my land it would avail you only so much if, when needed, you could not cast out a demon!' He felt guilty afterwards at this outburst, but it expressed too his sense of how real is the Unseen.[9] And as he left Britain he observed with frankness to his friend Charles Barlow, 'Your people have wonderful light, but oh so little faith!'

On his longer journeys in Britain Mr Barlow or someone else accompanied him, as when he visited Aldeburgh to call on the veteran George Cutting, author of the widely used gospel booklet *Safety, Certainty and Enjoyment*, which by that date had run to 30 million copies. Once, however, he excused himself for a week to visit London on business, during which, without telling his hosts, he broke briefly out of the very closed circle in which he was moving. That Sunday he called in south London at the Christian Fellowship Centre in Honor Oak Road, Forest Hill, to worship with an independent evangelical group brought together through the ministry of T. Austin-Sparks, a former Baptist minister. This friend, whose magazine *A Witness and a Testimony* he had been receiving and whom he had greatly hoped to meet, was away from home; but George Paterson and others welcomed him warmly, without realising who he indeed was or his special role in China. He enjoyed their fellowship and the preaching of the Word, and with them he received with gladness the Lord's bread and wine.

Two weeks later his stay in England ended. With this sole

exception he had remained exclusively within the very close circle of a single group of Christians, and had made no contact whatever with the wider field of evangelical church life and witness in Britain. James Taylor of Brooklyn, New York, an older man whose word carried everywhere almost pontifical weight with this 'London Group' of Brethren and who had been for some weeks in England, planned now to accompany him back across the Atlantic. Taylor was a skilled and penetrating interrogator and was delighted to find Nee very open and free with him about the Chinese work, outlining its local conditions and spiritual needs and asking much counsel. When it came to doctrine, however, and especially biblical prophecy, he found that Nee entertained ideas of the second coming of Christ which he could not approve and which on further questioning he could only regard as glaring error.[10] They reached New York, where Nee was received among the group with the greatest affection, and he addressed a meeting at Westfield on the subject of deliverance from sin 'which by most was thought wonderful' but which in Taylor's judgement 'was defective doctrinally'.

Meanwhile in Britain, by an astonishing coincidence, a senior brother of the group chanced to find himself seated in a train to Glasgow opposite a teenage girl who was diligently reading the Bible. Chatting with her brought to light the fact that she worshipped at the Honor Oak Road meeting. He probed further, and learned in due course that a very pleasant Chinese had been there at the weekend, and she described him. He was horrified: had someone failed to account for Watchman's movements? He resolved to investigate. That night George Paterson had a phone call from a stranger. 'Do you know a Chinese named Nee? Has he been in fellowship with you? Has he broken bread with you?' To each question George answered a matter-of-fact 'Yes', and then the phone cut off at the other end. He thought, 'Someone's in trouble.'

A cable went off to Taylor at Brooklyn, but by now Watchman was away at New Haven. His main reason for crossing the Atlantic had been to spend a few days with Thornton and Carol Stearns, who were home with their family on furlough from Jinan. That Sunday, in defiance of Taylor's expressed advice, he worshipped and broke bread, as he had done in China, with the Stearns family and some others in their home. 'He made no admission of violation of principles,' Taylor wrote in sorrow. Pressed as to his position in the matter, Watchman, who was by now under considerable stress, declined to say or write anything until he had taken counsel with his fellow workers in Shanghai. The facts, as Taylor saw them, were forwarded to Vancouver, where Nee was to attend special meetings.[11]

In principle the meetings of the 'London Group' were fenced off from all other meetings of Christian believers. Substantially anyone outside was debarred from fellowship with anyone inside it unless he agreed from that time forth to restrict his movements to meetings within the fence. This rule was carried also into ordinary social relations, and was later to be enforced with increasing rigour by James Taylor, Jr, until in the early 1960s the movement was agonisingly disrupted on this issue.[12]

In Vancouver, nevertheless, Watchman was welcomed most warmly and invited to speak at the planned meetings. He seems to have enjoyed real liberty, for at least one young Canadian found the Lord and, as by many also in Britain, he is still fondly remembered. While there he renewed contact with his dear friend C.H. Judd of the China Inland Mission, and called also on Lena Clarke who, having worked for 23 years with the China Inland Mission in Szechwan, had retired in 1929 and would now return in fellowship with the Christians meeting at Hardoon Road.

On the long, quiet voyage home across the Pacific, as if to set his seal on the way he was leading his servant, God gave to Watchman a fresh revelation of Christ as his life. For a long while he had been acutely aware of a failure in his conduct in the matter of pleasing God. Let him tell it again in his own words. 'When I was a young Christian I was commended by various people for the Christ-likeness of my life, but some years later I found to my consternation that my temper was often getting the better of me. Even when I managed to control it so that it did not actually flare up, it was seething inside; and to add to my distress and dis-illusion, those kindly Christians who had commended me for Christ-like qualities that formerly impressed them were not slow to tell me how unfavourably my present life compared with my past. I used to be so humble and so patient, they said, so gentle and loving – but now . . . ! The worst of it was that their criticisms were well founded. With my own tales of failure I could have far outdone them. But how had this state of affairs emerged? What was the trouble?'

Watchman used, he says, to think of Christ as a Person apart, failing to identify him in any practical way with the host of praiseworthy qualities such as meekness, patience, love, wisdom, holiness, that he himself felt so strongly the lack of. 'For two whole years I was groping in that kind of darkness, seeking to amass as personal possessions the virtues that I felt should make up the Christian life (rather as before my conversion I used to amass worldly things) and getting nowhere in the effort. The trouble was that I had been accumulating things, albeit spiritual ones, and

God had taken in hand to relieve me of them in order to make way for the life of his Son.

'And then one day in 1933 light broke from heaven for me. Reading again 1 Corinthians 1:30 I suddenly saw that Christ was ordained of God to be made over to me in his fullness. What a difference! Oh the emptiness of *things*! Held by us out of relation to him they are dead, for God is not seeking a display of our Christ-likeness but a manifestation of his Christ. Once I saw this, it was the beginning of a new life for me. He himself is the sum of divine things, and thus he was the answer in me to all God's demands, and that, not as a matter for my future discovery but as a fact for my present acceptance. My daily life as a Christian would be summed up thereafter in the word *receive*.'[13]

▲ An early photo of Watchman Nee, 1937

▲ Margaret Barber (standing) with Margaret Ballord at Pagoda Anchorage, 1928

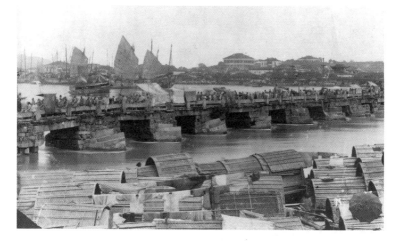

▲ Bridge of Ten Thousand Ages, Fuzhou

▲ Boys in middle school uniform, Trinity College, Fuzhou, 1930

▲ Trams and rickshaws, Shanghai, 1932

▲ Wedding of Watchman Nee and Charity Cheng, 1934. On left, bridegroom's sister (Mrs Ling), mother, brother (Hong-tsu) and father. On right,
bride's sister-in-law and brother (Samuel Chang) and eldest sister (Beulah)

▲ Wedding photo of Nee and Charity

▲ Rooftop in Shanghai, 1932.
Standing: Mayo, Powell, Faithful Luke, Phillips, Joyce, Dr C. H. Yu, House
Seated: John Chang, Mrs Mayo, Mrs Joyce, Watchman Nee

▲ Rooftop in Shanghai, 1932.
Seated: Dr Yu, Watchman Nee, John Chang, Faithful Luke with delegation of world brethren

▲ With T. Austin-Sparks, London, 1938

▲ Elizabeth Fischbacher (seated) with Mary Jones, 1960

▲ London, 1939

▲ London, 1939

▲ Watchman Nee   ▲ Angus Kinnear, 1938

▲ Three Chinese Christian leaders, 1935. John
Sung, Leland Wang, Watchman Nee

▲ Preaching band, Taiwan, 1953

▲ Preaching band, Taiwan, 1953

▲ K. H. Weigh and family, 1957

品璋大姊:

收到你四月七日的信,知道你沒有收到我通知你每次束西都已收到的信。你信上所提的束西,我都已经收到了,實在感謝你。

我身體情况,你是知道的,是慢性病,是器官病。發病就很难过,就是不發病,病依然在身上。只有發不發之分,没有好不好之分。夏天到了,多晒些太阳可以改變一点皮膚顏色,但不能改變病。但我維持自己的喜乐,请你放心。希望你自己也多保重一点,心中充滿喜乐。

　　祝你好

　　　　　　　　　述祖
　　　　　　　四月廿二日

P'in-tseng. Elder Sister.

I received your letter of 7 April. Knowing that you did not receive all those letters I wrote in which I mention all the things you sent me: All those things you mention in your letter I have received. I am really very grateful to you.

You know my physical condition. It is a chronic disease. It is organic. When it occurs the pain is severe (or, I feel very bad.) Even if it doesn't occur the disease is still there.⓵ The only difference is its being active or inactive.⓶ There is no such thing as recovery or non-recovery. When summer comes a little more sunlight can change the colour of the skin a little bit, but it cannot change the illness.⓷ But I maintain my own joy, so please don't worry (or, be at ease). And I hope you also take care of yourself, and let joy fill your heart.

　　　　　　　Wishing you well,
　　　　　　　Shu-chu.
　　　　　　　22 April 1972.

Heart amidst filled with joy

▲ A letter written by Nee shortly before his death (above) and translation below

13

New Horizons

B ack in China immense tasks awaited him. Correspondence between the Shanghai brothers and their
erstwhile friends in the West was to drag on for two
agonising years to its sorrowful conclusion, but it must not
be allowed meanwhile to divert them from the gospel outreach or the instruction of believers and the training of
God's servants. The strength of Watchman Nee's work lay in
the fact that every believer was an unpaid worker, and
everyone moving to a new city for business or in state service might make his home a place of prayer and a fresh centre of witness. The land itself was fast opening. From being
one vast maze of stepped footpaths clambering steeply over
hills and narrow tracks excellent for men and mules or a
wheelbarrow, it was blooming now with vehicle road systems and new railways. Rapid development of air flight
meant also that, for rulers and for those who could afford it,
fast travel about the country was becoming easier.

In the upstairs rooms at Hardoon Road, Watchman now
began to hold informal training sessions with a few of the
younger workers who were lodging there. He saw these
trainee brothers as the ones to whom these new fields of

work for God would one day lie open and gave talks to guide their thinking on church planting – that is, drawing new believers together in each locality as worshipping and witnessing groups.[1] He had seen much confusion in the West that had driven him back to the New Testament, where he found once more the simple lines first suggested to him in early writings of his now lost friends. Avoiding their legalism, he could seek to see in each town or village one such church congregation.

In January 1934 the third Overcomer Conference was held in Shanghai, at which he spoke on the centrality of Christ in Scripture and in the life of God's people. At this conference Witness Lee was able to be present from Yantai, as well as believers from cities in Jiangsu and Shandong, where assemblies of believers were fast springing up since Watchman's 1932 visit. The brothers date the work's several 'beginnings' in three four-year stages: Fuzhou 1924; Shanghai 1928; the north 1932.

But Watchman was restless. As himself a coastal dweller he had for some time wished to see more of inland China and especially the remote south-west provinces of Guizhou and Yunnan, there to gain a first-hand knowledge of the people, their life setting and their spiritual needs. Now in the spring of 1934 an occasion for this presented itself. A wealthy man named Ma had recently come to the Lord and at his baptism had taken the name of Ma Mu, 'Shepherd Ma'. From the Yangtze port of Yueyang he ran a successful trading business in Hunan Province with interests extending into Guizhou. A very straightforward brother, he possessed a strong Ford car and an adventurous spirit, to which was now added a new-found zeal for the gospel of Jesus Christ. Together the two planned a tour to the extreme limit of the just extended south-west motor road, and Watchman

now took the river ship to Yueyang to join him in the
venture.[2]

Loading the car with cans of gasoline and Christian
Gospels, they set out together on the circuit of the great
Hunan rice bowl, first south to the provincial capital of
Changsha and then north-west to Changde. They took their
time. Shepherd Ma did the driving, while at each ferry
crossing or wherever a few passers-by gathered, Watchman
Nee stood up in the halted car and preached to them Christ
Jesus as Saviour.

The navigable Yuan River has traditionally been the
route of trade with the south-west, and by now a well-worn
road led up its broad valley to Yuanling, as riverside rice terraces gave way to barley and wheat on the hillsides. This
city, where Ma had business contacts, lay within striking
distance of the Communist General He Long's Second Army
base at Sangzhi. However, the general was lying low and all
was quiet when they set out from there to climb on westward towards the distant Hunan frontier with Guizhou.
Some Hunan towns had down the years welcomed Christian outposts manned by European missionaries; yet still
so much of its populace was as yet unreached with the
gospel.

Guizhou seemed a province of more striking change, as
streets that until lately had stopped at city gates began to be
carried out into the countryside, and the newer contoured
roadway they were travelling hinted at more to come. But
there were maintenance roadworks to negotiate, and even
its finished surfaces were rough in the extreme. They were
well into the hills now. Shepherd was short-sighted so wore
thick lenses, and at the unfenced corners where a precipi-
tous drop awaited any false move, his arms, he declared,
'turned to putty'! At such times Watchman, with less

driving experience but steadier nerves, was compelled to take over the wheel.

At the provincial capital of Guiyang they were warmly welcomed by a group of believers meeting regularly in a home, and they enjoyed some good days of fellowship with them. Watchman shared with them some treasures from the Scriptures, and Ma was amazed to hear him give one long talk surveying Christian church history, full of dates, names and figures, without referring to a single note. Here at Guiyang, however, they themselves began to learn how uncertain was their way ahead. Some locals warned them that long stretches of the Yunnan road barely yet existed. What should they do? They had come so far: how could they now give up? Feeling, however, some inner assurance after prayer, they padded themselves against the cold and, having been commended to God by the church, they pushed on doggedly ever further into the mountains, where by now colourful azaleas and rhododendrons adorned the steeper valleys. Gasoline was in very short supply, so they conserved it by coasting the down-slopes on brakes alone. (Four years later, when being driven through Scotland, Watchman suggested we too might adopt this practice!)

Rain now gave way to snow, which lay white on the peaks as for some 200 miles they toiled on really high sections of a road nearing 6,000 feet, and once or twice crossed passes that approached 10,000 feet. Ma tells how the rhythm of the Ford's engine drummed into his mind the themes of Watchman's whistle-stop sermons. But Watchman himself, often taking the wheel at high altitudes with forceful Yunnan winds playing on him, found his heart now gave him severe ischaemic pain on exertion. (Had his earlier long illness taken its toll?) He was thus much relieved when the route dropped lower again and the going became easier. At length they came upon one more partial breach in its construction, and a long one. But some laughing tribal folk appeared and gladly came to their rescue with a very prolonged push through what was scarcely road at all, to set them back once more safely on the track beyond.

Here an engineer approached. 'Wherever have you come from?' he asked. 'Yueyang? But that's incredible! Then you are the very first long-distance travellers to make it over the route.'

Exhilaration now overcame their chill and fatigue as, after a needed break, they began the long, gradual descent eventually to the Gaoting plain, amid farmsteads and fields green with spring rice. This last stretch of the motor road was in fair shape and there were wayfarers passing back and forth on it. But approaching Kunming their fresh attempts at roadside witness were diverted by their hearers' questions about the vehicle. With the discovery that it had come through by road all the way from Hunan, it quickly acquired fame. Ma could have asked a good price for it!

They themselves, however, had a special interest in coming so far. North of Kunming across the River of Golden Sand (the upper Yangtze Jiang) lay Tibet. Back in Shanghai there were brothers out of Yunnan whom God was calling to evangelise the Tibetans, and Watchman wanted to see for himself what this would involve. A trek of several days brought them to a market in the mountains to which Tibetans brought their wares. Here Shepherd Ma recalls these people's extreme hospitality, always refilling his bowl long before he had emptied it, while Watchman, helped by an interpreter, sensed their spiritual darkness and need of the good news of salvation.

Their whole trip into the south-west was providentially

timed. It would have been quite impossible in the two years of civil warfare that followed. For in the autumn of this year 1934 the Communists under Mao Ze-dong and his lieutenant Zhu De, the opium addict transformed by Marxism, were forced by Chiang Kai-shek's encircling armies to break secretly out of their south Jiangxi base. Ever since 1929 these two had campaigned with success there in the south for a true peasant soviet in the villages. Now, expelled by overwhelming force, they began their historic 6,000-mile trek, with bag, baggage and archives, west into Yunnan, north up the Tibetan border, and east again into Shanxi. Other groups from Hunan, Anhui and north Sichuan made similar long treks to join them. The whole movement, known to history as 'The Long March', was to be a critical and formative experience in the evolution of Chinese Communism.

But long before these events Watchman was back in the great commercial city of Hankou, where he stopped to give to the believers a series of Bible studies on the Song of Songs.[3] These owed much to the Brethren commentator C.A. Coates and demonstrate an indebtedness to these writers he was always ready to acknowledge, whatever the strains that might afflict his relations with their successors.[4]

From Hankou he returned to Shanghai, where in late summer he appears in a happy photo with John Sung and Leland Wang. This meeting had been arranged by the Christian leader K.S. Li with the commendable aim of bringing together in a single team the gifts, methods and outlooks of these three so different men.[5] The encounter, however, was a passing one, each again going his separate way. Leland Wang disagreed with Nee's reliance on unsalaried ministers of the Word, as well as with his work's independence of the missions which, he feared, could only bring division and loss to the Christian cause. Yet in the light of subsequent events he was in later years to speak with generous approval of Nee's unflinching stand for his principles.

John Sung and Watchman Nee unhappily never quite hit it off, though each held the other in high regard and each reaped where the other had sown. Sung, who lived for only ten years after this, was a whirlwind evangelist who achieved results through dogmatic statement and emotional appeal. A friend describes him as 'cocksure and stubborn, constantly off at a tangent, a man whose every opinion was a conviction'.[6] Nee was certainly the more talented preacher; yet Sung was the one whom God used to sweep multitudes into the kingdom, and the revival that flowed from his preaching spread like a prairie fire.[7] Sung's converts generally stood firm, but he left their care to others. In the words of one observer, when he preached 'the sheep woke up and were hungry, and because there was no one to feed them Watchman's teaching ministry was timely in filling the gap'.[8] But in course of time Sung became outspokenly critical of Nee, while Nee privately expressed misgivings at Sung's theological immaturity and failure to provide for the permanence of his work.

14

Count It All Joy

At this point an unexpected and most welcome figure re-enters the story. On his return from England Watchman had learned that his schooldays sweetheart Charity Zhang was back in Shanghai, having achieved an MSc degree in biology at Yanjing University. Until now she had seemed outwardly the same pleasure-loving girl, at ease with current fashion and taste; but in her heart God's Holy Spirit had been at work. She attended several meetings at Wen De Li and there she met the Lord, and not long after that she asked for baptism. The older sisters witnessed that she was inwardly transformed, a fact which, when Watchman eventually met and spoke with her, he could joyfully confirm. Her presence aroused, too, his own long-buried affections. His Yunnan tour gave him time to weigh his feelings before God.

Seeing this, Charity's sister Faith (Mrs Bao) took a hand. Welcoming home the returned wanderer, 'Now,' she said, 'our dear Pin-hui has become an earnest Christian, serving the Lord with steadfast purpose. Would you perhaps consider marriage with her? I feel sure she would have no objections.'

Watchman was 30, Charity 31. Yet only after much prayer did he conclude that to yield to his heart's promptings was indeed God's will. And she agreed. Those black-coated swallows, messengers of love, had done their work! Then an urgent letter to his parents in Fuzhou sought their approval – and their help with the wedding arrangements. He-ping, recalling her blundering plans at Sitiawan, was struck with panic, but they set out happily for Shanghai, only to be met there by a host of rumours. Charity's maiden aunt Zhang Mei-zhen, it became known, was strongly opposed to the match of her brilliant niece with a penniless preacher. Angrily she wrote to him commanding the customary courtesy call, 'or I shall create hell for you!' whereupon he cancelled his planned visit, unwilling to play politics under threat. (A few others who idolised Watchman were also shocked that such a man of prayer could consider marrying a mere college beauty from Yanjing.)

But his mother went to meet Zhang Rui-guan, Charity's uncle and the family's legal head, who to her relief gave his full approval. She next invited Charity to accompany her to another city, there to take part with her in special gospel meetings. They shared a room for a week, living and praying together, and by the time they returned God had given her complete confidence that Charity was indeed his choice for her son.

Early in October nearly 400 believers gathered at Hangzhou, capital of Zhejiang, the ancient city of classical beauty, set amid steep hills and soft green lakes. A special conference had been arranged here by Philip Luan to consolidate the work in this very responsive region. Ever since Peace Wang had first visited the area for work among women, small local meetings had been growing up in eastern Zhejiang, and among those who now gathered were believers from such towns as Fenghua, Wenling and Zhoushan.[1] Others came from Suzhou in Jiangsu and from many more centres. Here for ten days Watchman expounded the Word in what was afterwards remembered as the fourth 'Overcomer Conference', and he was overjoyed to have both his parents present. The day following had been fixed by his mother for the wedding, and so slow was he to bring his mind round to the idea of being a bridegroom that he wore only his normal preaching garment, until his host came to his rescue and found him a coat.

Thus on the afternoon of 19 October 1934 (the anniversary of his parents' own wedding),[2] Ni Tuo-sheng was united in Christian marriage with Zhang Pin-hui in the presence of a large gathering of believers. They gave thanks to God, singing the hymn he had written for her ten years earlier; and afterwards they feasted at thirty tables of ten guests each.

Now the storm broke. They arrived back in Shanghai to find that Charity's aunt Mei-zhen had unleashed her fury in a public attack on Watchman. It took the form of a press advertisement in a secular national daily, harshly worded in scholarly Chinese. How, she asked, dare this poverty-struck preacher carry off her brilliant Pin-hui? Whence could he possibly afford to support, let alone satisfy, so cultured a young lady? If he could, it must be from foreign sources that he got his money. And there followed a veiled attack upon his morals, offensive enough in this context and readily seized upon by those who jealously resented his Christian influence. Not once but daily for a week the nationwide slander went forth, while handbills in the same vein were printed and distributed widely in Christian circles. One missionary observed, 'The one I read was so vile that I burnt it, and then felt I needed a bath.'

As one would expect, this wholly unwarranted public attack on him threw Watchman into deep depression. He was human, and trusting God he had followed till now a lonely pathway. His finding a new joy in partnership with Charity had been mercilessly twisted into an occasion for wounding them both and dishonouring the One they served. In their new home he retired to bed and would see no one. On principle he would never defend himself against such an attack, feeling that God might be using it to shape and discipline him;[3] but now they were in it together. It was a cruel beginning.

One forthright missionary lady called at the house and announced, 'He will see *me*, for I have a message to him from God,' and went in. 'No weapon that is formed against thee shall prosper,' she declared, 'and every tongue that rises against thee in judgement thou shalt condemn!'[4] And in an endeavour to lift his spirit Faith Zhang came and chatted in lighter vein. 'Does it matter what they say?' she teased. 'You have won a wife after your own heart!' For Charity was indeed a joy to him. Her Chinese, spoken and written, was beautiful and so was her English. She had a humble walk with the Lord Jesus that he could value highly, and would be the greatest help to him in his work. They would become the novella's traditional 'pair of king-fishers, close-knit in unswerving flight towards a common goal'. And as all agreed, Charity was beautiful!

They went for a brief 'holiday' to a remote country place where they could be away from it all – but not forsake the witness of the gospel. Together they read the Bible with open minds, sensing the need of a fresh anointing. There was a period in which Watchman seemed to be beset with problems. The painful interchange with the Taylorite Brethren was dragging on. His heart condition that had appeared in the Yunnan mountains began to recur. And he wrestled too with an inward problem concerning the indwelling of the Holy Spirit. On the Lord's Day they met for worship and prayer with a small rural group of simple believers. As sent there by God Watchman preached, but it only confirmed what he already knew, that something was missing. For a while now his preaching had lacked power and borne little fruit.

'I was facing a big problem,' he tells us. 'It concerned the question of personal enduement with the Holy Spirit for service. I was under a deep sense of a need of this, and also in some confusion of mind about the doctrine. Yet somehow, pray as I might, the Lord seemed unwilling either to answer my questions or to show me the way into the experience. I knew God had something for me, but it remained out of my reach. I must somehow get clear on this or I could not go on. It is no exaggeration to say that at that point my whole ministry hung in the balance.

'What God sought to give me I seemed unable to receive. I could not get through alone, and just then what I seemed above all to need was the fellowship of those senior to me in the Lord – but where to find it? Here we were far removed from other servants of God with anything approaching the knowledge of him that I enjoyed. He had sent us here. The handful of believers among whom we stayed were the simplest of country folk who knew so little of the Lord that they could certainly not, I felt, help me in this my difficulty. They would scarcely even have a sufficient foundation from which to pray intelligently for me in it, and certainly not enough to bring me through.

'But I was forgetting the Body! At last I reached an impasse. There was in fact nothing left but to call them in, if I was not to give up and go out altogether. So at my

request those simple brethren came to me in my need. I told
them what I could of my difficulty, and they prayed – and
as they prayed, light dawned! The thing did not need
explaining: the familiar Scripture itself became clear. It was
done, and done in such a way that it has never needed to
be repeated.

'Yes,' Watchman continues, 'God will bring us often to
places where we cannot get through alone. For the life that
asserts that "God and I are enough" is only in fact hindering
him. In that quiet rural scene the Lord had taught me how
those members of the Body which seem to be more feeble
are indeed to him most precious.'[5] The lesson would serve
him well in the future.

In November Watchman and Charity travelled south for
special meetings in Xiamen, and there the tide of blessing
again flowed. Watchman was greatly cheered one day to
meet, seemingly by chance, Li Guo-qing, the Fujian doctor's
adopted son who once spoke out of turn at Mei-hua fishing
village. He had gone on to Xiamen University and was now
an aircraft pilot. When Watchman asked, 'Do you still follow the Lord?' he replied, 'Mr Nee, do you mean to suggest
that after all we went through together there I could ever
forsake him?'

And among other rays of light to cheer him was the
return in January 1935 of Thornton and Carol Stearns.
After Watchman's 1932 visit to Qilu University, the emergence of a 'separatist' Christian group worshipping in the
town had raised questions about the orthopaedic surgeon
in a Union Christian university. Accordingly he resigned
and took up a challenging new appointment in Shanghai.
Here Caroline would become a friend of great help to Charity in coming days.

But there had come no solution to the problem with the

Taylorite Brethren in London and New York. It helped the Shanghai leaders, however, to formulate more clearly their own light from God on church relations. The Westerners had charged Watchman with having 'compromised the fellowship' extended to him by partaking at the Lord's Table (in Honor Oak and New Haven) with Christians who were governed by the principle that 'anyone claiming to be a believer was allowed to break bread without regard to the religious and other associations in which he was involved'. They sought therefore 'to enlighten the Shanghai brethren as to the principles of Christian fellowship and to help them to judge Nee's actions'. Occasion was also taken to call attention to his allegedly unsound views on biblical prophecy.

Their demand was one of separation from all other Christian associations prior to being received at the Lord's Table with them, whereas some in the Chinese meetings had long retained also their links with mission congregations without, till now, any questions being raised. To the Western brethren such laxity would not do, and the comparative immaturity of the Chinese movement was no excuse. The Brethren offered to them a century of written 'truth' and, as James Taylor put it afterwards in a separate letter to Faithful Luke, 'You are obligated to the Lord to embrace it, profit from it, and stand firmly by it.'[6]

From No. 36–38 Wen De Li, Lane 240, Hardoon Road their final long letter in English dated 2 July 1935 was signed and mailed off by D.C. Du, Y.A. Wu, W. Nee and K.Y. Chang. It was a humble and gracious appeal to Christian reasonableness and the Holy Spirit's rule, and it contained the following summary statement of principle:

- 'We must distinguish between "sins" (either morally or doctrinally) that hinder fellowship with God and "sins" which do not. We know definitely that sins like adultery, and disbelief in Christ coming in the flesh, would certainly put one out of fellowship, but as to the other "sins" – say, that of "bad association" and wrong interpretation of prophecy – fellowship with God is not hindered.

- 'The fact remains that many a child of God in the different systems whom we have thought unfit for fellowship, is having a closer walk with God and a richer communion with our Lord than we.
- 'It is the Spirit, and the Spirit alone, who can decide the question of one's fitness for fellowship.
- 'The reason why we receive a man is that God has received him (Romans 14:3). So the divine command is, "Now him that is weak in faith, receive" (14:1). We must receive all those whom God has received. This command is clear, decisive and embracing.'[7]

This, then, was a straightforward plea for open communion based upon awakened Christian conscience, but it was met from the West only with an entrenched exclusivism. A representative 'meeting of assembly character' was called on 30 July 1935 at Park Street Hall, Islington, when the formal break with the Chinese brethren was announced. Several who were present registered a profound shock to their better sense, but it was an authoritative decision, binding by consent on every meeting of the 'London Group' worldwide. The letter conveying this to the Shanghai brothers was dated 31 August 1935. It called into question the sincerity of the Chinese brethren's love for Christ, it charged Nee with lack of uprightness, and it stated that, had the principles outlined above been disclosed in 1932, fellowship then would have been impossible. 'We grievously failed in our lack of holy care in laying hands too quickly on those with whom we were insufficiently acquainted. We are unable to walk with you . . . This, of course, applies also to all those maintaining links of fellowship with you.'[8]

One of the letter's signatories was Charles R. Barlow, now a deeply sorrowing man. The Chinese too were left in a state of shock by the whole episode. Their disappointment in the sphere of Christian relationships and their grieved love were profound.

In the summer of 1935, Watchman and Charity went to Yantai in Shandong province. Elizabeth Fischbacher, a person much in demand as one of the China Inland Mission's gifted speakers, was holding revival meetings there in the town. She had learned that Watchman was passing lately through a period of spiritual barrenness, and he now shared with her some of the workings of his active mind. Himself open to a new experience of God, he agreed to attend her Yantai meetings. She herself shared a Shandong fondness for ecstatic accompaniment of preaching and prayer, and when her Chinese, or indeed her English, would not any more hold out she would pray and sing in the Spirit in other tongues. There was real substance and power in her preaching and Watchman came under its spell, responding to the appeal of the Word and entering into what was for him a quite new awareness of God's good pleasure. It is clear that he now found a further release that put an end to that barren phase in his own preaching. To Shanghai he telegraphed, 'I have met the Lord.'

To the autumn conference back there he brought a message on (a) the filling with, and (b) the outpouring of the Spirit of God, that cleared minds and led many into a like experience of divine power. The effect of this was that over a year or so a wave of spiritual release, some excitement and an emphasis on outward manifestations swept southwards through the churches – that is, in groups majoring hitherto on the mind rather than the emotions. Western evangelicals feared lest subjective experience might lead Christians away from the Bible text. But another acceptable avenue of release, said to have originated with John Sung, was already customary: to end prayer meetings with a brief period of simultaneous prayer when those whose petitions had been crowded out by limit of time could unload their burdens Godward. This practice could be a most moving outlet for the Holy Spirit when, under his control, massed prayer rose briefly in a crescendo and waned again to the silence of completion. Now, however, in the south rein was given also to extremes of excitement, with jumping, clapping, laughter, unknown tongues that conveyed no sense to hearers or even speaker, and a flood of dramatic healings, some surely real but not a few mistaken.

Late in 1935 Watchman and Charity again reached Xiamen where, due to a hitch over accommodation, the planned special conference meetings had at the last minute to be redirected elsewhere. At Jin-jiang (Tsin Kiang) between Xiamen and Fuzhou the dean of the Christian College, Wu Ren-jie (Lukas Wu, later to serve God in Manila), who had recently found the Saviour through interpreting for John Sung, now came to the rescue by opening his large home for the ten-day conference which nearly 400 attended. Watchman spoke on the victorious life and the outpouring of the Holy Spirit, and there was yet one more outburst of divine blessing. Thereafter Wu's household formed the nucleus of another worshipping and witnessing group, a pattern of spread that was to be reproduced in coming days widely across the land.

Witness Lee affirms that Watchman himself 'never spoke

in tongues'.[9] This may be so, but cannot now be proved. He certainly believed in the Holy Spirit's 'lesser gifts' to the church of healing and of speaking with and interpretation of other tongues. 'I have seen with my own eyes', he said, 'cases of instantaneous divine healing. We do not oppose this; we only contend with erroneous ways of healing.' And again, 'Some ask me if I oppose speaking with tongues. Certainly not, though I do question tongues which are obtained through faulty means.' And to this writer he recounted from experience a telling illustration of how, in one very confused village congregation, God had used this means to convey to them unpalatable facts which they needed urgently to face, but which the only otherwise informed person was under a vow not to divulge. This kind of thing, he maintained, gave meaning and purpose to the gift.

On the other hand, he was equally strong in affirming that 'not all speak with tongues',[10] and his teaching on the theme was always balanced. Indeed, a senior CIM missionary who a few years later attended his lectures on the Holy Spirit in Shanghai describes them as 'the clearest teaching on this subject that I have ever heard'.

Some revival methods, Watchman held, worked like spiritual opium. Addiction to them demanded mere repetition in an ever-increasing dosage. Elizabeth Fischbacher felt herself to blame for the loss of restraint that followed in the wake of these events and abandoned public preaching altogether, to discover in due course a richly rewarding ministry through her gifted pen. One or two leading co-workers were quite carried away by the emotional extremes of the movement; and a crisis came when a woman believer in Shanghai, under its influence, committed suicide from a high window. The conclusion appears to have been that the sovereign outpouring of the Spirit is indeed from God and subject to him, but if we let the experience become an addiction its true value is soon lost and we are on an empty road. Rediscovery of the Comforter's creative role in John's Gospel and elsewhere in the Scriptures offers a way to amendment.

When, after three years, the pendulum had swung back and the episode had run its course Watchman, talking with K.S. Wang in Singapore, observed, 'We find on looking back over this period that the loss has been quite large, the gain rather trivial.'

15

Rethinking

In October 1935, with the first straggling survivors of the
Long March, Mao Ze-dong emerged in northern Shanxi
to take up his new headquarters at Yanan as the undisputed leader of the Chinese Communist Party. Their
year-long feat of endurance was to become an emotional
high peak in the Party's annals. Some of its spectacular
episodes were already legends of Communist heroism and
invincibility: the breakout from the Jiangxi encirclement,
the secret crossing of the River of Yellow Sand, the forcing
under fire of the Bridge of Iron Chains over the Dadu River
at Luding, the ascent of the Great Snow Mountain, and the
nightmare traverse of the Sichuan swamplands. Sustained
throughout by political formulae and iron determination,
they emerged now at a key point on the fringe of the north
China plain, welded by their ordeal into a disciplined
nucleus for future operations. After so long under nearly
continuous military attack they had acquired a new self-
assurance as Chinese Communists in their own right, no
longer answerable to Soviet Russia.

Chiang Kai-shek's attempt to eliminate them had, at least
for the present, failed dismally and its abandonment in the

south brought relative quiet to that region. The Shanghai brothers who had felt called to the Tibetan borderlands found their way at last open to set out for Kunming in Yunnan. In the next year or so six made their way there. Among Tibetans themselves they met with a heart-warming response, but seriously lacked literature. Tracts and Scripture portions in the Tibetan language were therefore printed in Shanghai and shipped to them via Hanoi, where, to Watchman's disgust, the French government confiscated them. He arranged therefore for the plates to be flown to Yunnan and the printing done on the spot. Only thus after long delay was the need met.

Elsewhere in China the expansion of the work was set forward by two factors. One was the increasing demand among converts of whatever mission allegiance for Watchman's sermon transcriptions. The magazine and the Bible-centred booklets found their way into Christian homes everywhere, providing food for many who had been aroused spiritually by revivalist preaching but now had none to feed them. Nee's gift of explaining basic Christian doctrines in simple words went far to meet their need.

The other factor was, as we have seen, the spontaneous use of believers' homes. A prayer group would spring up where a believer moved by transfer of business or official service or by other displacement and at once this would become a fresh centre of Christian witness, drawing people, some out of paganism but not a few from various mission connections, into a simple church fellowship. They were men and women who had turned from their sins to the Saviour to give their all to him. As each small nucleus grew it was given 'elders' (*zhang-lao*) in the New Testament pattern to guide its activities and make provision for its ministries. It might in due course require larger premises, but its meeting place must be functional and never monumental and there was no thought of buying land for church buildings, or even renting halls, that did not spring from the expansion of the Holy Spirit's work in the believers themselves.

The movement also had 'apostles' (*shi-tu*, an envoy). These were full-time workers with a roving commission to evangelise the unreached, to establish churches where there were none, and to build up the believers. They themselves might move further afield, perhaps hiring a public hall for some fresh outreach in a new situation.

This meant that the activities embraced two concepts, the churches and the work. The work Watchman viewed (to use the English adjectives he himself coined) as *platformic*, the churches as *round-tablic*. To preclude if possible fresh sectarian divisions on grounds of doctrine or around personalities,[1] the churches were thought of as local units corresponding on the ground to secular administrative areas (villages, towns and municipalities). Besides being self-supporting and self-propagating, they were each locally autonomous, whereas the work was loosely coordinated by regions with Watchman and a few others acting as advisers to the mobile apostles in their areas, training them and themselves feeling responsible before God for the flow of their financial support. When an apostle found himself in any local church situation (but not when engaged in his wider work) he subjected himself to the local elders. In 1938 Nee stated that there were 128 such 'apostles' out in full-time service.

The whole structure and procedure had grown up over the previous decade by extempore application of their reading of the New Testament to situations as they had arisen. There seems no evidence that Nee ever met Roland Allen or even that he read his well-known writings, *Missionary Methods: St Paul's or Ours* (1912) and *The Spontaneous Expansion of the Church and the Causes which Hinder It* (1927); but it must be remembered that, whatever he may have read, he rarely if ever quoted Christian writers who did not share his own conservative evangelical position. His methods were still in process of development, and were thought of as secondary to the spiritual life and fellowship of the believers. Always conformity to Christ and witness to his saving power were the primary concerns.

The movement's strength lay in the quality of its manpower. Men and women joined it of their own free will, without the attraction of associated gain as offered, for example, by the mission educational system for a century and more. As Watchman has explained, what the Chinese saw and the missionaries took longer to realise was that, quite apart from the foreignness of mission patterns, they had unavoidably offered in the early days avenues of promotion in the church to men who had begun life as missionaries' house-servants and who, despite the splendid dedication of many of them, nevertheless constituted in practice a 'class' of Christians unlikely to inspire esteem among more cultured and intellectual Chinese. In the sphere of leadership, early missionary success could thus in the long term be self-limiting.

But here in the so-called 'Little Flock' meetings people met as believers to learn to know the Lord and serve him better. Some of the assemblies began to show a high preponderance of educated men, doctors, university staff, businessmen and army officers. Among the students who in Beijing in 1936 'composed almost entirely the regular congregation of the Christians Meeting Place in that educational centre' there were 'top honour students of Yenching,

Ching Hua, Peking Union Medical College, Peking University, and nurses in training in the Methodist and Presbyterian Hospitals. The missionary doctors said of them, "They are among our finest nurses, and they really seem to have something."'[2]

A quick survey of the extent of the work at this time suggests that within the movement there were already within China more than 30 local churches, some doubtless quite small, together with a few among Chinese overseas. But the feeling of observers about their spread was mixed. In the north-west province of Gansu in the early 1940s an Alliance missionary found reason to suggest that 'the further the movement got from its base the more it failed to distinguish between unfeigned love of the brethren and certain less admirable emotional expressions'.[3] He felt, as did others, that its adherents could be justly charged with spiritual pride, and that though in the coastal cities the movement flourished among the elite, there too it made 'unabashed efforts to prejudice members of established churches and divert even pastors if it could'. An English Baptist, writing of Shaanxi[4] Province, reports how 'in 1942 a group of earnest young men in Xian who studied the Greek New Testament and read Madame Guyon left the older churches to form a purified body called the "Little Flock", which re-baptised Christians who joined and which met for the "breaking of bread" and the preaching of the Word each Sunday. They were strongly anti-church and criticised different denominations of the Church in China as foreign accretions, yet do not see that their action in drawing away from the Church was setting up yet another denomination.'[5] And in the coastal province of Zhejiang, whereas some of the CIM missionaries might speak with warm appreciation of their excellent teaching and of the true Christian fellowship to be found among them, to others the rapid leakage of believers into their ranks from among the flourishing mission-related churches was a cause of growing concern. To them Watchman Nee seemed but a sheep-stealer. There is little doubt that he was at this time a thorn in many a missionary's side.

Of the original Fujian brothers several had already gone overseas as workers and Christian witnesses: Simon Meek in 1931 to the Philippines, Daniel Chen to Singapore, and Faithful Luke to Indonesia. In July 1937, at Meek's invitation, Watchman visited Manila and there and in Baguio addressed meetings of up to 100 for four weeks on the Christian life of victory, the fullness of the Holy Spirit and the practical fellowship of the church.

From Manila Watchman went on to Singapore, and then on through Malaysia again when the full-scale Japanese invasion of China began and thus was still away from Shanghai when on 14 August hostilities also broke out there. Chinese planes struck at Japanese shipping on the Huangpu and two jettisoned Chinese bombloads caused a massive death toll of their own civilians in a department store and on a neighbouring street. Marines landed to make a Japanese stronghold of the Hongkou suburb, while throngs of refugees swarmed into the Concession from the surrounding areas and set up 'straw villages' on every empty plot. Shanghai remained open from the south, however, and by this route within a month Watchman had found his way back to his wife. Their home was in an evacuated area, but she herself was safe with the sisters at Hardoon Road, though still within earshot of the land-fighting at Zhabei just a few miles to the north. Not for the last time their possessions had been ransacked, and when they found their way back there it was to miss, among other things, the Chinese Bible he had given her as a wedding present.

Satisfied that all was as well as could be, he was soon off again circumventing the battle area for a journey up the Yangtze to Hankou (of the triple city Wuhan). Here in November 1937 he called together as many full-time workers as could be reached, and gave them a course of addresses with open discussion on the lines of a similar conference he had urgently held in January that year in Shanghai. On these two occasions he abandoned for once his emphasis on the Christian's inward life in order to deal with more technical externalities. He had, he tells us, been led to see that Corinthian truths are no less precious than Ephesian ones, since the author of both letters was inspired by one and the same Spirit of God. Those who are acquainted with universal Ephesian truths cannot afford to make local Corinthian mistakes. He set out therefore to crystallise and codify the practical principles that together they had worked out from Scripture and used in living situations in the conduct of the work and the formation of local churches. Until now the workers had looked to his personal counselling, but with the disturbed state of the country he felt he owed it to them to define more clearly the position reached. This task completed, he returned again past the battle area to Shanghai, which by November was wholly under Japanese control, every house and hovel, every junk and sampan flying a Rising Sun to show who was master. Barbed wire, sandbags and barricades were everywhere and commodity prices soared. In December the southern capital, Nanjing, fell to the invaders amid unprecedented horrors. The 'rape of Nanking' would become legendary. Nationalist forces of government had begun their long retreat westward that was to end in the far isolation of Chongqing.

Full notes of the two series of lectures were shared around the fellow workers, which led immediately to a demand for their publication. With Charity's and Ruth Lee's literary help therefore, Watchman prepared them urgently for the press so that believers and workers throughout the country might share the values of the two occasions. By March 1938 the book was printed, appearing under the title *Gong-zuo de Zai-si* ('Rethinking the Work').[6] In his preface Watchman quotes Margaret Barber's observation that 'God's Spirit will only work along God's lines'. The book is in fact an examination from the Scriptures of some of 'God's lines' of church life and expansion as revealed to these particular men over this period and in this historic setting, and herein lies its value. 'The truths referred to in this book', Nee wrote, 'have been gradually learned and practised during the past years. Numerous adjustments have been made as greater light has been received, and if we remain humble, and God shows us mercy, we believe there will be further adjustments in the future.'

From his handful of missionary friends too there was immediate pressure for an English edition of the book, but of the wisdom of this he was not convinced. For his first title in English to be so untypical of his ministry as a whole seemed merely to invite misunderstanding. But anyway, in his search for the fellowship of older and wiser men he now had plans to accompany Elizabeth Fischbacher and two other CIM ladies on a visit to Europe. Before leaving this time he was overjoyed to be given by the doctors an absolutely clear report on his lung condition.

Taking Charity with them as far as Hong Kong to stay with the Nee parents out of reach of the war, they sailed by Anchor Line, and on arrival in the Clyde in July of 1938 Watchman went first to Kilcreggan to meet Mr T. Austin-Sparks. Until now they had only corresponded, but Watchman had been an appreciative reader of his devotional magazine, *A Witness and a Testimony*, and they quickly found themselves on common ground. It was here too that, arriving from a holiday in the islands and myself under a compulsion of God, I met him. We travelled south together to the annual Convention for the Deepening of Spiritual Life in Keswick, Cumberland, where the CIM ladies joined us. There on a morning of sunshine he attended the great missionary meeting chaired by the Rev. W.H. Aldis, Home Director of the China Inland Mission. As he sat near to a Japanese speaker on the platform the war havoc in China was fresh in everyone's mind. When his turn came he led the crowd to God in intercession for the Far East in terms that to many of us back there in the 1930s were a revelation. It was a prayer that few who were privileged to be present forgot. 'The Lord reigns: we affirm it boldly. Our Lord Jesus Christ is reigning, and he is Lord of all: nothing can touch his authority. It is spiritual forces that are out to destroy his interests in China and Japan. Therefore we do not pray for China, we do not pray for Japan, but we pray for the interests of thy Son in China and in Japan. We do not blame any men, for they are only tools in the hand of thine enemy. We stand for thy will. Shatter, O Lord, the kingdom of darkness, for the persecutions of thy church are wounding thee. Amen.'[7] While at Keswick he talked informally to mission candidates on the 'essential qualities of a missionary' and, from the Epistle to the Romans, on 'the Lord's work for our salvation; the Lord himself for our life'. Most significantly, at the end of the week he partook at the convention's vast united Communion service under the banner 'All one in Christ Jesus', thus publicly setting his seal upon the position he and his Chinese fellow workers had taken three years earlier.

Watchman now travelled to London and to the Christian Fellowship Centre at Honor Oak Road, Forest Hill, where his single previous visit had precipitated so acutely the issue of open fellowship. At once he felt at home there, with Mr Austin-Sparks and the other responsible men in the church. He made this his temporary base and it was there that the present writer spent with him some unforgettable weeks.

The church at Honor Oak was widely open to the Lord's people and had a clear missionary vision, but with an emphasis also upon the subjective work of the cross in Christian lives.[8] This, in the evangelical climate of the time, was felt to be somewhat negative and liable to divert active witnessing Christians to a too passive occupation with 'higher things'. Moreover, like Nee himself, Honor Oak was blamed for a drift of a few missionaries out of the historic Western missions in search of more spontaneous patterns of church life and testimony. Watchman had thus again opted to move in a flow slightly aside from mainstream church planting policies.

Those of us who were privileged to enjoy briefly something of a monopoly of his fellowship and ministry were immensely enriched by the experience. He was so easy to talk with, and his Eastern cultural background made discussion of our common heritage in Christ so stimulating. When he spoke in public, whether taking morning prayers or addressing a church meeting, his excellent English conspired with the charm of his mannerisms and his non-Western analogies to make him a joy to listen to. But it was the content of his addresses that won us. He wasted no words, but brought us straight to grips with some problem of Christian living that had long bothered us. Or he confronted us with some demand of God that we had shamelessly sidestepped, for on too many matters we Christians excel – as he engagingly put it – at 'dotching the itchue'. He displayed, too, the Chinese thinker's great care in his choice of terms and often gave back new meaning to our worn evangelical clichés.

Moreover he could see through us, and seeing, still be faithful. This was because always his object was to exalt the Christ he loved. Within a month of coming among us, skilfully, but with obviously deep concern, he put his finger right on one of our danger points; and that, sure enough, was our spiritual pride. He told us gently that God had shown him from experience that God trains his servants (whose sins have been met by his cross) by a principle of matching reward: 'Judge not, that ye be not judged, for the measure you give will be the measure you get' – that is, from God. We delight in the other clause: 'Give, and it shall be given to you; good measure . . .' but somehow skip the first one. He majors on 'Forgive'; 'Be merciful.'[9] No wonder, then, that notes of his talks to us have seemed, many years later in times of proving, to leap from the tattered notebook with fresh and startling relevance.

At that time I was a serious young missionary recruit preparing to set out for India in November, and with two other friends enjoyed long and valuable conversations with Watchman on everything from missionary finance to the book of Revelation. Never at any time did he so much as hint that I should leave, or not join, an established missionary enterprise. The best advice he gave me as the Lord's messenger in a foreign culture was to wear (metaphorically) for the first ten years one of the English learner-driver's L-plates that so delighted him when he first saw them in use on our cars. I came in due course to feel that for a Christian the ten years he suggested should be extended for life.

We were passing just then through the Munich crisis in Europe. As a foreign guest in Britain Watchman observed our anxious digging of shelters and distribution of gas masks, and then the outburst of emotional relief at Neville Chamberlain's return from Adolf Hitler with a vain declaration of 'peace in our time'. Because not directly involved he tasted, he says, that right kind of detachment that, on another level, the Christian, like Abraham, sometimes feels as a stranger and sojourner in this world.[10] Unknown to us he had his own private sorrows. At around this time news reached him from Hong Kong that Charity, who was expecting a child, had suffered a miscarriage. When her own letter came it was a brave one, but he knew how deeply she must have felt this blow with him away half around the world, and he wrote as best he could to comfort her. In fact, as soon as she herself was fit to travel, his mother He-ping took her off on a tremendous journey by way of Hanoi to Kunming to visit the evacuated believers in Yunnan Province. Alas, Charity was not in fact to conceive again and the Nees had no children.

In October 1938, at the invitation of Pastor Fjord Christensen of Copenhagen, Watchman was in Denmark for meetings at the International School at Helsingor, where he gave a series of ten addresses on Romans 5 – 8 which he entitled 'The Normal Christian Life'. These, supplemented with others on the same theme, were later to form a widely read book of that name.[11] To Watchman the so-called victorious life of current 'deeper life teaching' in the West was a wishful term too often used by the non-victorious for what in fact is real Christian living. Those who 'overcome',[12] he argued, are in God's eyes normal Christians; the rest are below normal! Moving on to Odense, Watchman gave another notable talk based on three key words – 'sit, walk, stand' – in Paul's letter to the Ephesians and again pointed us to a new plane of Christian living. It seems clear that he found, as have so many, much release of his spirit while among the Danes.

When coming to Britain he had planned to spend at most four months in the West, returning in November 1938 via the United States. However, the visit seemed incomplete without a fuller exchange of views with his new friend and counsellor T. Austin-Sparks on the subject of 'the church which is his body' (Ephesians 1:22f). Sparks saw and declared its heavenly reality; Nee's questions, as we have said, concerned the practical planting of that reality in the war-torn soil of China. When he reached Paris by way of Norway, Germany and Switzerland, a letter from his Shanghai co-workers urged him not to return without answers to this. It meant translating now into English his Chinese book *Rethinking the Work*. Happily Elizabeth Fischbacher was free to join him there with a colleague, Phyllis N. Deck, and undertake this task, so for two months she translated while Watchman abridged and edited and wrote another preface. At last in January, with the manuscript completed, he returned to London for a further four months based largely at Honor Oak, during which a mutually rewarding friendship with Mr and Mrs Austin-Sparks was cemented.

Here there were conference preachings once again, but not all the time. He found delight in tasting English family life, and where before he had been rather formal, now he would relax and play hide-and-seek with the children, folding himself easily out of sight into a cupboard in his long blue gown. Once, after preaching very effectively at a full conference, he joined a party of them for a picnic in the Surrey heathlands and is remembered by one as 'such fun to have around: not at all a very spiritual brother!' In the home he was astonished that all did not stand up every time Granny entered the room, and that on the other hand an adult would go so far as to apologise to a pet dog that had accidentally been trodden on. Out driving, with the frugality learned in Yunnan days, he insisted on switching off the car engine when descending hills. He took the children out too to Chinese meals, but himself found it necessary to support our bland English foods with soy sauce, of which he contrived somehow to keep a steady supply.

He had, of course, time to move around and at Sheringham in Norfolk he sought out Margaret Barber's friend of Norwich days, D.M. Panton, whose writings he had valued and to whom he tried to demonstrate his appreciation by, it is said, preparing two eggs Chinese-style for his breakfast. At another local church of the Open Brethren he met Mr (later Sir) John Laing, the constructional engineer, who recalled how Watchman graciously declined the offer of a gift from Western funds towards his work. And, most happily of all, he found opportunity for a private meeting of warm reconciliation with his long-time friend among the Exclusive Brethren, Charles Barlow.

In the month of May 1939, just before he left Britain, the English translation of *Rethinking the Work* appeared in London with the Witness and Testimony imprint, under the title *Concerning Our Missions*, and was avidly seized upon by many as a tract for the times.[13] This period, it must be remembered, was the heyday of interdenominational missions, some of whose long-established structures seemed by now sacrosanct. But already a few of their agents were facing honestly their inbuilt vagueness about what exactly to do with their converts. In some circles the view was gaining ground that only in vitally fresh communities could the

fruits of missionary labours be conserved, and to these readers Nee's strong emphasis on the local church, answerable
directly to God alone, came to them as a breath of fresh air.
Moreover, his distinction between 'the churches' and 'the
work' – a reasonable deduction from Scripture – seemed a
useful one. Besides this, there were passages in his book of
evident practical helpfulness such as his clear-headed chapter on finance.

When as a Chinese he rejected wholesale the plethora of
overlapping Western denominations, sympathetic readers
mostly nodded assent, but when they came to his strict
emphasis on 'locality' – one city, one church, worldwide –
there they stuck. It was a possible inference from Scripture
and no more. No New Testament writer affirms it as a principle and, as one Bible scholar shrewdly pointed out, in
writing to the one city which in New Testament times probably had a million inhabitants, Paul does not address his
letter 'to the church in Rome'.[14] Was Nee asking believers
in Western cities of many millions to return somehow to
first-century population figures in order to recover New
Testament practice?[15]

Many had thought through this problem for over half a
lifetime, honestly, humbly before God with the Bible before
them, and faced by the evidence of growing complexity
arising from centuries of fresh beginnings. Was there, they
asked, a way forward for us all that was not in essence a
retreat backward to the supposedly 'ideal' social conditions
of Asia Minor and the Levant? His friend T. Austin-Sparks,
for example, had chosen rather to emphasise the mystical
'Body' of Christ, and the freedom of the Holy Spirit to give
it today his own variety of expressions on earth, each a
'testimony' to the risen Head in heaven. 'To understand
the Church, the churches, Church order, the work of the

Church,' he wrote in his own copy of *Concerning Our Missions*, 'it is necessary to start from God's inclusive standpoint which is Christ. To know Christ in all His parts and ways is to know what the Church should be. Everything is "in Christ".'

Twelve months later in Shanghai we find Nee himself expressing to the church rather similar views. 'Our position is that, in any place, all who are the Lord's are therefore ours because we ourselves are his, and only those who are not his are not of us. If Hardoon Road ever comes to be a method of working in which concern for the local churches gives way to a mere concept of "localism", then may God have mercy on us and smash it, for it will cease to have spiritual value. We must never forget that all in whom the Lord has liberty are ours in him, and that in any place it is not even a spiritual local church, but the Body of Christ, that we are called upon to build up.'[16]

Though the understanding and warmth of fellowship between these two men was profound, on this particular issue they took a while to find themselves on the same wavelength. They were in no disagreement about the new wine, but Watchman's concern was with the wineskin to contain it.[17] His particular problem was one of accommodating to a sound, divine pattern the expanding and largely tradition-free work with which in the years to come he expected to have to grapple. But had he in the West sought more widely the practical counsel for which he had hoped, it must be admitted that, at the period in question, what he sought was everywhere in short supply.

Some months after his return to Shanghai he wrote back to his friend words which express his loneliness as a leader: 'You know, with the brethren here, because of their juniority, everything I say goes, despite their seeking to know the

mind of the Lord.' Then, of the link that in so short a time
had grown up between the two of them, 'The Lord has been
speaking to me,' he said. 'As a younger man, recognising
you as a senior brother in the same testimony, I think I need
this fellowship in a very real way.' Yet in fact, either they
corresponded but little, or very sadly the entire correspondence has been lost.

And still in China he was alone and always suspect. Less
than a decade later the godly Anglican director of perhaps
the finest mission in the land could describe him to me as,
from the foreign missions' point of view, 'the most dangerous man in China'. Some fine women of God had been a
strength and support to him by prayer and counsel in his
beginnings. Now he bore the care of a burgeoning movement of God almost single-handed. There never appeared
close to him again someone of his own stature, Chinese or
expatriate, to whom he could turn in time of need. It may
indeed seem to us something of a tragedy that even the self-
imposed limitation of his formal studies may have deprived
him of the stimulating and abrasive friendship of men
of like stature. He was God's watchman, God's sentry,
unsleeping at his lonely post.

16

Heyday

As he had done six years earlier, Watchman planned now to travel home via the United States. When he made inquiries at his embassy, however, they hinted that at some west Pacific ports the Japanese were using compulsory inoculations as a means of liquidating certain Chinese returning from the West. He then decided it would be wiser to travel all the way to the Huangpu River by British ship. The journey via Bombay and Columbo permitted a very brief stopover in India, but July 1939 found him back in Shanghai to the immense relief of Charity, who had feared for his safety in the now war-threatened West. They were delighted to be together again. Some months later he told a newly-wed couple that a marriage is like old shoes, ever more comfortable with passing time.

He arrived in a city that was a shadow of its former self, its high social life silenced under the miseries of alien occupation, and its once prosperous trade strangled by the constraints of war. From the devastated areas across the Suzhou Creek pestilence seeped into the foreign concessions. These were still kept open by the presence in the Huangpu of British, French and American warships, but were packed now with destitute refugees. As Watchman, inconspicuous in old gown and battered felt hat, moved in and out among the homes he encountered a callousness of spirit even more tragic than the prevailing hardships, for in the struggle to exist, unashamed self-seeking and opportunism prevailed to which not even the faithful seemed immune. 'I found many have already been hardened, to protect themselves,' he said in a note to a friend, 'and some have even been praising the Lord because they are not feeling anything of the sufferings around. As for me, I have to confess I am feeling every bit of them; only I am holding on to the Lord by standing in the kingdom. What has been happening around us is enough, had one a thousand hearts, to break every one of them. But my Father is God! I have never learned to love the word "God" as much as today. God!'

A rift had appeared briefly among the brothers in his absence, but the preaching gap had been filled by John Zhang, and more particularly by Dr C.H. Yu, the ophthalmologist. Dr Yu, short of stature and with delicate, refined features, was also musical and sometimes accompanied the singing with his violin. He loved the Lord and was sensitive to his Word, and as a speaker he showed promising gifts.

On the first Sunday morning of September 1939 Watchman called the church to prayer about the tense situation in Europe. Asking that several brothers would join him in leading the congregation, he says he 'marched into God's presence taking the church with him', claiming that nothing but his will should be done in this crisis. At the end of this very impressive hour in which many more took part he concluded, 'Well, Lord, you can never say your church hasn't prayed!'

Both the Monday prayer meeting and the Sunday evening 'breaking of bread' were now being divided between several homes in the city and here believers began to intercede strongly with God that he would set a limit to Japanese inroads into the Concession itself. To help clarify their thinking Watchman therefore gave, early in 1940, a talk, not to Chinese (or British or Americans), but to men and women in Christ, on the theme of God's use of world governments. All the way from Cyrus king of Persia to the Spanish Armada in Europe, he showed how God's ordering of secular history is essentially in relation to the destiny of his own people. Perhaps recalling his own prayer at the 1938 Keswick Convention, he told them, 'We must know therefore how to pray. It must be possible for British and German, Chinese and Japanese Christians to kneel and pray together, and all to say Amen to what is asked. If not there is something wrong with our prayer. We may remind God of what attitude Japan takes to him, but we must also remind him that in China Christians and missionaries have too much intimacy with the state. In the last European war there was much prayer that dishonoured God. Let us not fall into the same error. The church must stand above national questions and say, "We, here, ask for neither a Chinese nor a Japanese victory, but for whatever is of advantage to the one thing precious to thee, the testimony of thy Son." Such prayer is not empty words. If the whole church prayed thus the war could soon be settled God's way.'

Bible teaching at Wen De Li was seriously constricted by the still inadequate premises. An elderly sister in the meeting raised their hopes by offering a large building and land at only 40 per cent of current value. However, after the deal she then wished to dictate the form its development should take. When the brothers put to her the principle that God himself must lead them in how best to use a gift given to him, the offer was withdrawn. Instead the upstairs of the old frame building was remodelled as offices and more hostel space was found in the lane. Downstairs the many wooden pillars of the three (later five) properties called for various adjustments of the ground-floor space for tight-packed meetings. The hall had no heating and the floor squeaked loudly when walked on.

A missionary sister who had spent seven years among them describes the scene in 1940: 'On Sunday morning crowds gather quietly at 9.30 to hear the preaching of the Word, the women sitting on one side and the men on the other, the hall being wider than it is long. On the backless benches all must sit as close as possible to make the maximum use of the space, for outside the building on three sides more people sit at the windows and big double doors or listen to the loudspeakers, and there is even an overflow upstairs. As well as the poor, the educated and rich are here: doctors mingle with labourers, lawyers and teachers, with rickshaw men and cooks. Among the modestly clad sisters are not a few modern women and girls with fashionable hairstyles and make-up, short sleeves and daringly slit *cheongsam* gowns of tasteful silks. Children run about, dogs wander in, hawkers enter the lane, cars honk in the road outside, and the public address system is erratic. But each Sunday the word of the cross is faithfully preached. Sin and salvation, the new life in Christ and the eternal purpose of God, service and spiritual warfare – all are expounded and nothing is held back. They are given the strongest food and the straightest challenge.'

With Watchman's return to preaching an eager crowd hung on his every utterance. Standing there in his dark-blue cotton gown, he held their attention with his gentle manner, his simple but thorough reasoning and his apt analogies. No one ever saw him use any notes, for he remembered and could reproduce anything he read. To illustrate a thing visually he would draw a swift imaginary sketch in the air (which a young worker might reproduce on poster paper afterwards), and if to illumine some point he told a personal anecdote, it was nearly always a story against himself. His keen sense of humour sent frequent ripples of laughter round the hall and 'you never got sleepy in his meetings'. But from start to finish he never strayed from his subject. 'What matters', he used to say, 'is the effectiveness of the word proclaimed,' and unfailingly at the end he had left a clear and deep impression on the minds and hearts of his hearers.

Always Charity was present, quiet and reserved and preferring to be a little separated from the throng, but supporting him in all he did. Her second elder sister Faith (Mrs Bao) was, like the other women workers, more actively involved with personal counselling. So was Watchman's second sister Gui-zhen (Mrs Lin), who slipped away when she could from her other responsibilities in the town to give help behind the scenes with the sisters' needs. And always, too, in the background were Peace Wang, large, cheerful and reassuring, and Ruth Lee, small and bird-like, wise-looking and infinitely kind.

In the spring of 1940 Watchman gave the congregation a series of down-to-earth studies on Abraham, Isaac and Jacob under the title 'God's Dealings with His People', which was particularly telling in its later sections.[1] With his return from Europe he also brought to his preaching on the church a more mystical or spiritual note. 'The Church, the Overcomers and God's Eternal Purpose' was the theme of his first series of training talks, and these were followed through 1940–42 by an extended course for believers and co-workers in Shanghai on 'The Church, the Body and the Mystery'.[2] Witness Lee was among those then present and returned to his thriving Yantai congregation greatly enriched. In order to continue with them he was shortly to reject an attractive invitation for Bible training in the United States.

Nee's fresh spiritual emphasis on God's eternal purpose in his church and the overcomers was of particular interest to a number of missionaries from the West who were in sympathy with his work and who had already left their missions or were considering doing so. Some of them were sad that their long years of devoted service to the Lord had seemed so unfruitful. They were hoping to find in the new Chinese church setting the blessing of the Lord which was so evident there. In London, back in 1938, W.H. Aldis of the CIM had expressed to Nee his 'sincere hope that on your return to Shanghai it may be possible for there to be more and closer fellowship in service between yourself and those associated with you, and this Mission'.[3] This hope may have been realised in certain local instances, so close were they in evangelical spirit, but it is hardly surprising that on any larger scale it was due for disappointment. The regional directorates of the CIM and other missions continued to view Nee's work with caution, though the main ground for this was still perhaps his image as a sheep-stealer of their converts.[4]

It also needs to be said that with his preoccupation with the spiritual needs of Chinese potential leaders, Watchman had little time to give to finding ministry for those foreign women or fewer men who attended his meetings at Wen De Li. One exception was Dr Thornton Stearns, who had lately been invited to participate there as a church elder while he remained in his professional medical work. If there were others who waited at Hardoon Road for his guidance, doing very little, it might seem that there was paralysing inertia, but such inertia was never in fact a feature of the 'Little Flock' work itself and they were all steadfast together in prayer.

Some individuals may have seemed preoccupied with their growth in grace, making Bible study their first exercise, but most of the believers were very vigorous indeed in their evangelistic witness and outreach. They supported it too with imaginative follow-up of converts, for whose instruction Watchman now supplied a series of papers on the fundamentals of salvation. Even the Fuzhou gospel shirts continued as a feature of the street and village witness there. And in Wen De Li an extensive children's Sunday school work, for which there was not space in the halls, went on largely unnoticed in homes. Watchman's excellent gospel tracts have already been mentioned. Well written and brightly coloured, they invited distribution and discussion of their contents. Christian shopkeepers kept them ready at the cash desk or on display stands, like the one a visitor found in the midst of a long sales counter of glassware. Watchman's clear instructions to believers on how to introduce men to the Friend of sinners was supported by his own unremitting example, for though God might give to the church some to be evangelists, the instruction to Timothy to 'do the work of an evangelist' he held to be binding upon all.[5] 'Witness to at least one person a day' was his rule. He was thrilled therefore to discover that in a lane of twelve houses, when a maidservant believed, she decided to start work on the maid in the house on her right. Having won her to the Lord, she had worked on down the lane until, by the time the story reached his ears, six maidservants had found the Saviour.

Yet though these were, by general consent, some of the best years in the church in Shanghai, its witness went on in the face of an astonishing amount of criticism. They were charged with fickleness because the layout of the hall and the character of the activities was so flexible, and because special meetings would be put on at short notice when there was a burden on the preacher's heart and not at some obvious fixed season. From another angle there were attacks on Watchman's doctrine, and one respected missionary, while acknowledging that 'so many in China today are turning to Mr Nee as a teacher and leader to bring them back to the truths of the New Testament', felt it necessary to publish an attack upon his 'serious error' of usurping (in one of his books) the term 'apostle' for his pioneer workers and charging him with 'drawing away multitudes of disciples after himself'.[6] And a Chinese who claimed to have inside knowledge published a pamphlet averring that Watchman had access to a steady flow of foreign funds with which to support his work, and even attacking his integrity in their use.[7] Stature as a leader seemed but to invoke the proverb, 'He who raises his head above the heads of others will sooner or later be decapitated.' In more scriptural terms, 'All that would live godly in Christ Jesus shall suffer persecution.'[8]

In Watchman's private evaluation of the missions it was the Christian and Missionary Alliance that topped his list, and for a while he was on very friendly terms with one of its missionaries, who however then disappointed him by writing a magazine article criticising him and his work, as he felt, unjustly. He had, however, a philosophy of his own regarding self-vindication. 'If I proved myself right, my brother would be wrong; but what advantage would it be to me that my brother was proved wrong?' More seriously, he recognised that what we do to our brethren in the Lord will be the basis of his treatment of us in practical things. If we are gracious, he is gracious.[9]

For this reason he suppressed his feelings and, retiring from preaching, slipped away out of sight to Yantai for some weeks. There a friend found him in the depths of depression and, sensing his need of emotional release, challenged him: 'Have you tried praising the Lord?' 'I'll try it,' he said, and going out on the tennis court and summoning the full power of his now healthy lungs he bellowed, 'Hallelujah!' and again, 'Hallelujah!' The advice worked and he was shortly back on the platform again.

Someone in Shanghai had given him a baby Fiat which spent most of its life shut away in a garage, but into which he occasionally folded his long limbs and drove off on ministry with some colleague. Once, with Faithful Luke who was on a visit to Shanghai from Singapore, he drove to Hangzhou to enjoy the ministry of a young worker from east China, Stephen Kaung, whose gift as a Bible teacher, they agreed, held great promise for the future. Stephen was one of the workers based in Shanghai who in earlier years were privileged to receive personal training by Watchman, and whose ministry was now bearing fruit.

In Shanghai there were happy tokens, too, of God's loving care of the Nees themselves. One day they were invited to tea by a lady who surprised Charity by handing her a parcel. She opened it, to find Watchman's wedding gift to her, the Bible that had disappeared from their home after the Japanese Shanghai landings. This was the story. A China missionary speaking at a meeting in Ireland had exclaimed during his talk, 'If only I had with me a Chinese Bible, I could expound this passage so much more clearly!' To his surprise one was produced. 'How did you come by this?' he asked. A friend's son, it appeared, had been in the British forces in the Concession, and yielding to the looting instinct had entered an empty home and picked up a Chinese book. On the flyleaf he read in English, 'Reading this book will keep you from sin; sin will keep you from reading this book.' It must be a Bible, he thought, and kept it as a souvenir. The missionary in Ireland looked at the inscription and found beside it in Chinese, 'To Charity from Watchman' – names that he knew well. He asked and was readily given permission to return it to them.

Mother Nee, ever on the go, had left her husband in Hong Kong with the eldest daughter, Gui-chen (Mrs H.C. Chen), and was now staying for a while with Watchman and Charity in Shanghai. Though but a sister in the church she was still the dominating mother in the home. She was constantly out preaching, praying for the sick, witnessing to anyone from professional men to opium addicts. Yet she fussed over her son, concerned lest, when he himself was out visiting, nobody would think to give him anything to eat. This could have irked him, but he had by now come to terms with his ancestry and parental upbringing. 'Sometimes we feel we must have been born into the wrong family!' he had told co-workers in June 1940. 'But God determined whose child we should be. Joseph, with a special work to do for him, might well have wished for different brothers; but at length he could say, "God sent me before you to preserve life." Our whole life right through, and not merely since our conversion, is prepared by God to fit us for fulfilling his highest purpose. Samuel, Isaiah,

Jeremiah, Paul, all were God's men, prepared long, long before the need arose. So it depends not on human will or exertion but on God who shows mercy.'[10]

On Sunday 7 December 1941 the Japanese attacked Pearl Harbour in Honolulu. At 8 o'clock next morning, in a gentle drizzle of rain, as though heaven wept for Shanghai's five million souls, the Japanese sank the American and British gunboats at anchor in the Huangpu and stormed into the International and French concessions. The action was swift and complete. Barbed-wire barricades were flung across the roads, cars were commandeered, buses vanished, bicycles were at a premium, food prices quickly soared. As the refugee death rate rose and none who died in the city might be carried forth for burial, warehouses were piled high with coffins. Crime grew fast, and the Japanese did not care. Fear of their terrible retaliation protected them.

On 18 December 1941, in Hong Kong, Watchman's father died suddenly of a heart attack just one week before the Japanese occupation of that city. He was 64. His wife and others of the family were with him, but Watchman was not present. He was able, however, to travel there and make funeral arrangements. Ni Wen-xiu had died a true child of God.

Throughout the coming years, during which the Japanese extended their conquests in mainland China, to Singapore, Malaya and beyond, there were many instances of the gracious mercy of God shown to his people. For example, there is the following testimony of Faithful Luke and his family, who fled from Singapore.

When the Japanese invaded Singapore many refugees crossed the Causeway into the Malay States. Among them was Faithful Luke, Watchman's long-time friend and fellow worker. With his family of nine he went to stay with a veteran Christian, Mr Lee, in the small village of Gelang Patah, a few miles north of the border. Here they hoped to find safety.

The Japanese had taken Singapore and were advancing through the villages, massacring the entire population of each village as they went. They passed through Lee's village before daybreak on 4 March 1942 on their way to another village, but returned again the same evening. Faithful Luke was about to go to the local shops to buy a pair of slippers when the Lord spoke to him from Isaiah 26:20, 'Come, my people, enter thou into thy chambers and shut thy doors about thee, hide thyself as it were for a little moment, until the indignation be overpast.' With this warning he did not venture outside.

The Japanese soldiers went from house to house, borrowing blankets and mats, and saying that they could be collected in the morning in an open field between the school and the shops. They did not visit Mr Lee's home. Next morning the unsuspecting 'lenders' went to collect their bedding, but were bound, together with others as the soldiers went from hut to hut. The Lee household was in fervent prayer, while two young boys watched the proceedings through a latticework above the door. Even though Mr Lee's hut with its 22 occupants was close to the field, and somewhat larger and better looking than the other huts, none of the soldiers came to it. All of the captives, men, women and children of all ages, were killed without mercy.

The Lukes, the Lees and three other families (Tans, Chengs and Wus) were the only five Christian families in the village. These were the only survivors, the last mentioned two families not even being aware of the massacre because their huts too were not visited by the soldiers. The merciful hand of the Lord had blinded the eyes of the soldiers in the same manner as the Syrian army had been smitten with blindness by the prayer of Elisha.[11]

17

Withdrawal

One advantage the revivalist preacher of the gospel enjoys is his freedom to move on and leave to others the care, under God, of the fruits of his labours. By working instead as an apostle, planting churches and concerning himself with their upbuilding, Watchman had assumed a weightier spiritual burden and one that would tell heavily upon him during these years of political crisis and the breakdown of communications. Most serious of all was the moral responsibility he felt for the young full-time workers who, without assured salary of any kind, were scattered throughout the country faithfully telling the good tidings. His own early experiences in proving God for his practical needs had given him some understanding of the testings they went through in their costly service to him. As he put it after observing one of them passing through a severe trial of faith, 'To keep our hand on the plough while wiping away our tears – that is Christianity.'[1] So in a very rare letter to a friend in Britain he could say, 'Affairs of the churches and events of this part of the world are weighing heavily upon me. I am not buoyant, but treading on with trust in the Lord.'

It may be asked how this fast-expanding work, with some 200 full-time workers, extensive travels, a publishing programme, rented premises and plans to own property, was financially supported. The main principle was the voluntary tithing of personal income. This was at no time legalistically enforced, since the 'tenth' was seen as a token of one's giving oneself to God; but the principle of generous giving was taught and sedulously practised. As a result all Assembly Hall churches were self-supporting. There was, however, as we have seen, a distinction between the local churches with their eldership and the work with its mobile fellow workers who might not be answerable to any single local church. Yet these, when out breaking new ground with the gospel, might incur, over and above their family's livelihood, such outlays as the temporary hire of premises and the printing of Scripture portions and tracts. They were taught the life of faith and might receive gifts from the churches and from individual Christians, but for spiritual counselling and material support they were to some degree in the personal care of Watchman Nee himself. Some 40 of these were in practice his direct responsibility. The work's finances were handled therefore as a fund separate from local church offerings, controlled by him and two or three senior fellow workers.

The saving good news had brought into church fellowship many successful businessmen with their native flair for commerce, and some of these expressed their love for the Lord in generous financing of both the churches and the work's wider outreach.

In a penetrating talk he gave at this period on the mammon of unrighteousness Nee shows how, if today's wealth, like Egypt's, is to be spoiled in God's favour,[2] our money, honestly acquired, must in our hearts be brought, not sent, across the boundary that divides the world's currency from God's. We ourselves cross that boundary bearing it to him.[3] He did not discourage secular employment. Rather he followed the apostle Paul's instructions to Titus, 'Affirm confidently that those who have believed God should be careful to apply themselves to honest tasks.' 'Let our people learn to enter honourable occupations, so as to help cases of urgent need, and not to be unfruitful.'[4]

But with disruption of the Yangtze trade by Japan's occupation of the eastern seaboard many commercial interests were crippled, and in so far as resource for the gospel's spread depended on such as these the whole financial structure of the Lord's work was hard hit. Now in December 1941, with the outbreak of hostilities between Japan and the United States, inflation rocketed still further and Chinese commerce in the Concession almost reached a standstill. Any release and movement of funds for Christian enterprise became well nigh impossible. So it was that Nee now saw many of these loyal young 'apostles', God's messengers and their families, hungry, physically sick and nearly destitute. Ordinary church members were not much better off, and neither they nor he had funds left with which to come to their aid.

Thus it comes about that Watchman's story here takes an unexpected turn and one which some may feel to be, for him, out of character. Dismayed at this mounting problem, he had for some months sought God for a solution. Now early in 1942 he took a step about which he had been thinking since his return from England and to which he felt sure God had been leading him. This was, however, to raise big questions in the minds of some of his friends.

Watchman's brother George, with a natural teaching gift and a BSc in chemistry from St John's University, had some

while back set up as a research chemist with his own laboratories. He had also built up in Shanghai a manufacturing
and distributing pharmaceutical company, Nee Brothers, in
which some of the family had shares. It had not thrived,
since George was more scientist than merchant, but Watchman saw here something with potential. Non-warlike in
character, it could yet remain viable because any service to
medicine meets a wartime human need. Already in 1938 he
had sought my help to inquire in London about a business
licence for his brother to manufacture Sulphanilamide; and
on his return his father Ni Wen-xiu had pressed him, urging
it again not long before he died, to give time and administrative help to George.

In those days Chinese respect for parents was still high;
and now Watchman conceived the idea of floating an associate company to manufacture antibacterial and other drugs
and to turn over the excess profits to the work of the Lord.
So was born the China Biological and Chemical (CBC) Laboratories at 9 Jiaozhou Road, Shanghai. As manager he
invited from Hong Kong C.L. Yin, the one-time tuberculosis patient who years ago at Guling Sanatorium had rejected
his witness, only to be won for the Lord Jesus by John
Sung. At the outset Watchman, as Chairman of Directors,
left things to his able manager and merely kept a helpful
eye on the project, slipping into a modern-style gown to
attend business appointments and resuming his informal
dress and old slouch hat for visiting the saints.

Even his closest friends were puzzled at this apparent
change of direction. Faithful Luke tells how, with Daniel
Chen and Philip Luan, he called on Watchman and Charity
in their simple home at 13 You-hua Villas. As they sat in
the almost unheated room with the blackout curtains and
the windows pasted with anti-shatter strips, he put the

question many were asking: 'Why have you left the work of God to go into commerce?' Watchman replied, 'I am merely doing what Paul did in Corinth and Ephesus.[5] For me it is something exceptional, and it's only part-time. I give an hour a day to training the company's team; then I'm free to do the Lord's work.' And some of the team were his hard-pressed fellow workers who would themselves now mingle their gospel witness with paid employment. Yet when pressed he added ruefully, 'I am like a woman widowed who must go out to work from financial necessity.'

But soon his new way of life began to raise questions with some of the Shanghai church elders. Their image of him had become tarnished. Was he now in their eyes a renegade, or to change the metaphor, a ploughman who, looking back from the furrow, had deviated? How fit, they asked, was such a one to minister the Word? Towards the end of 1942 they asked him, as no longer a full-time worker, to discontinue preaching at Wen De Li. It is likely that Dr Yu, who was a sensitive man, demurred, for he himself retired forthwith from preaching. Watchman was downhearted and did not know what to do. 'I envy you,' he said to C.L. Yin as they sat together sharing a bag of his beloved Fujian oranges. 'You are free to do what you like in the factory, and if then you go and say a few words at the meeting they will acclaim you a very zealous brother. No one will question you. But me? Twenty-four hours a day they need to know exactly how I spend my time. I am a marked man.'[6]

To the rank-and-file of believers the shock of their elders' action was very severe, and with a few it raised speculation that there were more serious grounds for it than the ones given publicly. Ill-wishers pointed to his business lunches with people of the world, the kind of people to whom in the past his witness to Jesus as Lord and Saviour had often been most fruitful. Since the responsible elders remained silent, he felt his whole testimony to be in question; yet because of the many workers dependent on him he had no freedom to abandon the course he had adopted. There is no evidence that in the following two years the elders made any approach to him. For his part he recalled Margaret Barber's meekness in the face of his own tirades and once again he made no attempt at self-vindication, but accepted their action as a discipline from God who would in his own way justify himself.

Understandably Charity, who was actively helping him in the business, did not at once appreciate this attitude. One day she heard Watchman answer a phone call in which the voice at the other end went on and on at a high volume. Watchman simply listened to it all, answering now and again with, 'Yes . . . yes . . . thank you . . . thank you.' 'Whoever was that?' she asked, when he had rung off. 'It was a brother telling me all I have been doing wrong.' 'And were you guilty of all that?' she asked. 'No,' he replied. 'Then why did you not give him an explanation instead of just saying "thank you"?' she exclaimed impatiently. 'If anyone exalts Ni Tuo-sheng to heaven,' was the reply, 'he is still Ni Tuo-sheng. And if anyone tramples him down to hell, he remains Ni Tuo-sheng.' God is righteous, and to Watchman that was sufficient. He is known, acting true to character, to have ministered secret financial help to some of the brothers who were opposing him.

By the early months of 1943 the Japanese had made ready their Civil Assembly Centres, or internment camps, and to these the foreigners were led off in batches. Watchman did all he could for his friends among them, turning up thoughtfully with articles likely to be of help in the difficult days ahead, and he was especially concerned for Dr Stearns, who was in hospital and in fact too ill to go with his family into camp. On 16 March, the night before Elizabeth Fisch-bacher and Phyllis Deck were due to enter the Long-hua camp south of the city, the Nees entertained them in their little home with the solitary stove and the red and black curtains. Over a simple meal they prayed to God, proclaim-ing together his faithfulness; then the ladies returned late to their house at 17 Bedford Terrace. Finding she had left the key inside, Phyllis Deck climbed, as they sometimes did, on to a shed to reach a window at the back, and while doing so suffered a stroke and fell to her death. One of the most sane and godly of the missionary friends of the work, she died, it is said, still smiling.

For the CBC Laboratories Watchman had coined the Chinese name *Sheng Hua Yao Chang*, enshrining it, as a sales gimmick, in a clever couplet proclaiming the drugs' efficacy. Besides producing such basic antibacterials as Mercuro-chrome, they at length began to manufacture Sulphathia-zole, Sulphaguanidine, Vitamin B concentrates and Yatren. Of course there were problems he had not foreseen, and the demands of the project soon began to make inroads on his time, for in a business you are not your own master. There was commercial jealousy and cut-throat competition with the other big concerns, which were each fighting to come up with the first output of a new drug. There were com-plaints from shareholders, and incidents reported from sen-sitivity to the Vitamin B injections. Moreover, the family business was a weak link, bringing him into suspicion whenever it claimed as distributor the first batch of a new product. His organising and conciliatory gifts were called into play in handling what would at any time be a delicate operation, aggravated now by the conditions of war. As a result Watchman was frequently absent from Shanghai.

Now, having made arrangements with his brother George for the flow of remittances to the workers, he planned a longer absence. With the Japanese armies thrusting westward against Chiang Kai-shek's stronghold, it was nevertheless possible for a Chinese civilian, by using air travel and choosing his route, to cross the war front. He now set out for Chongqing, whence reports had already reached Shanghai of a spiritual awakening in the still free provinces. There the finest refugee universities and the shrewdest commercial and banking speculators in the land were bringing the far west swiftly into the twentieth century. As it was not part of Watchman's plan to be marketing drugs to the Japanese army, he began to investigate alternative lines of distribution in areas where the need was greatest. In this he was highly successful, soon obtaining Kuomintang government contracts that, by degrees, brought CBC up from one of the least to a place among the foremost of China's pharmaceutical importers and manufacturing wholesalers. He was to spend over two years in frequent travel between Shanghai and Chongqing, where he rented a small dwelling and Charity joined him, her young brother Samuel also having business interests in Sichuan.

A meeting of new believers in the city had been augmented by the influx of displaced Christians and was thriving under the ministry of Stephen Kaung, the young fellow worker whom we last met in Hangzhou. His gift for ministry had resulted in an invitation from the church in Singapore to help forward their work and witness. However, Stephen and his wife Mary narrowly escaped from there on 30 December 1941 in a small coastal ship before Emperor

Hirohito's forces crossed the Causeway and took Singapore in February 1942. He returned to China via India, and in due course found his new field of ministry in Chongqing.

Watchman did all that he could to help some of the refugee brothers with employment in the pharmaceutical business. From time to time he preached the Word with his accustomed clarity and vigour, and in Chongqing in 1945 he gave a series of talks on the 'Seven Churches in Asia' from Revelation 2 and 3. He equated these with the subsequent phases of church history in a way that reassured him afresh of the special place in each city of the local church in God's missionary strategy.[7]

But there was to follow a long spell when he preached very seldom or not at all. Although he excused himself on the ground of poor health, in fact it was also due to the demands of business and of frequent travel. His physique, fragile at the best of times, began to show marks of the stress imposed upon him, and ischaemic heart pain would sometimes warn him to go slower. It would then be the more direct work for the Lord that suffered. One day in 1945 his eldest sister's son Stephen Chan,[8] on a visit by river launch from his studies at Fu-dan University, met Watchman and Charity in a Chongqing street. Kind as ever, they invited him into a restaurant for a bowl of noodles, but he found them laden with anxiety about threats to the factory and with little time to talk. Leaving him to finish his noodles, they paid the bill and went in search of heavy capital to allow it to continue. Weighed down with these secular cares, was Watchman at risk of losing his old rest of spirit?[9] Surely it was time for a change; but two years more would pass before that became possible.

Meanwhile, he somehow contrived still to sustain his dual role by giving all possible time to reading and meditating on the Scriptures. This was his joy and release. Never before had he been so intellectually extended, and in the sequel back in Shanghai and Fuzhou the fruits of this study would eventually emerge.

In Japanese-occupied Shanghai the Hardoon Road meetings had struggled on for a while with diminished numbers. Then, partly from discouragement and partly to avoid joining the Religious Union sponsored by the occupying power, they had dispersed altogether to meet in believers' homes. This was a wise and essential precaution. The Japanese had instituted a blockade complex. At a signal, road barriers at every city block would suddenly be closed for hours or even days. In cases of severe reprisal they might even remain shut for weeks, causing unspeakable suffering since none might move out of the section in which he was trapped. Like other Christian groups in Shanghai, therefore, the Hardoon Road church survived, if at all, in private houses where those whom the Spirit moved took what lead and gave what support they could.

But the eight-year-long war was dragging to its conclusion. A final Japanese thrust southward from Hankou, effectively cutting China in two, nearly brought down the Kuomintang government in Chongqing. Then at last Japan, with her own home islands heavily bombed and the US land forces poised for invasion, accepted on 16 August 1945 the Allied terms of capitulation. Armistice with China was signed on 9 September at Nanjing.

With travel no longer a hazard, Watchman left Chongqing. At Christmas he was in Hong Kong, soon to arrive back in Shanghai, but still not to preaching, nor yet to a restored church. The saints were in spiritual need, but remained confused by rumours about him. It was hinted that he had misused church funds, or alternatively that he had collaborated with the Japanese. Even his close colleagues admitted to an unease about his secular employment. Clearly he himself could not interfere. 'I have put it', he told a friend, 'into God's hands.'

In the months that followed he began quietly making plans to detach himself from CBC. It had prospered lately through supplying essential drugs to Kuomintang military hospitals. Having satisfied the shareholders, he and George, as agreed, set aside a large accumulation of profits for transfer to the work of God and for future provision for the fellow workers. Next he travelled to Fuzhou, where the family home at 17 Customs Lane in Nantai had fallen vacant. It had a large garden and outbuildings and would adapt ideally as a centre of training for workers. As head of the family he now took steps to reoccupy it and with Charity's help to bring it into use for the Lord.

Back here in his boyhood surroundings he sought to adjust his thinking with fasting and prayer and with the Bible open before him. Throughout those difficult Japanese years he had not ceased to plan ahead for the extension of the gospel. The problem now was where to begin. The confusion in Shanghai required that he wait quietly for God to move. The faithful Dr C.H. Yu had returned to preaching at Wen De Li and in face of the odds was slowly drawing the believers together, appealing to them on the grounds of Christ indwelling to be reconciled one to another. Progress, however, was pathetically slow. Something more seemed needed.

Watchman thought now of his friend Witness Lee. Behind Japanese lines in Shandong, war conditions had not been so hard, and Christian gatherings in the coastal cities were now growing rapidly in numbers. Particularly was this so in Yantai, where Lee had been preaching the Word with great power and remarkable results. Now in mid-1946 Watchman wrote from Fuzhou presenting to him the needs of Shanghai and appealing to him to come to their aid. Finding God confirming this in his heart, Lee moved south with his family to Nanjing and from that base gave himself to the overdue task of recovery in that city and in Shanghai.

The message he brought reinforced that of Dr Yu. The living Christ indwelling them was his people's hope of unity, even as he was their source of life. But Lee was an activist and where Watchman as a profound Bible student had laid doctrinal foundations, Lee's more volatile temperament introduced something of the Shandong excitement and fire. This brought quick returns and in a matter of months confidence was restored and people were flocking again to the meetings, which soon snowballed in numbers. Lee was authoritarian and energetic, thriving on large numbers and with a flair for organising people. This gift he now brought to bear on Shanghai's confused situation. Early in 1947 the growing numbers attending were grouped on a district basis, and the pattern which developed in the ensuing twelve months was as follows. Twice a week they met at Wen De Li as their one 'church in Shanghai', on the morning of the Lord's Day for the ministry of the Word and on Saturday evening for fellowship. Three times weekly they met as *jias*, or 'families',[10] in 15 (later 24) separate locations for the breaking of bread on the Lord's Day evening, for prayer on Tuesday evening and for instruction of new believers on Friday evening. In addition there was a Wednesday evening evangelistic meeting centred in four of the *jias*. The elders remained in overall charge of the whole church, but each *jia* had a leading brother and a leading sister with several others, designated 'deacons in training', to help them with the charge of duties and to instruct inquirers.

It was soon found that people tended to wander from one district to another, so by June 1948 they were allocated to their districts with the injunction to 'obey them that have the rule over you',[11] and they had to apply for permission to change. By this date also, because of the rising numbers, the problem of pastoral care had become acute. The groups of from 40 to 200 believers in the *jias* were therefore subdivided again into sections, or *pais*,[12] of an average of 15 persons, often comprising those in a single street or lane. Each *pai* had two persons in responsibility to watch the believers' attendance at meetings and to care for their spiritual condition. This system conserved some values discovered during the church's dispersal under the Japanese, namely the intimacy of smaller meetings in which more can participate in prayer and discussion, and the development of spiritual gifts in those called on to take a lead. It is to be noted that there were no men's or women's meetings, no special meetings for students or other classes of the populace, since the church was without class. But in view of the apostle Paul's restrictions, the existence of gifted women preachers seems to have created a problem.[13] If they ranked as fellow workers they might exceptionally take special meetings. A young Christian in the Guangdong church hall recalls one day finding men suspending a large white sheet across the width of the hall. Asking what it was for, he was told that Ruth Lee and Peace Wang were visiting the local church. Since they must not here preach to men, the brothers would therefore sit behind the sheet and eavesdrop on their talks!

Evangelism was not the task of the preacher alone, but of the whole church. All believers were trained as 'counsellors'. At the end of a gospel address everyone turned and counselled the person sitting beside him, noting his name and address, asking him questions, letting him talk, and if possible, but without pressure, getting him to pray calling on the name of the Lord, for sometimes in that very act he would be saved. Western missionaries who saw this in action were impressed.

On Friday evenings there was exposition of the Word specially geared to those who had newly believed. In 1948 Watchman would be asked to supply 52 lessons of systematic instruction in Christian fundamentals, ranging from justification by faith to the practical principles of church life. These lessons were followed by each Shanghai group leader and came to be widely used in most churches.[14] The year's course was virtually compulsory for those who meant business with God, absentees being followed up and taken through the lessons personally at home. Those who came to the point of trusting the Lord Jesus for salvation soon knew what it was all about.

The effect of so much energetic organisation, however, meant that something of the earlier freedom in the Spirit began to be lost. A clock-in system was soon to be introduced at meetings which, together with a full index of believers' addresses, employment, family, etc., meant that anyone's failure to attend could be quickly followed up.[15] The Lord's Table was 'fenced' and believers from another locality were formally introduced and wore a badge with their name. No longer might you be accepted simply on your own testimony that you were born again and loved the Lord. In the past the Table had always been a place where conscience and the Holy Spirit's conviction were given full play in a man's heart. Now, however, your detachment from other Christian connections and committal to the Assembly Hall churches was first carefully examined.[16]

Witness Lee was careful to allay fears of 'organisation'. To him these arrangements were like a cup containing drinking water – mere vessels to communicate spiritual things. Yet this lost something of Scripture's personal tone. '*We* have this treasure in earthen vessels.' '*Your* bodies (and not your well-drilled formation) are a temple of the Holy Spirit.' Watchman's advice to a brother in 1940 was significant: 'Don't expect the Holy Spirit to be doing the same thing in Qingdao as in Shanghai: give him liberty!'

But here in this city, learning to 'walk in the Spirit' was too easily giving place to regimentation imposed by a firm authoritarian hand at the work's centre. Lee exhorted everyone in the church to be submissive. 'Do nothing without first asking,' he urged. 'Since the Fall man does as he pleases. Here there is order. Here there is authority. The church is a place of strict discipline.'[17]

18

Return

During the latter years of the war the Chinese Communist Party (CCP) had been conducting from their headquarters in the caves of Yanan a single-minded campaign against the occupying power. One of the legacies of their 1935 Long March had been the development of technical skill in guerilla warfare based on mobility and the absence of fixed bases. This strategy they next put into effect to confine the Japanese to the cities and establish close contact with Chinese villagers behind their lines. They had successfully applied their agrarian policy of land reform in considerable areas around the Yellow River and much of this remained effective after the Allied victory.

A second consequence of the March had been the emergence of Mao Ze-dong as undisputed leader. As the Party thrashed out its ambitious policies for the future his 'thoughts' too, as their ideologist, were now being treated as infallible guidelines.

The third legacy was an impressive self-discipline that bound together the disparate elements of the CCP into a unified force wholly convinced of the validity of its goals. Its frugal and abstemious way of life bore a striking contrast with the luxury indulged in by Chiang's Kuomintang leaders. As a result, whereas during hostilities many Chinese intellectuals and businessmen had chosen to migrate to Chongqing and the south-west, now the more idealist thinkers, eager for a clean-up of the country's internal disorder and corruption, had gone to Yanan for inspiration. It was thus known in Shanghai that in the north-west was an impressive body of men with clear-sighted plans for the future.

Since the war's end and Chiang Kai-shek's return to Nanjing, distrust between the Nationalist government and the Communist Party had developed into a hostility which even the skilled and sincere diplomacy of the United States General George C. Marshall had failed to allay. Chiang's extreme hatred of the CCP led him once again to launch a massive campaign of extermination which overran much of the area where land reform had taken root, and by March 1947 he had even captured Yanan itself. For a moment the Nationalists seemed to have triumphed. But it was an empty victory, for the Communist guerilla ethic made such a success largely meaningless. Mao Ze-dong's armies had merely stepped aside and were in fact poising themselves for a spring.

In the hearts of those bearing responsibility in the Assembly Hall churches the concern occasioned by Watchman Nee's prolonged absence from their ministry was very great. Already in 1946 Witness Lee had challenged the Shanghai elders: 'Were you in the Spirit when you made the decision to reject him? And what was the effect? Can you say it brought life?' 'No,' they had replied sorrowfully to each question. The remorse felt among the fellow workers and their patient search for a way back is well expressed by one of them in April 1947. 'Brother Nee's case was a mortal

wound to us, and words cannot tell how far the consequences go. The charge that he collaborated with the
enemy is entirely groundless and much else that has been
said was not based upon pure facts. This was the work of the
devil and shows our own spiritual deficiency at that time,
but we hope we may have learned our lesson. Objections to
his coming back to our midst have been gradually eliminated. He is ready, and there is a growing desire for his
return. The brothers here at Shanghai repeatedly visit him
in his home, and through such fellowship hearts are bound
together and barriers are cleared away. So we are waiting
for the right moment.'

Watchman too was content to wait. 'Time', he told a
friend, 'is the servant of God.' At his request two Christian
businessmen had been found to relieve him of his remaining responsibilities in the drug company, and in April he
was free to leave again for Fuzhou, expressing before going
his readiness to return to the church in Shanghai at any
time. In Fujian as elsewhere missionaries had been throng-
ing back to their stations and rounding up their scattered
flocks, but the number of foreign staff was less than before.
The missions therefore had superfluous holiday properties
in the Guling hill-station east of the city. Two of these were
for sale, spacious one-storey stone cottages protected with
typhoon walls on their ocean-facing sides. These Watchman
purchased for use as a long-term training centre for men
and women workers.

Here in the summer of 1947 a small group of workers
from Fujian, Zhejiang and elsewhere, including his old
school friend K.H. Weigh on leave from Hong Kong, joined
him for an intensive course of studies. In an initial series of
ten addresses Watchman returned to his spiritual starting
point, the foundation principles of his message of the cross.

Widely read since then under the title *The Release of the Spirit*, they are concerned with the principle of 'brokenness' as a condition of the release of divine power, and with the pivotal words of Jesus, 'Unless a grain of wheat falls into the earth and dies, it remains alone; but if it dies, it bears much fruit.'[1] They formed a fitting basis for a new beginning. But this was not all. In Shanghai God had greatly used him in recent meetings for newly converted students at a national university. Now in Fuzhou someone hired for him the large hall of the American Mission and immense crowds came from the area around to hear the former Trinity student. God seemed to be placing his seal afresh upon his servant's evangelistic witness.

Towards the year's end Witness Lee, who had till now concentrated his energies on Shanghai and Nanjing, yielded to pressure and paid a visit to the local churches in the famine-ridden southern provinces, ending in February 1948 with a series of meetings in Fuzhou itself. When these were over he and those with him, who included Peace Wang, came for counsel to Watchman in his home in Customs Lane, Nantai. Since the Allied victory the wider work had been left to care for itself and Lee had observed with concern the weakness and isolation of its scattered labourers. He strongly approved of Watchman's training programme and looked forward to discussing further with him the revolutionary methods of evangelism he himself had been free to develop in the Japanese-occupied north.

Churches in the coastal cities of Shandong had grown in size during the mid-1940s and Lee had conceived the plan of evangelism by migration. It is not certain whether this idea originated with him or from Watchman's observation of the remarkable fruitfulness of the wartime migratory movement to the south-west. Certainly for reasons of population and trade the Chinese had constantly emigrated, north across the Wall into Manchuria, west into Xingjiang, south and east across the Southern Ocean. 'Now', said the responsible brothers in Shandong, 'we have vast meetings here on the coast, and it is both impractical and unrewarding to maintain lonely pioneers indefinitely in the distant regions. Let a whole group of believers uproot themselves from Yantai and settle as a self-supporting economic unit in an unevangelised area. There let them become a nucleus of Christian life and witness.'

For precedent they found in Acts the statement, 'There arose on that day a great persecution against the church which was in Jerusalem; and they were all scattered abroad throughout the regions of Judea and Samaria except the apostles. They therefore . . . went about preaching the Word.' And again, 'They that were scattered abroad travelled as far as Phoenicia and Cyprus and Antioch . . . speaking the Word and preaching the Lord Jesus.'[2] Thus they began to cover the whole Syrian field and were already moving beyond. 'As yet', said the Shandong brothers, 'we have no such persecution, but even without one we can follow their example and disperse bearing the good news.'

Lee made a study of the matter and carefully worked out the details. Groups of families, selected as to personnel and representing a suitable cross-section of trades and professions – gardeners, shoemakers, teachers, nurses, barbers – were chosen and carefully prepared for their venture. (The barber's trade was popular. It required little equipment and gave ready scope for witnessing.) All these gave themselves to the church, who supplied their travel expenses and three months' living costs at their destination. By the end of that period they might be expected to support themselves in the new setting.

Back in the spring of 1943 two parties left the Yantai church, one of 30 families going north into Manchuria, another of 70 families to towns westward up the Baotou railway across Shanxi into Sui-yuan, far beyond the Wall. And there were smaller such movements in the centre of the country. Some in these groups suffered great hardships and the scheme was not wholly a success. Moreover, in May 1943 Lee himself came as a result under Japanese suspicion for espionage activities and underwent with great courage a month's interrogation with flogging and the 'water treatment'. Nevertheless, there was real spiritual fruit from the migratory experiment. A letter in October 1944 to Dr C.H. Yu in Shanghai from a brother Sun of the Shantou assembly, writing from a town on the upper reaches of the Yellow River, tells how they started meetings there on 5 December 1943 with a nucleus of seven brothers and three sisters. It then goes on to recount the baptism on 19 February 1944 of six men who had newly believed. 'There were no indoor arrangements, but they just could not wait to obey the Lord; so the only thing possible was to break the river ice which was two feet thick. Every day was icy cold, but on the one chosen it became suddenly 20 degrees warmer. With a changing-tent by the riverside no one was frostbitten or taken ill.' On 2 March they held a second baptism of four brothers and of one sister aged 66 who would never normally go out of doors in winter. This time there was more difficulty from lack of water under the ice and they had to search downriver for a deeper place. Again there were no ill-effects but only great joy, and the letter ended with words of exhortation to the Shanghai believers.[3] And this was a single one of many known centres where fresh life began to spring up by these means.

Now in February 1948 in Watchman's Fuzhou home

they discussed the application of these experiences to the scene of some confusion that Lee had found in the south. Might not a region like Guangdong or Fujian, Lee suggested, be evangelised best by collective effort from a centre such as Fuzhou? Watchman had himself been meditating along these lines and readily agreed. Jerusalem, he pointed out, became just such a centre. God's method was to concentrate his workers there, save many souls, establish a church, and thereafter disperse men from there to Samaria and to the ends of the earth. 'What we saw at Hankou in 1937 regarding Acts 13 and the principle of apostles going forth from Antioch was right as far as it went; but the book of the Acts begins not at chapter 13 but at chapter 1. Our failure in these few years is that we have had no structure of the work corresponding to the principle of Jerusalem. We should concentrate fellow workers for ministry in regional centres until local churches are fully established and thereafter transfer whole communities to other parts – unless, as in the Acts, the Lord arranges a persecution to scatter them abroad.'[4]

Somehow this came as a flash of new light to them all. They had come to him, Lee says, seeking to restore fellowship, but through him God gave them something more. Just as they had earlier come to see the churches in a strictly local city-by-city context, now they saw the work afresh in this broad geographical setting. It would mean for the apostolic workers an end to purely individualistic enterprise. 'We fellow workers then present', says Lee, 'willingly laid down our work, and we decided upon Fuzhou as our Jerusalem and starting place.' Several leaders were also present from the local church meeting at Tian Men Road, Fuzhou. These called their whole company of brothers and sisters together on 3 March, when 'they formally handed over the church and we fellow workers formally took it over. Thus', says Lee, surprisingly, 'the work and the church in Fuzhou had a new beginning.'[5] This statement appears a startling reversal of Watchman's earlier insistence on the local churches' complete independence of apostolic (that is, worker) control.[6] It is from this point in fact that the tighter authoritarianism makes itself felt throughout the movement, to become after liberation a feature of the churches outside China. Initially this gesture by the Fuzhou elders was perhaps in the main a generous act of reconciliation towards Watchman himself after several years of exclusion from its fellowship.

Sadly, however, the reconciliation in Fuzhou, scene of the work's very beginnings, was not complete. Since 1928 there had been two assemblies in Nantai with two sets of elders, quitting the 'one city, one church' principle that the movement held so dear. Chang Chi-chen, successor of John Wang, was senior elder of the group that met 'near the football ground', and though present in these discussions he stood out against the new ideas and, rightly or wrongly, would not at this time bring his fellow elders to break bread with the workers and representatives of the other group. This caused great sorrow to those who placed their hopes in a completely new beginning in Fuzhou; and though Watchman Nee himself made generous overtures, the situation remained unresolved.[7]

Lee was the bearer also of a conciliatory invitation from the Shanghai elders. They asked Watchman to lead a conference at Hardoon Road in April and May 1948, and he now felt able to accept. He arrived there to find over 30 elders and others from the Shanghai and nearby churches as well as 60 workers from all over China waiting to greet him. These latter included some from Shandong who had seen the Communist land reform in operation at close quarters and who entertained no illusions as to the hostility of the Party cadres to Christian faith.

Watchman went aside first of all with the Wen De Li elders and in the presence of God made full confession of his own failings over the past few years. With this act of reconciliation fellowship between them was at last fully restored. Among the fellow workers he was now welcomed back into a novel setting. Some kind of hierarchy had been established among the top echelon which gave to them an order of seniority, expressed by a row of chairs on the platform, on which the elders sat during meetings. One of the believers from that time affirms that Watchman never occupied one of these chairs on the platform. If he was in the meeting then he would be speaking on the platform, but more often he was away on other ministry.

But the slogan 'Bow to authority' was in fact to become a new and, to many, very disturbing feature of the work from now on. To us today it seems so entirely out of character with his past teachings and way of working that one wonders if it could possibly have originated (as a few have thought) in a change of mind in Nee himself, or whether, at a time when he was spiritually vulnerable, he was caught off balance by the enthusiasm of others.

All present were now ready to rededicate themselves for cooperation with God in the much-talked-of migratory invasion of inland China. Watchman outlined to them what was in his mind. 'When, in his Acts of the Holy Spirit, God scattered the people abroad through persecution there were some thousands of believers in Jerusalem, and there was a constant movement outward. Yet when Paul returned to Jerusalem there were the same large numbers of believers. We must not remain stationary, but must move out and make room for others, for as many will be added as move out. Today [in the late 1940s] China has about 450 million inhabitants and only one million Christians. Give all Christians the same training, then send them forth, and we shall see the church proclaiming the gospel everywhere. We need not wait for persecution. Whether by persecution or not, go forth we must. For many of us half our time has gone. The remaining half must be spent in taking a straight course. If we are not faithful the Lord will choose others to go this way, but that would take at least another 20 years. We must save those 20 years for God.' As a first priority he laid special emphasis on the unevangelised north-west, Gansu, Qinghai and Xinjiang. 'I believe', he concluded, 'that within a short time the whole of China can be won with the gospel. Let us give our all for this.'

Thereafter he addressed the packed church congregation, so many of whom had waited long to hear him, and one of his first messages to them was from the words of Jesus, 'Render to God the things that are God's.'[8] The effect was explosive, first of all in the turning to the Saviour of a large number of hitherto uncommitted men and women. Within the month as many as 200 new believers were baptised and brought into the church. The meeting place which could only hold 400 was strained to accommodate over 1,500 believers, with people sitting on the stairways and in the parlours behind the building or standing in the lane. Urgent plans were made to purchase land for a new and larger meeting hall.

It was already known that Watchman had handed over the entire CBC business to the church. In the prevailing euphoria and the rush to consecrate themselves to God, many now began to bring gifts of cash, small and great, and pour them into the church offerings for the extension of the work. Others arrived with substantial gifts in kind. Already there was growing disillusion with the high taxes, unchecked inflation and economic chaos promoted by the corrupt Nationalist government, and this had produced in many a revulsion from the world and its ways. There were those therefore who turned over whole businesses – printing works, ink factories and the like – as outright gifts for the church's use. Such giving up of wealth by Christians had not been seen hitherto in China. It was Acts 4 over again with all its strengths and, too, with room left for its possible abuses, as when for example families were not of one mind in an action taken. The slogan 'Render to God' was passed nevertheless from one coastal city to another with revivalist fervour, and much spiritual blessing accompanied the fresh consecration of lives to the Lord Jesus.

The trouble was, however, that from now on the churches attained an unexampled material prosperity. They began to command extensive funds and to operate businesses. Even the CBC itself, instead of being quickly disposed of, had been retained for the church. This was just at a time when 'capitalist' was to become a term of opprobrium and when, in a state without any concept of ethically conceded charities, the mere possession of wealth was going to arouse immediate suspicion. The case for ideological reformation of the movement seems almost, by this ill-conceived development, to have been presented to the Communist Party 'ready made on a tray'.

Now the Fuzhou training programme was resumed. By the middle of June 1948 over 100 young fellow workers from various cities were gathered for this in the green seclusion of Guling Mountain. Simon Meek and Lucas Wu from Manila and Faithful Luke from Singapore were among those invited from overseas. A welcome to join them had even been extended via Samuel Zhang in the Chengdu meeting to two young pioneers, Geoffrey Bull and George Patterson, who were, however, by now headed for the Tibetan border. In April Watchman had written to a friend in the West, 'Yes, I think China has a need for missionaries. But for them to be useful as divine blessings they should learn to be subject and to be one with the local assemblies. As the brethren here are learning to see the authority of Christ as Head in the Body and to cease from independent ways, it will be my hope that brothers from abroad will be likewise. We are almost "spoiled" by blessings everywhere, so send everyone you can spare.'

The wooded valley of Guling, high above the Buddhist monastery of Boiling Spring, commanded an extensive view of the Min Estuary from Pagoda Anchorage to the ocean and was an ideal setting for spiritual preparation. Here the group settled down to long, disciplined study. Watchman and Charity had a tiny cottage of their own, bright with flowers, where he waited upon God and set in order the thoughts he had amassed in the years of his withdrawal and comparative silence. His output in the months that followed was immense, and covered such varied themes as the qualifications of a Christian worker, the ministry of God's Word, the principles of spiritual authority, the problem of sickness, the promised 52 lessons for new believers, the local church's business affairs, the new principles of extension of the work of the gospel and how to study the Bible.[9]

At first, grieved by the Fuzhou situation, Faithful Luke would each Sunday do the long journey to Nantai and back in order to break bread with the local church, walking sorrowfully down the endless stone steps with their vista of green rice fields and reddish-brown villages backed by hills, then on past the black city walls of old Fuzhou and across the Bridge of Ten Thousand Ages to Nantai. Evidently for a while Watchman had still felt uncertain of where he stood with all the gathered workers; but soon Luke could assure him that all was indeed well, so obtained his agreement that they might meet thereafter for the Lord's Table in a little prayer hall set amid Guling's terraced fields.

When Watchman addressed the workers it was as if floodgates long under pressure had opened. He would walk up and down with his hands behind his back, just speaking from his heart. After his talks he would invite questions, and his answers were valuable, never evasive but always frank and to the point. Every morning there would be one session given over to individual testimonies in which a worker would speak for half an hour, after which others were invited to give their criticisms, and finally Watchman would sum up for the benefit of the one concerned. The whole training programme was conducted under a strong sense of urgency. The political future in the nation was quite unknown. In his first editorial in May to a new Shanghai magazine, *The Ministry*, Watchman had written, 'These days are critical beyond anything we have thought.'

In the north the capture of Yanan by the Nationalists the previous year had proved an empty victory. The harsh brutalities they inflicted on innocent villagers whom they had 'released from land reform' were their undoing. Such acts exposed their brief gains to erosion by Communist guerrillas, who worked skilfully behind their lines to win peasant affections. In late June 1947 Mao Ze-dong had been able to launch units of his People's Liberation Army on a counter-drive through Henan that by September had penetrated to the Yangtze valley. Other units were redeployed to the east and north. Early in 1948 Manzhouli (Manchuria) was severed from China and by the same autumn many cities of Henan and Shandong had fallen without a struggle. Disciplined and well led, the Communist troops had unbounded faith in their cause. Chiang Kai-shek's forces by contrast were disheartened through self-loathing, ignorance of their trade and tyranny from above, and were swiftly losing what stomach they had had for civil strife. Soon whole regiments and even divisions were deserting or surrendering without a fight as discipline and loyalty to their Generalissimo ebbed away.

It was against this background of uncertainty that the Guling training programme soldiered on. In the winter months there was a break for review and for a conference of workers at Hardoon Road. Watchman and his colleagues found Shanghai troubled by hunger and economic distress, skyrocketing inflation, robbery and mob violence. Harsh police controls and repressions were making life hazardous and many of its citizens now longed for peace at almost any price.

At Wen De Li Watchman shared in the ministry of the Word under conditions of great solemnity and found people waiting on his every utterance. Much time was spent by the church in prayer, pleading that God would so control events that doors would stay open for the gospel. Nee went into close conclave with his workers and elders, making known to them his inner conviction, reached after much prayer, that in the event of a turnover of government to the CCP he himself should remain in Shanghai. He had read Marx and Engels and was sure that the Communists would behave very differently from the alien Japanese, and that conditions for Christian witness under Marxism would be intensely difficult. The church might no longer be free to serve the Lord, even in suffering, and might face entire elimination. But his personal calling was to serve Christ in China and to bring him to the Chinese people. Chiang Kai-shek and his ministers might retreat, but not the church of God. To the few workers present he said, 'When the older ones fall, you younger ones must continue to go forward.' He added his further recommendation that, if circumstances forced a movement of population overseas, Witness Lee should be prepared to go with his family and work for the spread of the gospel among the Chinese dispersion. Lee agreed to hold this plan before the Lord. Then the party of trainees returned to Fuzhou to resume their studies in Guling.

19

Consistent Choice

On 31 January 1949 the Communist Eighth Route Army entered an undefended Beijing. By April the armies of liberation were grouped on the muddy north bank of the two-mile-wide Yangtze. Nearly half a million Kuomintang troops were deployed along the southern bank facing them, supported by a powerful navy and air force. Yet when on 20 April Mao Ze-dong and Zhu De gave the order to cross the river and liberate the south, the flotillas of junks, rafts and sampans went over almost unopposed. Nanjing, the southern capital of the past three decades, had yielded to the realities of the situation.

Watchman had already telegraphed from Fuzhou instructing Witness Lee to move with his family from Shanghai to the new field of work in Taiwan. He had also sent Charity with a small party of ladies to Hong Kong. Faithful Luke had left for Singapore and Simon Meek and Lukas Wu for Manila. With the People's Liberation Army driving rapidly southward, capturing an average of three cities a day, it was now decided to break up the Guling training course prematurely. The workers descended to Fuzhou and those from the north were flown to cities where they might be swiftly over-run and thus get back to their churches. Witness Lee now arrived to report briefly on the situation in Shanghai before departing to Taipei. The new light-construction hall at 145 Nanyang Road was, he said, completed and would seat 4,000. The 52 lessons for new believers were now in print. There was much economic distress, but the meetings were going on in life and they were proving God's faithfulness in fresh ways.

In May it was clear that Shanghai was about to fall and Watchman knew he must return there. The liberating army that entered the city on 25 May was impressive in the extreme, disciplined, well fed, well clothed in their olive-green uniforms, thoroughly indoctrinated with Communist convictions, and led by officers who lived and dressed as simply as the rank-and-file. To everyone's relief there was no looting and no violence, a hint of the social clean-up that was to follow. For a short while Watchman resumed the care of the church with weekly Bible studies and instruction for the workers and helpers on a wide range of subjects and needs. In addition he set aside time for a new phase in his own education. He had long ago assimilated the outline of Marxist doctrine and well understood its anti-religious character. He was on friendly terms too with several convinced but hitherto secret Party members in the city, one of whom, Charity's sixth uncle, lived close to his home. He now met this man several times for talks, with the object of discovering what were the Party's future plans regarding religious groups. He foresaw collision between the authorities and the rank-and-file believers on certain issues of Christian life and walk, and the CCP might well prove hostile to the church's programme of nationwide evangelism.

But this was the honeymoon period that for two or so years followed liberation. Party members quietly observed the Christians, watching for leaders of influence and gift, and while appearing indifferent made their calculations for the future. Thus Charity's uncle made warm promises to help Watchman, personally guaranteeing that if he stayed on in Shanghai he would be unmolested and need have nothing to fear. It is probable that like so many others Watchman was deceived by the Party officials he encountered into thinking them reasonable men who could be dealt with wisely.

That summer, while Shanghai suffered typhoons and floods, the heart of the Yangtze valley fell to the Communists with the capture of the Wuhan metropolis. By October the Nationalists had lost Guangdong, and Guiyang and Chongqing fell a month later. On 1 October 1949 the People's Republic of China was proclaimed in Beijing with Mao Ze-dong as Chairman and Zhou En-lai as Prime Minister.

During those weeks Watchman had seized the opportunity to visit Taiwan and encourage Witness Lee and the handful of fellow workers who had accompanied him there. The many Chinese refugees were disheartened by severe difficulties of housing and employment, but in his few days there Watchman gathered several hundred together for meetings and the nucleus was formed of a new church in Taiwan that under Lee's guidance was to go from strength to strength.[1] Drained of strength himself, however, and oppressed with many cares,[2] Watchman went on now to Hong Kong to join Charity at Diamond Hill in the Changsha peninsula of Kowloon. While there he held a series of meetings for young people and saw the beginnings of revival in this until now none-too-thriving local church.

He returned to Shanghai in the early months of 1950, during which period, on 6 February, that city was heavily bombed by Nationalist planes based in Taiwan. The electricity plant was hit and for some time light, power and running water were severely rationed. Back once more in Hong Kong, he placed in charge there as elders two men of opposite temperament, James Chen and K.H. Weigh, to work together for the Lord's sake. He helped them with plans to secure on Observatory Road in Kowloon the site for a new church meeting place.

In that month of May 1950 Witness Lee joined him there to report on developments in Taiwan and was assured that he was right to return there and carry on. Before they said their last farewells in June, Lee tried earnestly to dissuade Watchman from returning to Shanghai. 'But Brother,' he protested, 'it has taken so long to build up the church there. Can I possibly desert them now? Did not the apostles remain in Jerusalem under just such conditions?'[3] With Lee's experience of what the CCP had done in its Shandong communes, they reviewed therefore their own recent plans for gospel outreach and discussed how, perhaps, Christians living communally as a visible church might disarm suspicion and ensure continuity of God's work. But again on their last evening Lee lovingly renewed his personal appeal to Watchman. 'If you go back,' he said, 'it could be the end.' Watchman, however, had received from the Shanghai elders a telegram telling of their many problems and pleading for his early return. Peace Wang, who was present, added her support to their plea. 'The Lord sat as king at the Flood,' she reminded them. 'He sits as king for ever!'[4] Nevertheless, Lee took him aside yet once more to appeal earnestly to him alone. At last Watchman exclaimed, 'I do not care for my life. If the house is crashing down, I have children inside and must support it, if need be with my head.'

To test his loyalties yet further, news now came from his birthplace in Shantou of the call to glory of his mother, Lin He-ping. Yet even so this did not weaken his resolution and he instructed his eldest sister, Mrs Chen, to attend to the funeral arrangements while he himself left for Shanghai. He went partly to stem a movement of evacuation of believers to Hong Kong that earlier he had encouraged and partly to carry through what the brothers controlling the pharmaceutical company (chaired by Witness Lee) had finally agreed upon, namely, its disposal to a concern operating from Manzhouli (Manchuria).

On his arrival back in Shanghai he called Charity to join him there, and soon after spoke to the workers on 'buying up the opportunity because the days are evil'.[5] He confessed to the opportunities wasted in the past and went on, 'No servant of God should be satisfied with present attainment. Anyone who is content with what is, is a loser of opportunities. I believe those that God is now giving us are far beyond anything we can conceive. Every day God is giving us new openings, and the aggregate who can assess? Today is 7 July 1950. To redeem the time is to seize today the opportunities God has appointed for us today. When the church buries a talent there is serious loss. We think that because the meeting place at Nanyang Road has just been completed we can settle down for the rest of life. We have our preaching there and 10 or 20 souls are saved, and we think we have done so well. But if the Lord's intention was that we win 1,000 souls in one day, then 900 souls have been lost! When God moves let us move. As soon as the door opens slightly, enter in, for the trouble with opportunities is that they do not wait for us.' And he went on to suggest that there were whole groups of Christian believers in other movements, such as the Shandong-based *Ye-su Jia*

Ting ('Jesus Family') with its principles of communal living, to whom in the present crisis they might go out in fellowship. 'We can learn from them,' he said, 'for they are ahead of us in the way they have all things in common; but as regards the truth of the church, no doubt we can be of help to them. If this be truly God's opportunity, may we not miss it.'[6]

It seems clear that Nee believed some degree of cooperation with the new government on the lines of Romans 12 to be both possible and necessary, depending of course on how the clause in the constitution was applied that guaranteed freedom of religion. The Assembly Hall churches were circularised urging believers not to emigrate but to stay in China for the Lord's sake. They should be prepared to give up material comforts and, as good Christians and good Chinese, to cooperate sincerely with the state when called upon for such public work as road-building and irrigation works. Only, they must not act in conflict with the Bible nor deny their Lord.

This worked well at first, but a knowledge of Marxism–Leninism should have warned them that first impressions are illusory. Communist policy is relative, conditioned by three things, time, place and circumstance, and when any one of these changes the policy may change. Attitudes therefore may alter in a night, and there is no such thing as the Party keeping a promise.

In some coastal cities it was realised that the sheer size of the meetings might lay them open to criticism and this again emphasised the need for dispersion for the gospel's sake. In Zhejiang Province several groups of volunteers had therefore disposed of their possessions and pulled up their roots, moving out to depopulated areas of Jiangxi. Here they had established agricultural settlements to bring the land under cultivation. They built their own simple mud-walled houses and from the first lived a rigorous communal life governed by a strict routine which left ample time for personal devotions and nightly group edification in spiritual things.

There had been much enthusiasm about this move, especially when they won a few Communists to the Lord. 'Our day has come,' they thought.[7] But in June the government's well-tested agrarian policy of land reform became law. For the next year or so, whereas the cities enjoyed some respite, the villages were upheaved by mass meetings, popular trials (and in some cases executions) of landowners and rich peasants, and the redistribution of land among the poor peasants and labourers. All other work came to a standstill and all country churches were closed for the duration. The migrant Christians were not exempted from the re-education and struggle meetings and from a deliberate perversion of their motives. In due course they were to find, as did the Jesus Family, that they were no less suspect with the Communists for doing the right thing for the wrong reason than for not doing it at all.

Missionaries in Hunan at about this time describe how, when their congregation had scattered and they themselves were on the point of leaving, they were courageously befriended by a brother of a Little Flock group that had lately migrated into the area. In spite of dangers Watchman was conducting meetings by the light of a broken pressure-lamp (which they were able to replace for him with a better one). Police came and told him, 'You cannot carry on your services any more,' to which he replied, 'We have to, you know! Our Bible says we must not stop assembling together.'[8] 'Then if you must, may we attend?' 'Certainly you may!'

And a missionary in Zhejiang wrote, soon after leaving, of conditions in that province, 'The influence of the Little Flock permeates the country. It has begun to lay a new and strong emphasis on evangelism. It has never had any affiliation with foreign missions, and this is a great asset in the New China. May it not be that this movement is God's specially prepared instrument for the present time? It is close-knit, yet unobtrusive and adaptable in organisation; it is wholly indigenous, deeply spiritual, and with a kindling missionary fervour.' A letter received a year or so later spoke of the possible union of the different groups of Christians in the town, and she comments, 'This would mean a union under the leadership of the Little Flock, and it is perhaps the best provision against the present difficulties.'[9]

During 1949 most missionaries with evangelical vision had tried to remain in their outposts in hope of continuing their witness under the new regime. But in May 1950 there took place a series of meetings held, in the Communist manner, late at night in Beijing between the Premier Zhou En-lai and three liberal Protestant leaders, led by Y.T. Wu of the Shanghai YMCA who for ten years past had secretly been a Party member. The purpose was to work out a Christian Manifesto for the Protestant Churches, of which Zhou treated the three present as representative leaders and founder members of a new Christian movement whose principles he now, with every show of cordiality, dictated to them.[10] The 'Direction of Endeavour for Chinese Christianity in the Construction of New China' which emerged required the church in all its activities to accept the leadership of the People's Government. Cooperation in the state's Common Programme of reform was to be the price of religious freedom. Zhou virtually commanded the dismissal of foreign personnel and the refusal of foreign funds. Had not

Leighton Stuart, the missionary head of Yanjing University, served as US ambassador to Chiang Kai-shek,[11] and were not all missionaries imperialists?

The men called to this conference formed the Preparatory Committee of what came to be known as the 'Oppose-America, Aid-Korea, Three Self Reform Movement of the Church of Christ in China'.[12] Its object was to make the church self-governing, self-supporting and self-propagating, where 'self' was the antithesis of 'imperialist'. It was made answerable to the Religious Affairs Bureau, set up under the atheist Committee of Culture and Education in Beijing. Its slogan was 'Love your country; Love your Church', with a studious avoidance of the offending name of God. Its periodical *Tian Feng* ('Heavenly Wind') rapidly became the official, and for very long the only, published organ of Christian communication.

In the months that followed, there was a nationwide drive to obtain signatures to the Christian Manifesto approved by Zhou En-lai, and with its publication in the secular press on 23 September it quickly became clear that the work of missionaries would in future be seriously restricted, if not rendered impossible. Indeed, their presence in the field was becoming an embarrassment to the Chinese churches on whom every pressure was being brought to join the Three Self Movement. Within the year 1951 there took place the nearly total evacuation of all those who, after the Japanese War, had returned with such high hopes. The century-long association of Chinese and foreign Christians was thus cruelly and abruptly broken.

Some missionaries leaving the country through Shanghai, or held in that city awaiting exit permits, attended the Nanyang Road meetings. These left enriched, heartened by the movement's evangelistic zeal, and moved by Nee's own warmth of personality and sustained helpfulness in Bible exposition. One such visitor observed, 'Most Christian services, you feel, are helpful at some point, but these are helpful right through!' At about this time, Leslie T. Lyall invited Watchman to meet several CIM colleagues at his Shanghai flat for a discussion of the future. How should they occupy themselves in the interval before they might be asked to return? 'Translate for us some really solid commentaries such as those by Dean Alford,' was the reply. 'We have so little in that category and we need it badly. And come back as teaching elders in the assemblies; not again as evangelists. Evangelism in future must be the task of Chinese believers.'

A Chinese pastor attending the Nanyang Road hall at about this time heard Watchman, he says, speak for a whole week on Romans 1:1. 'Each evening he delivered a different sermon of outstanding quality; but when you put them all together you got a single long and well-composed thesis. It was simply marvellous.'

On 1 January 1951 he gave to the church a New Year message on the significance of God's blessing disclosed in one of Jesus' miracles. As one of the last talks we have from him, its essence is worth recording here.

'All service is dependent upon the blessing of God. We may be very conscientious and very diligent, we may believe in his power and may pray to him to put it forth, but if the blessing of God is lacking, then all our conscientiousness, all our diligence, all our faith and all our prayer is in vain. On the other hand, even though we make mistakes, and even though the situation we face be a hopeless one, provided we have the blessing of God there will be a fruitful issue.

'Consider the miracle of the loaves and fishes.[13] The

point was not the quantity of material in hand but the blessing that rested upon it. Sooner or later we must recognise that what counts is not the state of our treasury or the number of our gifts. It is from the blessing of the Lord alone that man derives his sustenance. One day our own resources, our power, our toil, our faithfulness will all proclaim to us their vanity. The tremendous disappointment of future days will lay bare to us our own utter inadequacy. This lesson is not easily learned. The hopes of so many are still centred, not on the blessing of the Lord but on the few loaves in their hands. It is so pitifully little we have in hand, and yet we keep reckoning with it; and the more we reckon, the harder the work becomes. My brothers and sisters, miracles issue from the blessing of the Lord. Only let that be upon the loaves and they will be multiplied. Where the blessing rests, the thousands are fed: where the blessing is absent, much more than "two hundred pennyworth" is insufficient to feed them. Recognise that, and we would cease to ask "How many loaves have we?" There would be no need to manipulate and no need to dodge; there would be no need for human wisdom and no need for flattering speeches. We should be able to trust the blessing of God and wait for it. And we should often find that, even where we had bungled things, somehow all was well. A little bit of blessing can carry us over a great deal of trouble.

'What is "blessing"? It is the working of God where there is nothing to account for his working. For instance, you calculate that a penny should buy a pennyworth. But if you have not paid your penny and God has given you ten thousand pennyworth, then you have no basis for your calculations. When five loaves provide food for five thousand and leave twelve baskets of fragments, that is blessing. When the fruit of your service is out of all proportion to the gifts you possess, that is blessing. Or to be rather extreme, when, taking account of your failures, there should be no fruit at all from your labours and still there is fruit, that is blessing. Many of us only expect results commensurate with what we are in ourselves, but blessing is fruit that is out of all correspondence with what we are. It is not just the working of cause and effect, for when we reckon on the basis of what we put in we merely bar the way for God to work beyond our reckoning. If, on the other hand, we set our hearts upon the blessing of the Lord, we shall find things happen that are altogether out of keeping with our capacity and that surpass even our dreams.

'A life of blessing', Watchman concluded, 'should be our normal life as Christians, and a work with the blessing of God upon it should be our normal work. "Prove me now herewith, saith the Lord of hosts, if I will not open you the windows of heaven, and pour you out a blessing, that there shall not be room enough to receive it."[14] Here in Shanghai at the beginning of 1951, this is still the Word of God.'

20

The Trap Closes

For two years Shanghai's city thoroughfares were bright with processions of workers and young people bearing paper flags and large red silk banners. To the throb of drums and the chant of slogans, *Yang-ko* dancers swayed and pirouetted before massive portraits of Chairman Mao. But in the streets and lanes, intensive organisation was in process. Neighbourhood revolutionary committees had been organised; and there was constant inspection of workplaces and homes, everyone informing on everyone else. Human privacy was invaded by the zeal of cadres trained in indoctrination, while ready at hand to act on information received were the regular municipal police, with the secret police lurking in the shadows behind them. There were 'tiger hunts' to search out and destroy vicious capitalist tigers who preyed upon the people's wealth. To live as a Christian in such circumstances called for faith and courage of a high order.[1]

Letters in early 1951 spoke of enlargement of Watchman's ministry, but there were other affairs too to claim his attention. From 16 to 21 April Premier Zhou En-lai called a conference of 181 church leaders to allay the alarm caused by the sudden cutting off of overseas funds.[2] An edict in December had meanwhile required all receiving foreign subsidies to register full details of sources, amounts received and the conditions of their use.[3] Watchman was required to attend this meeting, as an observer representing a group of 'self-governing, self-supporting and self-propagating' churches. True, they had received contributions in the church offerings from visiting missionaries, as well as casual overseas gifts towards the gospel work, but there was no demand on them to register as the tools of imperialism. He was there by government design 'for the benefits received through this experience'.

In Shanghai the meetings could continue 'mostly as usual' and all the fellow workers were labouring urgently to redeem the time. But 27 April was Black Saturday[4] in Shanghai with the arrests of many thousands of intellectuals and others, followed by a programme of thought reform of writers. Quite a few Christians were among those taken in and 'some co-workers have been in bondage and suffered for the Lord; but most are safe and well. Only all are under trials.'

On 2 May 1951 *Tian Feng* published a summons to the Christian church in China to take part in accusation meetings. Strong persuasion was exerted on whole congregations to engage in self-criticism and reform. 'Propagandise well, accuse minutely' was the slogan.[5] Only this would qualify them to join the Three Self Patriotic Church. They must publicly denounce and purge out 'imperialist elements and their stooges' hidden within their own ranks and leadership. Some groups were shown whom they should accuse among their leaders; others were told to find them for themselves. YMCA Secretary L.M. Liu published an article on 'How to Hold a Successful Accusation Meeting', appealing to Matthew 23 (Jesus' attack on the Jewish Pharisees) as precedent, and urging Christians to overcome their inhibitions by attending and learning from secular political meetings. 'Many Christians have the old-fashioned idea of "being above politics", therefore we must hold accusation meetings to educate everybody. To hold a successful big accusation meeting is one of the important tasks that every church must do well to wipe out the influence of imperialism.'[6] But no New Testament preacher or writer in fact takes Matthew 23 as a precedent. Essentially that chapter is unique to Jesus himself.

To show the way, the Three Self Patriotic Movement (TSPM) organised a huge meeting on Sunday 10 June for the public denunciation of the departed Christian missionaries. It was held in the Shanghai dog-racing stadium. Carefully chosen 'accusers' representing leading Christian groups addressed an audience largely of church congregations. With rehearsed speeches and every show of indignation and hatred they vilified their brothers in Christ, both missionary figures of the past and former colleagues. The whole performance was designed to bring loss of face, not merely to the missionary-sending nations but, in the long term, to Christianity itself.[7] And any Christian's non-attendance at the meeting was carefully noted. Thus the movement gathered sway as Christians turned against one another in this self-degrading form of persecution, and woe betide those churches who stood apart from the exercise. Urging its further intensification, *Tian Feng* was able to announce on 11 August that 63 big accusation meetings had been held since May. The Christian churches were accommodating themselves to the niche prepared for them in the new society, in which 'Three Self' was ultimately to mean control by the state, financial dependence on the state and propagation in line with the ideology of the state.[8] No wonder that letters in July reported, 'The assemblies are now in a very trying situation, and so especially are those who bear responsibility like brother Watchman Nee,' who was reported to be once again ill and on his back.

Meanwhile the People's Government was pressing on with its highly successful programme of moral clean-up aimed at eliminating crime and prostitution and all forms of corruption. Claiming to be the people and to rule in their name, the Party sought to achieve country-wide what the missionaries had tried to tackle man by man and yet to do it using not legislation but popular persuasion. In November 1951 the state instituted two such ethical campaigns that were to occupy the country in the coming months, the *San-Fan*, or 'Three Antis', opposing corruption, waste and bureaucracy in the civil service, and the *Wu-Fan*, or 'Five Antis', opposing bribery, tax evasion, theft of state property, shoddy work and stealing economic secrets for private speculation in the field of business. Posters everywhere called the public to repent and confess,[9] and there was a rash of accusations and false charges and an outbreak of suicides. This was a pointer to what lay ahead, and as if to underline it, Watchman had been notified that the transfer of the China Biological and Chemical Company (CBC) to its prospective purchasers was suspended by government order pending inquiry into its accounts and tax payments.

Then in the 30 November issue of *Tian Feng*, the official Three Self Christian periodical, there appeared an article by a member of the Little Flock congregation in Nanjing entitled 'A Revelation of the Secret Organisation and Dark Doings of the Ci-tang Road Church'. He wrote, 'I am a believer who from the outset has belonged to the Ci-Tang Road Church (in Nanjing) and who regarded it as the purest of assemblies until I was indoctrinated regarding the Three Self Patriotic Movement, when I saw plainly what a vile place it is. I have long been deceived, but today I stand on the ground of love of country and love of religion, and with emotions of unqualified wrath I expose its professed "spirituality". In order to conceal the true anti-revolutionary nature of this movement, those in responsibility at Ci-Tang Road persistently and emphatically affirm that it is a "local church". As a matter of fact we have been utterly misled. From its very inception it has been subject to the Shanghai assembly and is strictly controlled by Watchman Nee. It is an organised system of nationwide and occult character. Watchman Nee has an involved, secret system for controlling 470 churches all over the country, with Shanghai as his administrative base. Shanghai governs these indirectly through "central churches" established in large cities such as Beijing, Hankou, Qingdao, Fuzhou, etc. The dark, mysterious control Watchman Nee exercises over the churches goes quite beyond the sphere of religion. To facilitate his totalitarian control he disseminates anti-revolutionary poison and dominates the thought of church members. He shamelessly terms himself "the apostle of God"!'

To a group of workers who wondered what action Watchman would take in self-defence, he recounted his four-fold experience of being disciplined by God's hand of love: his excommunication at Fuzhou in 1924 and the revival that had followed; his grave illness attending the difficult choice between the role of popular preacher and the less attractive pursuit of Christian witness through the local churches; his withdrawal from ministry during the Japanese War and the spiritual enrichment with which he had returned; and now this attack upon him and, by implication, upon them all. No doubt in every criticism there was some element of truth. But why retaliate, he concluded, when each time the Lord's rebuke had proved so instructive, his chastening so spiritually fruitful?

Above all he urged them, 'when we are depressed through evil report let us give way, not to the depression but to the Lord. Of course we are depressed, for Christianity is a paradox: we have this priceless treasure, but we have it in vessels of clay.[10] What counts for God is the quality of the treasure, not that of the containing vessel. God does not remove our weakness; instead he bestows there his strength. Herein is the glory of Christianity, that no human weakness need limit divine power.'

Communist cadres were by now attending Nanyang Road and trying to stir up demands that the church stage their own accusation meeting. At length early in 1952, under extreme pressure from the Three Self headquarters, a meeting was called at which two of its representatives were allowed to address the assembly. Their speeches charging imperialism in the church's leaders brought only a bewildered silence. No one spoke in support. At length someone plucked up the courage to say, 'Is it not true that Paul counted all things but loss for Christ? Should we not therefore count even our honoured People's Government the veriest refuse that we might gain Christ?'[11] At this a cadre, planted in the meeting, burst out, 'Watchman Nee ordered women to cover their heads in prayer. This is despotism!' Designed to be inflammatory, the charge merely backfired on the accuser. Brothers demanded to know who was this outsider who had put the question. The Three Self spokesman got up and announced, 'Obviously you are not ready for self-reform and need training in this. I put Mr Watchman Nee himself in charge of your re-education.'

All in the church now saw what they were up against. No

doubt the fellow travellers had suffered a setback, but they would bide their time. Watchman, after talking things over with Charity and with his fellow workers and elders, gave himself up to one thing, the preparation of biblical material for believers. Ruth Lee and her assistants took down in writing everything he had to give. To one group of young people, for instance, he talked at length on the proofs of the existence of God. There were series, too, of a practical character, on Christ as the righteousness, the wisdom and the glory of God for the believer, and on the power of his resurrection. But that was not what had been ordered. Now therefore there were new government demands, this time that he leave Shanghai. Financial questions outstanding in the pharmaceutical business with which the church was still saddled required his presence in Manzhouli (Manchuria). So the pressure to buy up the opportunity intensified to the point of desperation. Together the team worked all day and long into the nights, recording his expounding of the Lord's Word, until, that month of March, they were getting only two hours sleep nightly.

One member of the Nanyang Road meeting recounts that as a young man at this time he sought spiritual counsel concerning a personal failure. Despite the extreme pressure Watchman was under, he nevertheless took time to speak to him and shared instances of failures in his own life, and how the Lord brought him through them. The brother received much encouragement, and could say of him, 'He was such a humble brother.'

At length the state's ultimatum could no longer be resisted. He gave a last word of exhortation to his beloved brothers and sisters in Christ, adding, 'Tell them in Hong Kong to dissociate all secular business enterprise from the church.' Sorrowfully he took leave of Charity. Then with deep misgivings he set out for Harbin. Very little was then heard of him until his public indictment four years later in January 1956.

In his fiftieth year he had in fact been arrested in Manzhouli by the Department of Public Security on 10 April 1952,[12] and at his first inquiry, either at Harbin or in Beijing, he was charged as a lawless capitalist 'tiger' who had committed all the five crimes specified in the *Wu-Fan* campaign against corrupt business practices. He was warned that the Sheng Hua Company would be required to pay a fine of 17,200 million *yuan* in old currency (equivalent to nearly 1.5 million US dollars). He neither accepted this unfair accusation, nor did he have the funds to pay such a fine. So he remained in prison, and the company was in due course confiscated by the state.[13]

Initially in all such cases the conditions of imprisonment were harsh in the extreme, without, it is probable, actual physical violence but with threats, poor food, sleep deprivation, vermin and a constant pitiless drain upon physical endurance. His Bible, of course, was confiscated at once. No communication was allowed with anyone outside.

He is said to have been offered the chance of reinstatement as a public Christian figure if he would lead his immense following into step with the People's Government within the Three Self Patriotic Church. The experience of others at this period makes it certain that, if he was thus in demand, fierce attempts were made to re-educate him into acquiescence in the national neurosis, a supine renunciation of all freedom of thought. We have ample documentation of the thought reform methods then in use: the long hours of questioning by relays of interrogators, the political lectures, the vigilant scrutiny by relentless warders, the occupation of his cell by convinced and converted 'fellow students', and the strident speak-bitterness of the group struggle meetings.[14] That no change of heart took place and no confession worth using emerged speaks volumes for the keeping power of God. So far as is known, the confession obtained amounted to an admission that he had used paid employees to set the Fuzhou properties in order without participating himself in the physical labour involved. But he will have been required to write and rewrite the chronicle of his life in endless detail, for from this, piece by piece, the criminal case against him was built up and he was confronted with 'evidence' that was compounded by a process of mind-deadening repetition.

There were precedents. Already by February 1952 a confession of precisely the kind they sought from Nee had been wrung after imprisonment from Isaac Wei, son of the founder of the indigenous True Jesus Church, bringing the adherents of that large group into step with the state. The same year the Jesus Family, envied for its communal success but vulnerable by reason of its rural situation, had been treated to the alternative, namely forcible dissolution and the disgrace of its leaders with 'convictions' of espionage, counter-revolutionary activity and licentious living.[15] The Party would not tolerate in China a 'centre of darkness' where the right thing was done for what in their eyes was the wrong reason. If no 'imperialist' links could be proved in a truly indigenous movement, its leaders must be arraigned as common criminals. And this therefore was the fate now in store for Watchman Nee.

Meanwhile, with his withdrawal from the scene the fences were temporarily lowered by the Three Self representatives. Elders of 'Little Flock' assemblies everywhere were assured of an unconditional welcome if they would join the steady flow of churches into this 'mountain stream which, the further it flows, the clearer and broader it becomes'. 'The door is still open,' they were told, 'and we are extending friendly hands, hoping the day will arrive when we will unitedly dwell together.' With Watchman out of their reach they had no strong spiritual counsellor to turn to, and one by one they capitulated,[16] most of them very soon to regret the step.

In the city of Wuhan, to take a single instance, the 'Little Flock' congregation had joined the Three Self Movement as early as 1951 and submitted to the prescribed 'learning' programme. But then one of their preachers, He Guang-tao, led them out again. 'We withdraw from the movement', the police charges report him to have said, 'purely for reasons of religious belief, for the believer and the non-believer cannot bear the same yoke.' Thereafter the elders declined to receive cinema tickets and other learning material from the Religious Affairs Bureau and gave a cool reception to its officials sent to report to the church on the government's religious policy. Many other local churches followed their example. *Tian Feng* reported[17] that in 1954 He Guang-tao called a conference at Wuhan of preachers from meeting places all over central China, encouraging them in the faith and urging them to lead their congregations to independence of the Three Self Patriotic Movement and to pray for those churches which had not yet withdrawn. In the four years following Nee's arrest many churches were to find again their spiritual feet in this way, the church in Shanghai withdrawing from the movement late in 1955. They were to bring down wrath upon themselves as a consequence.

But meanwhile the work at Nanyang Road continued somehow to move forward with influence and power. Services for worship were able to continue and even, for a year or two, special evangelistic meetings at the New Year holi-day. Because of the general uncertainty of life, opportun-ities for personal witness were greater than ever before. The work of the Church Book Room somehow continued with a flow of publications, mostly now anonymous but recog-nisable as Watchman's Bible expositions.[18]

In the spring of 1952, following a compulsory course of Marxist indoctrination of all students, there had been a remarkable Christian awakening in two of the colleges and many were born again. This led to a series of summer and winter conferences that continued for several years using the Nanyang Road hall as a venue, and new Christian fel-lowships sprang into being in every Shanghai college, not excluding, it is said, the School of Political Studies. Saying grace at meals served students as one means of recognition. Prayer disguised as conversation between two or three with unbowed head in an open space might go undetected, and the three-quarter-hour respite immediately after the weekly mass political indoctrination gave a chance, with cadres off their guard, for a larger hurried meeting. Here, at risk to their future careers, some prayed aloud who had never done so without a prayer book and there took place that true ecumenism under pressure which, one of them affirms, 'Watchman Nee had always prayed for'.[19] This pat-tern of student revival was, it is said, being repeated widely over China.

July 1955 saw the public attack in the *People's Daily* on the faithful fundamentalist preacher Wang Ming-dao of Beijing. This Daniel of a man was greatly loved by students, who composed nine-tenths of his congregation, and an attempt upon him in the form of an accusation meeting ten months earlier had backfired with an 'Oppose the Persecu-tion of Wang Ming-dao' movement. His magazine, *Spiritual*

Food Quarterly, ever loyal to the Scriptures, was still in production and widely influential. Watchman Nee greatly respected him as a man of God, but was less happy with his church with its constant turnover of students, passing through, rather than being built together as a spiritual house for the Lord.

Wang Ming-dao had firmly rebuffed all Three Self overtures and from the Party standpoint the trouble was that, as an independent preacher who neither served nor headed an organisation, it was difficult to frame him on any 'criminal' charge, so political implications must be sought in his Christian testimony alone. These were found in the courageous pamphlet he produced in June 1955 entitled *We shall be Steadfast because of Our Faith*. The story of his arrest on 8 August has been told elsewhere. A few of his former supporters were found ready to put themselves in the Party's good graces by accusing him of treasonable intent. With his imprisonment and subsequent forced 'confession' under extreme mental stress, one more Christian rallying point was eliminated.[20] Released a year later in a state of nervous breakdown, he recovered sufficiently to withdraw his confession publicly, whereupon he was imprisoned for an indefinite term. The field was now clear for the major storm to break.

21

Ordeal

On Wednesday 18 January 1956 there began in the Church Assembly Hall at Nanyang Road a series of meetings called by the Religious Affairs Bureau at which the whole congregation was required to be present. They ran consecutively for twelve days, lasting all day, and believers were excused employment to attend them.

At these meetings items from the list of criminal charges to be brought against Nee and those associated with him were progressively made known to the believers, who were encouraged to express their views. Accusations of imperialist intrigue and espionage, counter-revolutionary activities hostile to government policy, financial irregularities and gross licentiousness had been accumulated in an indictment running to 2,296 pages. The object of this preliminary exercise was to prepare the church members with data and to arouse their indignation in readiness for a mass accusation meeting to be held at the month's end. Opportunity was given for the elders and senior sisters, already informed of what was required of them, to admit their own complicity and to lead the church in its denunciation of Watchman as an enemy of the people. Two elders made statements that were considered inadequate. Dr C.H. Yu, Ruth Lee and Peace Wang declined to make any accusation at all.

On Sunday 29 January Watchman's case came for summary hearing before the Shanghai Court of Public Security. The hearing was brief and in private. The charge was that from his hiding in the Christian Meeting Place in Nanyang Road he had conducted systematic counter-revolutionary intrigues against the People's Government. His crimes were listed under five headings. He and his accomplices had supported imperialism and the Nationalist regime; they had opposed popular movements; they had corrupted youth; they had sabotaged production; and Nee himself had acted licentiously. The charges were read and he was allowed to answer only 'Yes' or 'No'. No explanation was permitted. He denied the one really substantial charge, that of spying and sabotage. To the others he is reported to have remained silent. The hearing completed, the case was referred for judgement to the High Court with a strong recommendation for severity.

The same day Dr Yu and the two women were taken into custody along with several others,[1] and in the next week 30 more workers and responsible brothers were arrested locally while a simultaneous sweep of the churches country-wide drew in some 1,000 key men and women throughout the movement. (Later estimates put this figure twice as high.) These all disappeared from sight, and their wives and children, debarred from visiting them, were left without support.

Next day, Monday 30 January, the promised accusation meeting took place at the Tian Zian Theatre on Fuzhou Road. It was convened by the heads of the Public Security Bureau and the Religious Affairs Bureau and a total of 2,500 persons were present, including, probably by order, all the Protestant pastors. Attendance was compulsory for all the Nanyang Road church members. The chairman was Luo Zhu-feng, Chairman of the Shanghai Religious Affairs Bureau. The charges were now proclaimed publicly in detail and backed by an exhibition of photographs and other documentary 'proofs'. Relating to this astonishing event I have been supplied with the list of named persons from all classes who spoke out and of agencies who contributed evidence supporting the charges against Watchman Nee. Omitting their personal names, here is the army arrayed against him.

Inquisitors against Ni Tuo-sheng[2]

Various Professions: President of the Revolutionary Communist National Party. Vice President of the Women's Association of Shanghai City. An elderly housewife in Shanghai. A medical school student. An engineer of the Shanghai Biology Department. A Vice President of the Chinese Education Association in Shanghai. General Manager of a pharmaceutical factory. President of a medical school. A pharmaceutical clerk. A doctor. A labour worker. A Vice President of a medical school. A Chinese doctor.

Various Religions: A Catholic. A Turk. A Buddhist monk. The Chairman and Vice Chairman of the Three Self Movement.

Christians: A famous Christian leader. A Christian farmer in Jiangxi Province. Manager of a Chinese Christian Association. A Christian lady. A Christian.

News Media: Three Commentaries of the Daily News. A Commentary of the Shanghai News.

Communist Organisations: The Shanghai Committee of the Three Self Movement. Official inquisitions in Chin-an and Chian-ning. A proclamation of the Shanghai political officials. An appeal of the Shanghai people's district attorney. A proclamation of the Shanghai police department. The official critique against Ni by the government. The published document accusing Ni as a spy of the Nationalist Party. An inquisition by the government. The proclamation of the victory of the government over Ni.

The following summary of the charges against him is compiled from official reports of various stages in the month's proceedings. As far back as 1941, it was alleged, Nee had engaged in transmitting to the American air force and to agents of Chiang Kai-shek information on the Communist army movements and secret plans. The real purpose of his last visit to Hong Kong in the spring of 1950 had been to report on the success of the Nationalist bombing of Shanghai's electric and water supplies on 6 February and to encourage more of the same thing. He had further informed Chiang's emissaries of the schistosomiasis (blood-fluke) epidemic among units of the Liberation Army in Jiangsu and Zhejiang provinces, and had advised the dropping of larva-infested snails into the Zhejiang rivers and lakes, along with the withholding of raw materials needed for manufacturing curative drugs.

Nee was further charged with being a lawless capitalist who had profiteered in the pharmaceutical trade. Under cover of his China Biological and Chemical Company he had imported raw materials from abroad to sell to other manufacturers, and by bribing tax officials had evaded the foreign exchange regulations covering such deals. In this way he had stolen from the nation some 17,200 million *yuan* (old currency). From July 1950 to August 1951 under cover of the same company he 'had stolen state secrets' by leaking news to private concerns that the People's

Government was placing orders for military purposes, and by passing on details of secret technical procedures. Furthermore, he had indirectly been guilty of sabotage. Fires and explosions in the Shanghai Dye Works during 1955 and the current month of January 1956 were attributable to his having, five years earlier, detailed to these factories Christians trained by him for the long-term task of destroying production.

Nee was, it turned out after all, a running dog of the imperialists. He had failed to register the Christian Meeting Places as a foreign-subsidised mission on the specious ground that they were purely Chinese. All the time he was hiding his imperialist dealings. Since 1921 he had in fact received gifts and legacies towards the work from missionaries, from the Exclusive Brethren, from the Christian Fellowship Centre in Forest Hill, London, and from individual donors overseas. Moreover, when the China Inland Mission withdrew from the country it had handed over to Nee a number of church buildings, thus confirming that he and they 'were one in political thinking'.

Since long before liberation Nee had 'carried on under the cloak of religion well planned and organised counter-revolutionary activities against the new society'. Assuming the role of founder of the Christian Meeting Places and aided by his clique of reactionaries hidden there, he had set up his 'emergency plan' for China, conducting training sessions for all church officers. In these, through lectures, sermons and discussion meetings, he pursued his subversive activities. He had incited Christians to oppose the great enterprise of national liberation by instructing them to fast and pray that, just as Pharaoh's host perished in the Red Sea, God would drown the People's Liberation Army in the Yangtze River. In 1950 he had incited Christians in all the

Meeting Places to sign their names openly attacking land reform. Yet before its introduction he had tried to anticipate it by carrying out a 'land reform' of his own, giving away to his own church his extensive holdings in Fuzhou. This was merely a cover for his criminal activities.

Even now his harmful influence was being felt. At a time when, under the able leadership of Chairman Mao, China was embarking on the bright path towards Socialist construction, Nee's associates were teaching that these were what the Bible calls 'the last days'.[3] They had impaired the will of the people by, for example, attributing to the judgement of God the Wuhan flood disaster in the summer of 1954. They gave credit to young people who flunked school examinations in political studies, and discouraged Christians from participating in big self-criticism and accusation meetings on the ground that Christianity is above politics. In his March 1956 address to the National Conference of the Chinese Christian Church, Dr H.H. Cui in Beijing forcefully attacked this last valuation: 'For the past hundred years the dexterously planned strategy against Chinese Christians of applying poisonous ideas of "religion above politics" has been the malicious scheme of the missionaries of imperialism.'[4]

Much was made of the counselling of young Christians, many of whom Nee and his followers were said to have corrupted with their pernicious advice. For some young people they had helped arrange marriages, or in other cases had advised against a particular match, and not all were satisfied. The prosecutor instanced one whose husband 'had turned out to be an espionage agent now imprisoned by the Government'. Other young men and women had been lured into handing themselves over for training to serve the Lord, 'only to be given work that was hard and humiliating'. Worse still, they had been discouraged from joining the People's Voluntary Army, and Nee had thus posed a threat to the Resist-America Aid-Korea Movement. Quoting 1 John 2:15, he had taught that young people should not love the world. (A transcription of his teaching on this theme may have been used here as evidence.[5]) In this advice, it was argued, he was plainly being dishonest, since what he really loved was the discredited world of Chiang Kai-shek's banditry.

Nee and his clique had harboured many Kuomintang agents – underground workers, army generals and escaped landlords – and had absorbed them into the Christian Meeting Places as preachers, elders and deacons where they had been engaged for him in carefully planned subversiveness. In 1950 they had been instructed to take cover in productive labour and to outdo even non-Christians in their supposed zeal for such state projects as roadworks, but the sole object was in this way 'to set forward his emergency hidden plot'. Several of these 'underground workers' were named in the charges: 'Chen Lu-san, a former police chief and counter-revolutionary bandit, Lu Si-guang, whose hands were dipped in the people's blood, Li Yin-xin, and a great many others' (clearly some of them in the Nationalist state employment before they had given their lives to God), and these were now identified as Chiang Kai-shek's 'undercover agents'. Between 1949 and 1951 Nee had, it was alleged, posted such men to Christian Meeting Places in Kunming, Chongqing, Suzhou and other cities 'to expand his counter-revolutionary influence under the guise of gospel migration and preaching the Word of God'. Through such means he had hurried into action his conquer-China-with-the-gospel plan whereby evangelism became an effective cloak for political propaganda. Madly he had announced his aim within 15 years to cover China with 'good news' that should do better than a Communist revolution.

The most shameful step in this plan had been his 'Render unto God' campaign of April 1948, with its fraudulent appeal to Christians to follow the example of the book of Acts and to hand over themselves and their possessions to God for the gospel's sake rather than to the Communists for (as he was charged with stating) death and destruction. This deception had spread like a bush fire through the nation's nearly 500 Christian Meeting Places, netting an estimated US $500,000 in cash and sale of goods. This was of course nothing but a political stratagem to enlist cadres and funds for his counter-revolutionary programme.

Finally, for the benefit of simple God-fearing believers, Nee was charged with being a 'dissolute vagabond of corrupt and indulgent living' who frequented brothel neighbour-hoods and had always been a shameless and indiscriminate womaniser. He had confessed, it was claimed, to seducing over 100 women, Chinese and foreign. No evidence for this was produced.

Here in the Tian Zian Theatre on Fuzhou Road, the long, shoddy recital of the case against him dragged out to its con-clusion. Then the chairman, Luo Zhu-feng, called upon the Vice Mayor of Shanghai to give the main address and Xu Jian-guo stood up. After alluding to the facts of the arrest in April 1952 (not until now made public), he went on to dis-cuss the government's religious policy.

'The People's Government guarantees freedom of reli-gious belief,' he assured them. 'Unfortunately some counter-revolutionaries slyly emphasise the difference between materialism and idealism in their writings and thus arouse the people's emotions and disrupt their unity. The question before us today is of counter-revolutionaries hidden within the Christian Meeting Places. The opposition of Nee and his gang to the Three Self Movement is not a matter of religious principle. It has had its own secret purpose.

'Religion is religion and faith is faith, they must not be mixed up with a person's private counter-revolutionary ideas and used as a cover behind which to spread the poison of hatred towards country and people. Every Christian should enter positively into the struggle to expose these arrested men's crimes. We still have serious questions about a number of others also, but for the present we let them alone to see if they will repent and show a new attitude. Through our investigations of the past few years we have a great deal of information on file, which we will use if need be. Those who do not heed this warning must take the consequences. And you who are members of the Christian Meeting Place should not be afraid of washing your dirty linen in public, but should vigorously seek out and expose all offenders.

'This struggle has just begun. We will not draw back until we have completed it victoriously and rooted out every counter-revolutionary hidden within the Little Flock.' Following the Vice Mayor's oration the meeting was closed.

One of the accusers was a young female medical student, previously a rather zealous believer from the Nanyang Road meeting. The faith of all was being tested to the limits, whether to stand fast or to yield as Peter had done in Caiaphas' courtyard.

As an old school friend and fellow worker of Watchman observed at the time, the charges against him were not religious but political and moral. 'It is one thing to suffer as a Christian; it is quite another to suffer as a criminal for sins not committed. Shall we not ask God the righteous Judge to intervene in the forthcoming High Court trial to clear his own Name, deliver our brethren, and cause that his Word in China be not bound? And shall we not pray for their enemies, who are the Lord's enemies, held captive by Satan?'

On 1 February 1956 the Shanghai municipal government took the unusual step of publishing in its *Liberation Daily* an official statement of Watchman's arrest on 10 April 1952 and stated that he and two others, Zhang Zi-jie and Ni Hong-zu, were held in the Shanghai First Place of Detention. Zhang was a fellow worker from Qingdao. Hong-zu was the fourth brother, the eighth child in the Ni family, and did not claim to be a practising Christian. He was known to have been a senior political agent of Chiang Kai-shek, and had been enticed back from Hong Kong with the Party's promise that his personal finances in Shanghai were protected and would be restored to him. He was eventually executed as a traitor. Unquestionably the public association at this moment of the two brothers' names was designed to give credibility to the charge against Watchman of espionage.

On 2 February Bishop Robin Chen published a statement in *Liberation Daily* denouncing Nee and his accomplices and emphasising how glad he was that this stumbling block to faith had at length been removed. The same day at Huai En Church the bishop presided over an enlarged meeting of the Shanghai Council of the Three Self Movement. It was addressed by a dozen clergy and church leaders who engaged in 'furious reprimands' that echoed the official charges and praised Chairman Mao and the Communist Party for their 'perfectly correct and necessary action' in imprisoning Nee and his group. These fierce wolves in sheep's clothing should be given the severest punishment. The meeting passed a resolution that spoke of 'the grave and momentous sins of these evil leaders in their traitorous rebellion against the government' which had aroused Christians to 'an unprecedented righteous indignation'. Their teachings were incompatible with Christian doctrine and all Christians who had been deceived and poisoned by them 'must without exception be required to engage in studies designed to elevate their patriotic conscience and uncover their sins'.

One woman speaker at this meeting described Nee as an anti-revolutionary profligate and shameless adulterer. 'We women, hearing this, could not but hate him,' she said. Taking its cue from this, the Shanghai *Liberation Daily* featured next day a cartoon bearing the caption *Jiao Chu Lai*, 'Render Up'. It depicted two levels or floors of a house. On the upper floor people were pressing forward to where a masked man sat on a stepladder, urging them to pour their possessions into a great funnel labelled 'Render unto God the things that are God's'. Every kind of gift was going in, right down to that of the coolie who had stripped off his shirt and the little jacket of his weeping child. On the floor below, to which the receptacle extended, it was differently labelled 'For the Work of Counter-Revolution'. Here from the funnel's outlet a stream of gold and silver, watches and jewellery and money gifts came pouring out at the feet of the admiring Ni Tuo-sheng, who relaxed with a prostitute seated in his lap.

By such calculated measures was Watchman dethroned if possible from his place of affection in the Christians' hearts. Few dared openly to speak his name, but silently many Christians all over China supported him in prayer.

Pastors and evangelistic workers throughout Shanghai were now instructed to organise study in small groups from 5 February onwards to acquaint Christians everywhere with 'the crimes of Ni Tuo-sheng'. At Nanyang Road all meetings other than Sunday worship were closed to make way for this special indoctrination. For guidance *Tian Feng* of 6 February devoted eleven pages to a review of Nee's case. Its editorial was headed, 'Drive the Cruel Wolves out of the Church', and ran, 'From the recital of their crimes, it can be seen that this gang has been destructive of our economic reconstruction, dangerous to the people's livelihood and social order, and a threat to national safety. Their presence within the Christian church has been a dishonour to the holy name of the Lord, a blot on the church's reputation and a corruption of gospel truth. They are very clever and devious, and like to talk about holiness. Their own actions however are far from holy, and the life of Ni Tuo-sheng himself is too adulterous to repeat.

'Brothers and sisters of the Christian Meeting Place: we are very happy that this gang can never again disturb and harm our beloved church, and so without hindrance we may now unite freely in mutual love. Fellow Christians, let us celebrate our common victory and consider it cause for rejoicing. It is only by exposing and expelling such wolves that we can purify the church so that it may glorify the Lord.'

Subsequent issues of *Tian Feng* maintained the flow of invective. That of 29 February told also of another big denunciation meeting at the Nanyang Road Hall with more than 3,000 'Little Flock' members present, including representatives from Nanjing, Changsha, Suzhou, Wuxi and other places. Their presence was designed to give weight of authority to the election of a governing committee of 14 who should take the place in Shanghai of the imprisoned leaders. This meeting proceeded with much more emotional pressure than the one on 30 January. Hesitations and questionings had in some degree been overcome and *Tian Feng* reported that all were ready to join in a frenzied demand for vengeance. Its 15-page report of charges and denunciations was followed by a devotional article entitled 'Now abideth faith, hope and love, these three'.[6]

A large number of delegates from the Church Assembly Halls now attended the second national conference of the Chinese Christian Church held in Beijing from 15 to 23 March 1956. Here the Chairman of the Three Self Movement, Y.T. Wu, gave his report of progress since the previous conference in July 1954. At that time, he said, 'just as we were going ahead in full confidence, a little group, on the empty pretext of its being a "question of faith", opposed the Three Self Movement and broke up our unity.' He described how, during the national campaign in late 1955 and early 1956, 'some counter-revolutionaries hidden within the church were uncovered. Under the cloak of religion these men acted as spies, spread rumours, and disrupted the central campaign of the Chinese people. Within the church they used the pretext of "faith" to oppose the Three Self Patriotic Movement, trying with a religious slogan to confuse their fellow Christians, to corrupt youth and to destroy Christian unity. Their exposure removed the obstacle to the unity of the Chinese Christian church. Today all Christians are united on a wider and firmer basis than ever.'[7]

Soon opportunity was given for the 'Little Flock' representatives to make their public confessions and join the ranks of the Three Self Patriotic Movement. In a later speech the Anglican Dr H.H. Cui stated, 'Elder Yan Jia-le of the Beijing Little Flock and Miss Xu Mei-li of the Shanghai Little Flock have made accusations in this very conference. Who has ever been compelled to make accusations? We simply could not do otherwise but grasp such opportunities to reveal and accuse these proponents of imperialism and anti-revolutionism when we fully recognise their horribly criminal acts.' He spoke of the 'hidden claws of the wolf under the sheepskin' of those whom the West chose to describe as 'brave Christian leaders'.[8]

On the last day a letter from the committee of the TSPM was sent out to all Chinese Christians, which included the following paragraph: 'We remember that in the national conference of the Chinese Christian church of July 1954 there were still some believers who did not understand the meaning of coming together in the Three Self Patriotic Movement. They took a destructive attitude and tried to prevent the union of Christians. But today the situation is very clear: we see now that the obstacle to union at that time was the presence of counter-revolutionaries hidden within the church, who, wearing the cap of "faith", tried to destroy the patriotic movement against imperialism. Now they have finally been exposed, and the deluded brothers and sisters have come to realise the true situation; and so the grace of brethren living together in harmony has now finally descended upon us. Brothers and sisters, let us together before the Lord rejoice and give thanks.'[9]

Provincial conferences followed, that for Zhejiang being held at Hangzhou, the place where Watchman and Charity were married. When this conference was thrown open for speeches, members of the Assembly Halls were especially eager to stand up and disavow their former attitude and to join in condemnation of their imprisoned leader. According to incomplete reports, the 'Little Flock' had at this time 362 places of worship and 39,000 members in this one province of Zhejiang. These figures were interpreted as indicating that China-wide its members made up some 15–20 per cent of the whole Protestant church in China, and that they may have become its largest single denomination.[10] It is certain, however, that many of these were congregations founded by the China Inland Mission and subsequently absorbed, with other independent groups, into the ranks of the 'Little Flock'.[11] In Anhui Province it was officially reported in March that 'as many as possible of those who had been perverted by Ni Tuo-sheng's widespread influence had been re-educated, and the remainder arrested'.

By mid-April reorientation of the church at Nanyang Road, Shanghai, was pronounced complete. Its formal 'entry into the TSPM' took place on 15 April at a meeting with representatives of the other member churches. The themes of the meeting were 'The Clarification of Our Faith' and 'How to Participate in the Three Self Patriotic Movement'. Bowing to 'the desires of the masses', the church publicly announced its 'rebirth'. It was addressed by a representative of the Religious Affairs Bureau and several church leaders made speeches of welcome. The whole Protestant church in China was now, it was claimed, united under a single authority.

Afterwards, however, the *Tian Feng* reporter plaintively observed, 'But a small number of brothers and sisters who had been deeply affected by the anti-revolutionary poison were still uneasy and could not in conscience agree, thinking that the question was one which involved their faith.' So the authorities set to work to close the boltholes. All informal Bible classes, prayer meetings and other unauthorised activities in private homes were actively proscribed. Independent evangelists and preachers were classed as outlaws. Freedom of Christian worship was loudly proclaimed, but it was a conditional freedom, reserved for those under state surveillance within the approved fold.

Throughout these proceedings Watchman Nee himself had of course remained out of sight. On 21 June 1956 he appeared before the High Court in Shanghai. As before, and as in all such cases, it was not a public trial but simply a public meeting to condemn him. It lasted five hours. During the hearing it was announced that he had been excommunicated by his own church. He was found guilty on all charges and was sentenced to 15 years imprisonment with reform by labour, to run from 12 April 1952.[12]

22

Last Years

When the storm broke in Shanghai in January 1956 Charity had been amongst those 'wanted'. She was, however, under strict medical care in hospital. With high blood pressure resulting in retinopathy, which threatened her eyesight, and a heart condition, she was too ill to attend the accusation meetings or to produce the confession demanded of her. But by June, at the time of Watchman's sentencing, she was herself in prison. At the year's end her confession was still not completed.

She was released a year later in 1957 under strict home surveillance to begin her long vigil. She lived now in a room off the Xu-jia-hui (Siccawei) Road not far from the First Medical School. Few dared visit her and to do so openly took great courage, for she was related to a criminal reactionary and so was herself without civil rights. One of Watchman's nieces and her husband cared for her as best they could, but association with her could be dangerous. Her neighbours rarely talked with her; but now and again a Christian student or one of the believers would seek her out, usually after dark, to escape detection. Avoiding mention of her husband, they would speak together about the

Lord Jesus and then unite in prayer. Always the visitor went away uplifted, amazed at her fortitude and inward rest of spirit, for she was a woman with considerable inner resources.[1]

Although not now in prison, she suffered more than many prisoners. Twice a day, morning and evening, Charity was ordered to sweep the alleys. As a reactionary she could be beaten and spat upon by any passer-by, even by a child. Once after a denunciation meeting in which she was criticised, she said to a young relative, 'We have been made a spectacle to the whole universe, to angels as well as to men. The Bible told us of this so clearly.'[2] When put on a stand and harangued publicly, she always stood firm and kept silent, never bringing the name of Jesus to shame. Praying in her heart, she relied on her God.

Day by day, year after year, almost all who saw her called her scornfully 'White Hair', and everyone knew that the old white-haired woman did penal labour under surveillance and got treatment unfit for human beings on account of her and her husband's faith. Her patient bearing of this for the name of the Lord Jesus could not fail to become an effective witness for all to see.

Then in 1966, with the start of the Great Cultural Revolution, she was made to suffer even more until her life became for her a nightmare. Her health by now was very poor, but from the beginning to the end she kept her eyes fixed on the Lord Jesus who himself went unprotesting 'like a lamb to the slaughter, and as a sheep before its shearers is dumb'.[3] One summer's day in 1966 the Red Guards put her in a small cell and she was interrogated and severely tortured. Those outside the cell could hear the sounds as she was whipped by a leather belt, intermingled with shouts of threats and abuse. They felt as though their own hearts were being lashed – but through it all she remained silent. After a long time she was brought out. She was covered in wounds and her eyes, because of the beatings, were swollen like steamed bread. The lenses of the glasses on which she was very dependent had been broken.

She was humiliated in every possible way; she was publicly denounced and paraded through the streets many times. On one occasion she and two older Christian sisters had to hold up their hands for a long time with shoes on them. They had to wear dunce caps on their heads, and boards with slogans hung round their necks. For several hours the Red Guards tried to force them to deny their faith. But they kept silent. After further humiliation the Guards fiercely challenged them, 'Do you still believe in Jesus?' Each of them replied 'Yes'. Then the Red Guards picked up leather shoes from the ground and threw them at their faces and bodies, and shouted, 'Because of your obstinacy you will go and see your God.' Praise God that he was with them and gave them strength in their time of persecution. Afterwards they spoke of their joy in being counted worthy to suffer for their Lord.

The Red Guards also searched Charity's home and confiscated any Bibles and hymnbooks which they could find. She had taken trouble to hide some. Later, the children of neighbours climbed the wall and found two Bibles under the eaves. This was reported and a further charge was added to those already made. 'After I became a Christian,' said one of Charity's nieces, 'I discovered a hidden Bible and was jubilant because none were available. This small book became very precious to me.'

Charity remained in Shanghai during the long years while Watchman was in Tilanqiao Prison. She was allowed to exchange letters occasionally and to visit him once a month, taking with her some food and daily necessities sent from Hong Kong. While he was in Qingdong Farm she visited him once only. He was feeling guilty that he had left her on her own so frequently soon after their marriage while he travelled widely preaching, and he was therefore so much hoping that they would have time together when he could care for her. Just when this looked possible in 1967, his sentence was prolonged by another five years because he would not recant.

At that time, by order of the Great Leader, all students who graduated from middle school were sent to rural areas to be farmhands, educated in the Party's Principles through hard field labour. 'In 1970 I was assigned to a rural area,' says one such student, 'and Mrs Nee prayed for me every day that I was there. Before I left Shanghai for that remote place in the spring of 1971 she said to me with tears: "The Lord Jesus is our precious Saviour. Whatever happens to you, follow him." In that country place I received from my Lord wonderful guidance and experienced his abundant grace. I think my experiences there are inseparable from her prayers.'

To Watchman's great grief Charity passed away on 7 November 1971. Having had a fall in which she fractured some ribs, probably due to a stroke, she died after three days. With her high blood pressure, Charity had expected that one day she would suffer either a heart attack or a stroke. She had always hoped that she would be received by the Lord quickly if she had a stroke so that she would not be a burden on others and could avoid suffering over a long period. Thank the Lord that he heard her prayer. She went to him peacefully and painlessly in hospital. A sister whom she had not seen for 17 years came to be with her at the end and to arrange her funeral. Her faith never wavered. Only seven months later Watchman himself was to join her in the presence of their Lord, a more wonderful experience than if they had been reunited in their tiny home in Shanghai.

Many years later it was learned that the Shanghai Public Security Bureau (Police) had issued a document in August 1986 stating that the charges made against Charity during the Cultural Revolution had been investigated and found to be untrue. Thus, 15 years after her decease, Charity was absolved from all charges made against her.

It was some years after the writing of the first edition of *Against the Tide* in 1973 that reliable information about Watchman Nee's last years and death eventually emerged from China.

So what of Watchman Nee himself from 1952 to 1972?

After his arrest in 1952 Watchman was kept in prison for four years without contact with his family or friends. It was only in 1956, as we have seen, that he was brought before the High Court in Shanghai for sentencing. The sentence of 15 years' imprisonment with reform by hard labour was to run from 12 April 1952.

He was imprisoned in the Shanghai Municipal (Tilan-qiao) Prison and he was now allowed to appoint one relative as visitor, so that after those long four years Charity was permitted to see him again. This monthly supervised interview took place in a hall with an open-mesh barrier between them and lasted for half an hour. They could now also exchange letters once a month, strictly censored. Everything possible was done to make him renounce his faith in Jesus Christ – hard labour, brainwashing and physical torture.

The forbidding First Municipal Prison in Shanghai where he was incarcerated backed onto the Suzhou Creek and

Charity had to cross the city to Amoy Street in the old International Settlement to reach it. It had been built by the British in 1912 in traditional style with hideous grey walls. Turret stairways led to each of the five floors of its seven blocks. Watchman's single cell measured 9 feet by 4.5 feet. As furniture it had only a wooden platform on the floor to sleep on. The padlocks on most of the doors had been made in London. Outside the door was a gallery 200 feet long onto which the cells opened like cupboards with windows in their facing walls. Due to bedbugs sleep was difficult.

The day was divided into eight hours of labour, eight hours of education (indoctrination) and eight hours of rest. He rose at 5.00 a.m. to mingle with the throng of lost and sullen men at work in the prison factory or at exercise in the oppressive quadrangles that were devoid of any vegetation. There was no prison uniform and the prisoners' own clothes were worn and tattered, or, if the wearers were diligent, a mass of patches. They made a drab and depressing sight. Meals, prepared by the women prisoners, were three a day, two of them solid (for labour) or light (for non-labour) and the third of gruel. Though they included fresh vegetables and occasional meat, the heat of summer brought to light the prisoners' cage-like ribs and prominent veins. Clearly they lived barely above subsistence level. They were allowed an occasional hot bath and a fortnightly haircut. In winter with no heating the extreme cold called for many layers of clothing to stay alive.

As officially a criminal against the civil code, but in their eyes a counter-revolutionary, Watchman received the same educational reform as a political prisoner. Lectures were given in politics, current events and production techniques and filled waking hours. In each section there was a library of approved books, newspapers and films. During much of the time there was a blare of political propaganda over the loudspeakers.

As in due course Watchman's circumstances became known outside, small quantities of food, clothing, soap (which was severely rationed) and money were sent to Charity from Hong Kong and could be taken by her, once she was released from prison, for his use. It was learned that his mind was clear and he was being kept occupied. At times, heavy labour was his occupation, but he was allowed writing materials and part of his reform through labour meant employment in translating from English into Chinese such scientific textbooks and journal articles as were of value to the authorities. He could buy approved books for this purpose, and at a later date two volumes of a medical dictionary were purchased in Hong Kong and sent for his use. It is practically certain, however, that he was never allowed a Bible. For that source of spiritual comfort he depended on his prodigious memory.

The summer of 1956 had seen the beginning of the 'Hundred Flowers' period of relaxation of thought, but a year later, at the time of Charity's release, there followed the phase of 'Blooming and Contending' with its harsh Rectification Campaign against liberal thinkers. Nevertheless, a student visiting the church at Nanyang Road found in 1957 a throng of courageous people proclaiming, 'The Lord is my strength and song: and he has become my salvation.' There was a morning service, in the afternoon the breaking of bread, and a meeting for young people in the evening. She says it was most refreshing. That July there was a five-day student conference in the meeting hall.[4] Indeed, that summer witnessed a widespread Christian awakening throughout China, fed it would seem by the stimulus of the carefully preserved writings of Wang

Ming-dao and Watchman Nee. Many students were also taking very seriously the exercise of committing large portions of the Chinese Bible to memory against a day of trial.

In November of the same year the first of Watchman's popular writings, *The Normal Christian Life*, appeared in print in Bombay, India, based on his ministry in Europe in 1938–9. It is unlikely that he was ever aware of those writings' wide spiritual fruitfulness outside China.

With January 1958 came Mao Ze-dong's Great Leap Forward, aimed to make the nation's production 'faster, better and more economical'. Guided by his infallible thoughts as interpreted by the cadres, the Chinese people threw themselves into overtime effort in everything from close-planting of rice seedlings to the backyard smelting of pig-iron. Physical exhaustion from this led inevitably to the dwindling of church attendances. The year had begun, too, with an intensive campaign of socialist education of Christian pastors, designed to identify them as members of the exploiting classes, 'parasites on society', and to draft them into productive labour. *Tian Feng* was full of reports of the wicked things discovered, such as faith healing and the casting out of demons. Imperialism was said to have raised its head again, and there were the usual baseless charges of immorality. Lists were supplied of pastors sent to prison or to work in the mines. Many Christian leaders who had mistaken the Party's temporary strategies for its ultimate aims and had joined in the early denunciations now found themselves in their turn denounced. 'One did not know', says a close-up observer, 'whether to mourn over those accused or those who made the accusations.'[5]

The corollary to this was the unification of worship, for which a campaign was now set in motion. Everywhere congregations were fused and church buildings were made available for secular use. By September the churches in Beijing were reduced in number from 64 to 4, and in Shanghai from 150 to 20. The Nanyang Road hall became a factory for making woollen scarves. Compulsory reform of the 'Little Flock' included the abolition of its women's meetings and of its weekly breaking of bread with the personal interviewing of members before it. Hymns were to be unified and approved by the State Church Committee. In all churches preaching on the theme of the last days and the Lord's return was banned, as also was mention of the vanity of this world. Teaching should favour church union and socialism. All books used in the interpretation of the Bible were to be examined and judged, and those containing poisonous thoughts rejected. Buildings and church property as well as church accounts were to be handed over to the Standing Committee of the State Church, namely the Three Self Patriotic Movement.

Inside the First Place of Detention, where pressure to step up productivity was no less strong, a quietly defiant song of praise was rising to God. A foreign prisoner in another block tells us how he himself contrived a year or so later to sing each morning, before the loudspeakers came on, four or five songs that he had composed from Scripture and had memorised. This gives credibility to the report of more than one prisoner released in the summer of 1958 saying that the singing of hymns was frequently to be heard also from Watchman's cell. Those who remember his pleasant baritone voice, or who are familiar with the many lovely hymns he composed or translated into Chinese, will feel this story is wholly in character and will even have some idea of what he sang. They will be reminded, too, of the first-century occasion when 'the prisoners were listening'.[6]

The trial and denunciation of Ruth Lee and Peace Wang

took place that summer of 1958. They had steadfastly refused to accuse Watchman Nee, and were each given 15 years' imprisonment to run from January 1956. In due course it was known that they were employed under harsh conditions of labour, making cloth shoes. Dr C.H. Yu had also resisted every inducement to denounce Watchman, even when his wife and son were sent to persuade him to accept release by doing so. He was by now suffering from cancer and was too ill, when the time came, to stand trial. A little later, when out on parole, he died in one of the former upstairs offices at Hardoon Road, firm in his faith to the last.

The New Year of 1959 saw no firecrackers, no gay new clothes, and of course no evangelistic meetings. *Tian Feng*, now a bi-weekly and the last surviving 'Christian' magazine, limited itself to propaganda articles. People everywhere had been exhorted to 'hand their hearts over to the Party', and all were now fully occupied with being productive. But by the time that three Chinese mountaineers, spurred on by Mao's strategic thinking, had placed a small plaster bust of the Chairman at the summit of Zhumulangma (Mount Everest) in May 1960, China was already plunging into economic crisis. A combination of gross mismanagement and natural disasters had compelled food rationing and brought near-famine conditions in many areas, and Mao's Great Leap Forward policy was having to be reversed. Naturally enough the famine penetrated into the Places of Detention. In 1962, when two frail and aged 'Little Flock' elders were released after serving ten-year sentences, it was said that Watchman weighed less than 100 pounds (45 kilograms). Eighteen months later he was ill in the prison hospital with coronary ischaemia and was relieved from manual work for a while. Drugs which were advised were allowed to be purchased in Hong Kong and sent to him.

In June 1966 the Great Proletarian Cultural Revolution exploded on the nation, taking by surprise even the shrewdest of observers close to the heart of affairs.[7] It appears that the personal ambitions of the present generation of privileged administrators were thought to be threatening the collective interest. Mao Ze-dong himself feared the CCP was forsaking its ideals, and concluded that the only sure and true way forward was 'continuous revolution'. On 18 August at a mass parade in Beijing Mao's student Red Guards received the blessing of 'our great teacher, leader, supreme commander and helmsman' upon their crusade for ideological enthusiasm and purity. Armed with his 'thoughts' (*The Little Red Book*) they attacked the nation's leaders, from Vice Chairman Liu Shao-qi down, as bourgeois Soviet revisionists. In Shanghai within months the administration was in upheaval and the Municipal Committee had fallen. Factories closed, vituperative posters covered every blank wall, clashing crowds filled the streets, and no one knew a moment's privacy. On one occasion Red Guards appeared at the gates of the municipal jail and, charging Fu Wei-ren the governor with revisionism, burst into and took over the building for a while. Storming through its cells and lecture rooms, they violently molested some of the inmates. There is evidence that in this episode Watchman was knocked down and suffered a fractured arm. This episode may lie behind the stories of his physical mutilation circulating in the West, in which it was affirmed that because he would not stop testifying to Christ the Communists cut off his hands and his tongue, later found to be untrue. Certainly from now on the New Thought took precedence over all other studies in the reform of the prisoners, and the selection of approved books in the prison library was freshly made to conform with it.

In April 1967 Watchman's 15 years were completed. Frequently throughout this period the loudspeakers in the First Municipal Prison had warned prisoners, 'If you have a five-year or a seven-year sentence, and when your term is up we are not satisfied that you have changed, you will be given a further five or seven years.' So while many around the world were praying for his release, and although Charity, who was now in poor health, was confidently expecting it, perhaps few others were so hopeful. Postcards were exchanged between his sisters in Hong Kong and Shanghai. 'Is elder brother at home?' 'Elder brother is not at home.'

The year 1967 also saw the distribution of 86 million copies of the four-volume *Selected Works of Mao Ze-dong*, 35 million *Quotations* (*The Little Red Book*) and a further 100 million *Selected Readings and the Poems*.[8] Now it became even more dangerous for someone to possess a Bible.

From this year on church services were discontinued throughout the country and the few remaining pastors and clergy were ordered to return to their native villages. All religious buildings of all faiths were 'secularised', and anti-religious propaganda was posted on their walls. *Tian Feng* suspended publication indefinitely.

In September word was received by the elders at the Church Assembly Hall in Hong Kong, apparently from high authority in the People's Republic, to the effect that Watchman and Charity might be ransomed out of China if a considerable sum of US dollars was deposited in the Hong Kong branch of the Bank of China. There was some precedent for this. A political prisoner with his family, reported in Beijing to have 'defected to the West', was widely believed to have been bought out for a very large sum by just such a mutual

agreement. So great was the love felt for Watchman by
Chinese believers in South-East Asia and beyond that very
quickly the ransom was collected and placed on account as
specified. Then in 1968 word came from the same official
source that the deal was off. The money was released intact
for return to the donors. We may ask ourselves what lay
behind this reversal of plan.

Assuming that the offer was real and that it reached
Watchman, he was certainly fit to form a decision one way
or the other, since a letter in his handwriting which found
its way to Hong Kong with a refugee affirmed that he was
in very good spirits and reasonable health. It is therefore
held by the young fellow workers who had been closest to
him that, like those earlier men of faith who 'disdained
release',[9] he himself turned down the proposal. This is
inherently probable. By staying firm to his principle of
cooperation with the state in things neutral – study, labour,
translation work – he would do least harm to the image of
Christians as loyal Chinese, 'subject to the governing
authorities'.[10] His model behaviour might even help to ease
the lot of others, whereas for him to 'defect to the West'
would certainly involve them all in an appearance of
compromise.

But there was another aspect. He was not, after all, in the
hands of unscrupulous men, but of God. The men doubtless
knew in their hearts that he had been framed and that his
'crimes' were fictitious, but that was their concern. What
mattered was that God was handling him in his own way,
and that God could say, 'Blessed are you.'[11]

At some point early in his life Watchman had learned the
lesson of 'brokenness' whereby the Christian, being once
touched by God as to his own strength and permanently
crippled there (as was Jacob at Jabbok), discovers in that

experience the ever new strength of God. When he is weak, then, in God, he is strong.[12] 'I cannot hold thee, but I can plead with thee. I have no faith and can scarcely even pray, yet I believe!' And when that is so, God, because he is being leaned on, must act. Watchman never sought to graduate from that school. 'We shall always be learners,' he said at Wen De Li, 'but at some time we shall learn that fundamental lesson, and after that nothing will be the same again. There is now no way of not being a cripple. From that point begins a knowledge of God beyond anything we have ever dreamed.' Once he made the point most tellingly by taking a biscuit from a plate and snapping it in half, then fitting the two halves together again carefully. 'It looks fine,' he said with a smile, 'but it's never quite the same again, is it? You are like that. You will yield ever after to the slightest touch from God.'

Watchman's inward peace derived thus from a sense of destiny, which in this life is perhaps God's greatest gift to a man. In 1950 he had elected to return from Hong Kong in the conviction that God had a task for him in the new China. It would be wholly consistent for him to feel now that, whatever the appearances, this was still where God could use him and therefore wanted him to be. 'Nothing hurts so much', he used to say, 'as dissatisfaction with our circumstances. We all start from rest, but there is another rest that we discover when we learn from Jesus how to say "I thank thee Father, for it seemed good to thee".[13] God knows what he is doing and there is nothing accidental in the life of a believer. Nothing but good can come to those who are wholly his.

'To what are we consecrated? Not to Christian work but to the will of God, to be and to do what he pleases. The path of every Christian has been marked out by God. If at the close of a life we can say with Paul, "I have finished my course," then we are blessed indeed. The Old Testament saints served their own generation and passed on. Men go, but the Lord remains. God himself takes away his workers, but he gives others. Our work suffers, but never his. He is still God.'

As 1967 approached and Watchman's 15-year prison term neared its end, the government made it plain to him once more that in order to be released he must renounce his faith in the Lord Jesus Christ and make a written declaration to that effect. As he refused to comply, his sentence was extended for a further five years.

In 1970, in his sixty-seventh year, he was secretly moved from the city's prison to Qingdong Reform-through-Labour Farm in Qingpu County, a suburb of Shanghai. Here his translation work will have ended, and now he was put to more physical tasks with the fieldworkers in the open air. His compliance had become urgent for the government, as with the near-ending of his sentence they had already leaked publicly a rumour that 'Ni Tuo-sheng has renounced his faith'. His refusal, of course, brought on him fiercer persecution. Around this time they shut with him in his small cell two rogue criminals who for a promised reward used incessant pressure to make him recant. Force was called for and his fellow prisoners in the camp later described how his cotton-padded jacket seemed beaten to shreds. His ischaemic heart condition had flared up and he was in considerable discomfort.

Charity was allowed once only to visit him there and this was to be their last meeting. Suddenly there was no more news of him – only silence. Her letters to him were refused and the family waited in vain for some word. He had in fact been sent away under escort to a yet more miserable and now further off place of exile: Baimaoling Reform-through-Labour Farm in Anhui Province. This was a mountainous area where at that time famine was rife and many were short of food. The long sequence of oppressions cast upon him one after another could not totally deject him, believing as he did that God who knows our end has an ultimate purpose of good, for our part in which he is preparing us. God never destroys hope.

Then on 7 November 1971 Charity went to the Lord. At first the family were hesitant about letting him know, since his health was so poor and his cardiac condition so precarious. However, early in 1972 his eldest sister-in-law, accompanied by her grand-daughter, made the long journey by rail and road to the camp and it was immediately clear how ill he was, this being confirmed by other prisoners as having been the case for some time. The sad news brought him great grief. Charity had been his one point of contact over all the years and he was so sad that he had been able to give her so little help or care during the many years of essential travel for the work's sake, followed by his 20 years of imprisonment.

After his visitors had left they were able to correspond with him frequently, and Charity's eldest sister now sent small parcels to him, from the gifts received from Hong Kong. Watchman's 20-year sentence was completed on 12 April 1972. In a letter that Watchman wrote on 22 April to his sister-in-law he said, 'You know the chronic heart condition is always with me. When there is an attack it is distressing, but when there is no attack of course it is not so difficult, but the condition remains . . . I have joy within . . . I hope you also are experiencing this joy.'

It is known that Watchman was in discussion with the prison authorities about where he could move to on his release. He was told that he could not live in Beijing or Shanghai, but only in a small village or town, and all this subject to someone being willing to receive him and, of course, approval from the appropriate higher authority. In further letters written in May to his sister-in-law and to his nephew-in-law, he expressed his desire to return to the company of his relatives. He was still hoping to be released but was aware of the burden his care might be for others and the risks entailed to them. His nephew-in-law, who had cared for Charity, was now willing to take responsibility for Watchman. Charity's sister was intending to come to visit him again, and in a series of letters written late in May he made mention of this and requested her to bring some small items to him.

Then on 26 May 1972 he was transferred from Maple Peak to White Cloud Mountain Renovation Group, an even more remote place, ten miles further on the other side of a mountain. We may ask, why was he moved again, to a more inaccessible place, and at a time just before his release? Was he considered such a threat that he was 'never to be released'?

On 30 May he wrote a short letter, his last, to his sister-in-law. 'You do not need to come any more' (indicating that he knew he would very soon pass from this world into the presence of the Lord). Then he added, 'In sickness I retain joy in my heart.' These were triumphant words: the last cry of victory. Throughout 20 years of suffering and imprisonment the enemy of souls had been utterly defeated. He ended the letter, 'Short letter but deep affection. Wish you well,' and signed it *Shu-zhu*, his childhood name that was always used among his family.

In June the family received a brief message from the farm notifying them of his death. The same family pair made the

journey again, accompanied by a male relative. The authorities claimed that he had suffered a heart attack, but no
death certificate was issued. By the time they arrived he had
been cremated and they could only see his ashes. They were
told by other prisoners that he had become very seriously
ill, was put on a tractor and sent some 40 miles over rough,
unmade country roads from the outpost workplace to the
farm's hospital. A healthy person would have found the
jolting along such a road most unpleasant. For him it must
have been agony. Somewhere along the road to the hospital
he passed away.

The family members were shown a piece of paper that
was found beneath his pillow with several lines in large letters written by a shivering hand. He wanted all his life to
testify to this truth even unto death: 'Christ is the Son of
God. He died as the Redeemer for human beings and was
raised up from the dead after three days. This is the biggest
thing in the Universe. I shall die for believing in Christ.
Watchman Nee.' The cadres in the farm would not give it to
them, but the younger visitor memorised the words. They
also mentioned that he had written a lot in a 'reactionary'
diary which doubtless contained new discoveries of the
truth that he had found in the prison years. They would not
hand this over either, but his relatives were given his only
possession – his old jacket torn by many beatings. In this
was discovered another slip of paper hidden in the lining
which said, 'Only God is ever living – only God is everlast-
ing.' This statement of truth must have served as his
encouragement and comfort through those long years.

The exact day of Watchman's death is not certain, but it
is believed to have taken place on 30 May 1972, the date of
his last letter. He is recorded as having been cremated on 1
June 1972. His ashes were buried by his nephew-in-law in

his home town in Haining, Zhejiang Province. In May 1989 both Watchman's and Charity's ashes were finally laid to rest side by side in the Xiang-San Cemetery at Suzhou, where two simple tablets were erected.

Although God did not fulfil Watchman's final wish to come out of prison to join Charity, he prepared more wonderfully for them – together reunited in his presence.

> 'I have fought the good fight, I have finished the race, I have kept the faith. Finally there is laid up for me the crown of righteousness, which the Lord the righteous Judge will give me on that day, and not to me only but also to all who have loved his appearing.' (2 Timothy 4:7–8)

> 'To him who overcomes I will grant to sit with me on my throne, as I also overcame and sat down with my Father on his throne.' (Revelation 3:21)

> 'And they overcame him by the blood of the Lamb and by the word of their testimony, and they did not love their lives to the death.' (Revelation 12:11)

23

Unhindered

Through the discovery and spread of his devotional writings in the West the name of Watchman Nee became during the 1960s one more rallying point for prayer on behalf of Christians in China generally. Yet this interest in him was quite new, and it is disconcerting to compare it with the suspicion he had earlier aroused in those evangelical mission circles where his work encroached upon established interests. Some of his readers began to feel they had more in common with indigenous Chinese witness such as his than with the foreign missionary enterprise that had so sadly failed to read the signs. One heart-searching admission of this failure was to come from an Anglican missionary after the forced departure from Fujian. He described Nee's work as 'both a real and an expanding fellowship', and admitted that 'such movements began as protests against our errors. What he saw as the tragic opposition between the catholic order and the freedom of the Spirit would not have happened if we had not exported to China our own torn and mutilated Western post-medieval Christian traditions.'[1] But a Chinese observer in the West could hopefully see in the suspension of the foreign mission endeavour a prelude to a richer evangelical future. 'It is reasonable to expect', he wrote, 'that a new type of missionary movement will be started in China.'[2] Can it be said, we may ask, that to such a future Watchman Nee made any positive contribution?

He had been born into an age of revolution. Once won to Jesus Christ he saw the need to work out afresh for himself in a Chinese context the Christian programme of life and witness, free of irrelevancies, and he settled for the Bible as sufficient. Reading it constantly through and through, he hoped thereby to escape the danger of selectivity, and he expected problems arising from action upon it to find their solution in fresh encounters with the living Christ who is its theme. Thus, to quote a missionary's comment, 'The movement of which he was the leader had tremendous appeal as an embodiment of the gospel not only radically biblical but also radically Chinese.' That is to say, in the context of contemporary China it may be one of God the Holy Spirit's original movements in history. As a mere technique transferred to another setting it could disappoint.

When it came to ecclesiology, his chief weakness (but one in which down the ages he has had plenty of company) lay in treating as mandatory the principles he had derived merely from New Testament example. His insistence upon the geographical *locality* of the churches (one secular city: one local church administration) may have opened the door too readily to state control just because it led to so rigid and centralised a structure.[3] By contrast, his rediscovery a decade or so later of the first-century fact of migration evangelism seems truly inspired in its timing. By it, ideas of Christian flexibility and opportunism were planted in the minds of many whose destiny was very soon to be a forced dispersion. As the Party began to uproot and scatter the population, seeking by that means to liquidate religious faith along with all other forms of dissent, these more fluid and pragmatic concepts of Christian life and witness were destined to come into their own. You have then what might be termed the extempore church, a people one in Christ but scarcely at all organised, becoming increasingly versatile in its worship and witness and learning from the Holy Spirit, not merely how to survive under fire in new situations but how, as one people, to do battle there for God. Like Jacob at Bethel (the house of God), its members had heaven opened above them, a direct access to God, and a glimpse of his very real heavenly host.[4]

Watchman's most valuable contribution to the survival of faith and of lively biblical thinking in China may lie elsewhere. His unforgettable teaching on the Christian's walk with his God contains seed 'with life in itself'. The grain of wheat may die, but will not remain alone. The Word uttered will not return empty, but will accomplish the thing for which it was sent. 'Erudite and profound, comprehensive and thorough, he is one of the best preachers I have ever met,' says a Chinese pastor of the Alliance Mission.[5] And in the words of a Western missionary, 'There is no doubt that Mr Nee was a man raised up by the Lord to inject the truths of the gospel into the very bloodstream of the Chinese people. His words stuck like burrs. His books and tracts ran everywhere. If one was asked to draw up a shortlist of the most influential Chinese Christians there have ever been, it would be hard to leave him out.'[6]

But what did Watchman Nee achieve by electing – if indeed he had any choice – to stay in China, shut up, as was Paul, 'like a common criminal'?[7] What message have his final years to bring to us?

First there is his situation itself. It can be argued that this is what Christianity is all about. 'You will be dragged before governors and kings for my sake, to bear testimony before them and the Gentiles' – thus Jesus warned the Twelve. 'What you are to say will be given you in that hour; for it is not you that speak, but the Spirit of your Father speaking through you.'[8] This was borne out in their experiences in the book of Acts, and as F.F. Bruce points out, it establishes also Paul's true motive in appealing to Caesar. 'If Caesar in person heard Paul's defence, what might not the outcome be? It would be precarious to set limits to Paul's high hopes, however impracticable they might appear in retrospect to us who know more about Nero than Paul knew in AD 59.'[9] To Paul, imprisonment was not punishment for preaching the gospel but a platform for its preaching,[10] and others throughout the Christian era have made this their experience. Madame Guyon, the story of whose life had so influenced Watchman in his early years, wrote of her official interrogation under threat of the scaffold in 1688, 'Our Lord did me the favour which he promised to his disciples to make me answer much better than if I had studied.' This aggressive outspokenness for the kingdom calls forth always that response from God that lies behind the final word of the book of Acts – *unhindered*.

In May 1968 a Chinese visitor to a Western capital asked for asylum. The story he told to the authorities there was that he had at one time been a prison guard in the Shanghai First Place of Detention and that through Watchman's witness to him he had found Jesus Christ as Saviour. If this offers a glimpse of what Chinese Christians are today achieving through 'the word of their testimony'[11] – and it may indeed do so – it must prompt also a further consideration.

In his discourse on the last days Jesus uses, to us by

implication, the identical words about witnessing before the authorities that he used earlier to the Twelve. There is, however, a significant addition, for sandwiched between the two sentences quoted above is the familiar statement, commonly thought of in the more usual context of world mission, that 'the good news must first be preached to all nations'.[12] In other words, the classic setting for proclaiming the gospel of Christ today is often the criminal court and the interrogation room. For by the very nature of his task the interrogator himself is wide open to the witness of his victim. His role is to ask questions and to search for motives and causes. He may believe himself to be the aggressor holding all the weapons in his hands, but before God he is a lost and dying man. The prisoner, aware of the man's need, is the one ideally placed to confront him with the news which 'is the power of God'.[13] This does not mean that, even if falsely prosecuted, the defendant gets off. Our Lord Jesus himself was held on fabricated criminal charges, and it took a trial and an execution to call forth from his judges, from a fellow prisoner, from his executioner and from the common people the admission that he was a faultless man. We are not faultless. We are afflicted, perplexed, persecuted, struck down, always carrying in the body the death of Jesus, so that the life also of Jesus may be manifested in our bodies.[14]

This privilege of fellowship with Christ as overcomers with him in a spiritual warfare, through participation in his triumph over death, had long been Watchman's ambition for his fellow Christians. Back in the 1940s he found himself intrigued by John's stormy symbolism in the book of Revelation of a woman confronted by a hungry red dragon when she is about to give birth to an infant boy. This child, to the dragon's discomfiture, escapes being devoured by

finding his place at the very throne of God: another figure
of our resurrection union with Christ, since 'they' (who are
represented by the child) 'love not their lives even unto
death'.[15] Some may feel that the attenuated and serpentine
dragon of China has little in common with John's Grecian
symbolism – though a Chinese believer with the character
for 'dragon' in his name often prefers to change it at baptism. Yet to Chinese believers today, as they claim their right
of access to the throne of grace, the concept of a disappointed dragon – and a Red one! – must surely possess a
certain charm.

In his night-long meeting with the founders of the Chinese Christian Three Self Patriotic Movement, Prime Minister Zhou En-lai made clear the Party's position on freedom
of Christian witness. 'We are going to let you go on trying
to convert people, provided you also continue your social
services. After all, we both believe that truth will prevail.
We think your beliefs untrue and false; therefore if we are
right, the people will reject them and your church will
decay. If you are right, then the people will believe you; but
as we are sure that you are wrong, we are prepared for that
risk.'[16] It was a winning presentation of a quite ruthless
intent, and it already has its answer in the assurance of
Jesus to his church that against her even the bars of death
will prove fragile. She will rise again.[17] When Jesus said
this, he was himself about to put those bars to the test.

A quarter of a century ago I wrote at this point in the first
edition of *Against the Tide*, 'It is certain therefore that we
shall see in our day the reawakening in China of a vital
Christian faith.' 'The old superstitions are reviving,' com-
plain the discouraged Party watchdogs – and they should
know! History has already begun to take a new turn, and
'the tide' to change, since then.

Open collision is inevitable. For God's children the Christian life is not generally lived out of sight or underground, for 'quite openly' is the other adverb with which the book of Acts concludes. 'Christianity is not a religion of recluses and mountain retreats; it is social and bound up with the community; therefore it must be a challenge to Communism.'[18] The evidences are now widespread that the Spirit of truth is still at work where once Wang Ming-dao, Watchman Nee and so many other faithful men and women witnessed to the saving work of the Lord Jesus. Their testimony is even now bringing conviction to a world whose unseen ruler is already judged.

Appendix A
Christianity in China

What conceivable place – if any at all – had Jesus Christ here in this Celestial Empire, so long ruled with High Heaven's mandate (save for rare interludes) by a sequence of great imperial dynasties? Does there exist in Christianity any discernible Asian link or divine trend eastward?

Jesus had commanded his disciples to go into all the world and make disciples of all the nations. To this end, the Holy Spirit was given on the Day of Pentecost to indwell the believers and give them power to be his witnesses.

The coming of the Holy Spirit had been on a very public occasion, because Jerusalem was crowded with visitors. Those moved by Peter's immediate appeal included pilgrims (whether Jews or converts to Judaism) drawn there to the Jewish festival of Pentecost from as far off as Greece and Italy in the west, but also from Iraq and Iran in the east. What impressions did these carry back home? Even for mere spectators among the listening crowds, something of it must have remained alive in their memories. Yet oddly, after that the book of Acts in the Bible tells us mainly of the westward movement of the good news. Simon Peter, the disciple who once denied Jesus, but then bitterly repented and was restored, set out early, as did missionary colleagues such as Paul, Silas and Timothy, and planted groups of believers in cities along the roads laid by imperial Rome. Paul even hoped to reach furthest Spain.

We are thus easily misled into thinking of Christianity as somehow European in its roots and outlook, with little or no connection with east Asia and Han China.[1] However, to counter this impression the Bible also has one episode of an African pilgrim returning from Jerusalem to Ethiopia and being converted to Jesus and baptised while on his way there.[2] In fact, by the second century there are whispers of a far wider ranging of the good news.[3] Coins of all the Roman Emperors from Augustus to Nero covering the New Testament story have been found in extreme southern India, confirming the existence of sea trade with Egypt. The south Indian state of Kerala is home also of an extremely early Asian tradition not recorded in the Bible. This tradition says that Thomas Didymus, the disciple who, until he met Jesus afresh in person, publicly questioned the fact that he was risen from the dead,[4] later travelled by sea to Cranganore in Kerala. He was a witness to this very same good news of the risen Jesus. Before his own murder by spearpoint in Chennai (Madras), he led many leading Indians to trust and love him. Their heirs, who still serve him widely across Asia, remain convinced of the truth of this tradition. And an old Malabar liturgy of theirs reads, 'Through St Thomas the kingdom of heaven took wings and sped its flight to the Chinese' – suggesting that the message of Jesus found a reception, if no more, at least among Chinese traders and the crews of their visiting ocean junks.

Yet the Bible itself lacks any detailed record of such eastward moves on the part of the Twelve or of others close to them. (Luke, the author of its book of Acts, joined the apostle Paul moving from Antioch not eastward but west to Rome.) However, later sources tell us that, quite early, unnamed traders from the same Syrian Antioch took the good news eastward into Iraq (where so long ago men of Babylon conspired to defy God, provoking him in response to move Abraham to trust in him). The outcome of these men's witnessing reassures us, for here also, as in the West, their word was warmly received. By the second century, with Ctesiphon (now Baghdad) as one of several larger centres, many local groups of believers in Jesus sprang into being. God was quietly moving, and in the third and fourth centuries his churches began to appear further on round the Gulf into Iran. The outlook was indeed promising. Eventually, however, the conversion of the Roman Emperor Constantine I, with his new capital at Constantinople from AD 330, made Christianity an official state religion of the whole area, with all of such a system's weaknesses.

In Italy, Egypt and west Asia scholar bishops had early designed *creeds* or doctrinal summaries of the Christian faith, starting originally from the baptismal confession supplied by the risen Jesus himself in Galilee.[5] Slowly, as the Greek Scriptures were collected, they derived from them a consensus on major doctrines; but doing so they watched one another, suspicious that heresies might arise among some of the remoter outgoing missions and their leaders.[6] However, it is their rather stormy records that open for us a window onto what is real living history.

Early in the fifth century one Nestorius of Antioch, a true man of God with a strong Christian following in his native Syria, was taken from them and made briefly (428–31) Rome's patriarch of Constantinople (now Istanbul). While he was there ill-wishers charged him with too eagerly stressing the dual nature of Jesus: that is to say, his real deity and no less real humanity equally present in the same Person. Nestorius could well have challenged his opponents by reading aloud to them from the New Testament Letter to the Hebrews, 'We have Jesus the Son of God who has gone into heaven. Being also human he is able to sympathise with our weaknesses, having been tempted in every way just as we are, yet without sin. So we may receive mercy and find grace to help us in our time of need.'[7] This is a priceless reality that in some Christian quarters was being lost sight of. Unhappily, however, envy and personal rivalries among his critics displaced clear thinking and aroused strong enmities, and in 431 this led to scandalous scenes at the church's General Council of Ephesus. Without anyone clearly stating a supposedly 'correct doctrine', the Council declared Nestorius to be a new Judas, a traitor and heretic promoting falsehood. They deposed him from office, excluded him and his fellow Syrians from the Empire and condemned him to spend his remaining years in exile.

This was cruelly unjustified, for he was but mending a flaw in current Christian thought. Twenty years later, in 451 at the Council of Chalcedon, the clear-thinking Roman Pope Leo II restated Nestorius' true doctrine in a fresh form of words, and affirmed it as the church's orthodox view.[8] There had been no real cause to condemn him. Exiled to Petra in Arabia, he endured prolonged tortures and a savage martyrdom (in 440) in upper Egypt.[9] But under God's hand this sorry episode enhanced among his Syrian colleagues their love for peoples yet further east and their fresh initiatives to reach them. Denied fellowship in the Empire's Roman Church, they now went on their way and in due course spread the gospel east across Iran, both down into

India and north along the Uzbek and Kazak trade routes, there to meet the laden camels of China's merchants with silk and fine metalwork. By around 510, when in the far west Christianity was at last spreading into pagan England, Nestorian missionaries were already resident in China's capital, Xian, proclaiming likewise their good news of Jesus who brought to man the love and forgiveness of a just but merciful God.

Here in China, Nestorian (Da Qin) records are sparse, but there are enough. It is in the Tang Dynasty of able and vigorous rulers (618–907) that we hear further news of them. In 635 a Nestorian from Syria named Alopen arrived in the capital of the great Tai-zong Emperor and was well received. An imperial edict of three years later gives the Christian faith high commendation: 'We find this religion excellent and separate from the world . . . beneficial to the human race and worthy of being spread all over the Celestial Empire.'[10]

Alopen's own coming is recorded 150 years later on the great Xian Monumental Stone, a 9-foot inscribed slab of black marble set up a century and more later in 781 some 30 miles from the Huang-he River. It may have fallen, or been buried by Christians, 60 years on when the dynasty turned hostile, only to be unearthed in 1623 by men digging foundations. This furthest east monument of early Christianity stands preserved today in Xian's 'Forest of Tablets'. Beneath a cross on its face are engraved 17,000 Chinese characters, with more also in Syriac, summarising Christian doctrine. It is strangely weak, however, on the one central item: the death and resurrection of Jesus. Were they by now treating that focal fact as a 'mystery' too sacred for public display, lest its brave statement invite contempt and vandalism? Doing so one fears they would blunt the sharp edge of their witness and perhaps even signal their mission's eventual end.[11]

Elsewhere too in China documentary fragments survive, with Syrian worship songs and passages from the Old Testament in the same Chinese script as that on the monument. We know the Nestorians translated the Bible into Chinese; and more recently in one of the famous cave temples in Dunhuang there came to light a hoard of ancient Christian manuscripts, including a list of 350 books used by them in Tang China. Among the hoard were portions of a four-Gospel outline of Jesus' life and ministry, and the immensely popular Psalms of King David.[12] Now, amazingly, news has recently come of the discovery near Xian itself of Christian relics and other tangible evidences of a thriving Christian community within a large monastic compound of around the time of Alopen. This very important site at Louguanrai is currently being excavated and may yield much new information.

So in trading cities across Asia from Baghdad to Beijing, Nestorian churches had displayed a living and active faith in Jesus Christ, along with a true concern for the poor. They had survived both Zoroastrian animosity in Iran and the dynamic eastward pressure of Islam after the death of Mohammed in 632. (Since then, however, Arab forces had raced westward across North Africa into Spain, and eastward, and had now reached the northern Turkic races as far as Xinjiang.) But in the end Mahayana Buddhism, at the peak of prosperity with its rich shrines and ceremonies, now rivalled Christianity as a competing world faith and edged it aside into private backwaters. Then, in 841 the Tang dynasty turned fiercely hostile. The Wu Zong Emperor issued an edict dispersing monastic groups of all non-Taoist faiths and sending their priests off into secular employment.

From data on the Xian Stone it seems that some 70 monasteries and 3,000 church buildings may have been destroyed.

From Han China itself Nestorian Christianity now largely fades from view as an active witnessing force across east Asia. For somewhat longer it would find a north-western home among the Uygur Tartars, to win imperial favour again when those Mongols themselves ruled China. But slowly the Da Qin flame would die. Theirs had been eight centuries of heroic Christian witness. Just a few of them survive today in the Kurdish mountains. It remains for us now to describe concisely the near-empty 1,000 years from 840 to 1840 that follow, until the Protestant period with its fresh arrivals from northern Europe.

We begin with four centuries of absence. The Tang period ran on to its end and lesser rulers followed, until in 1271 the Mongols burst in from the north with their Yuan dynasty. Meanwhile, the Christian West had alas reverted to means quite alien to the spirit of Jesus and his kingdom 'not of this world'.[13] Already Emperor Charles I of France (747–814) had taken the sword to force pagan north Europeans to convert – or face slavery or death. Soon, with its 'Crusades' (1096–1204), Christian Europe would bring arms in the cause of religion back to the east Mediterranean in an attempt to reclaim from Islam ancient Israel's Holy Land. Mounted crusader knights and their pagan mercenaries 'committed murder and rapine while bearing the cross before them, the cross which is the one thing that should have dissuaded people from war'.[14] And this was to prove a spiritual disaster. The crusaders were forced to flee, only to leave behind a lasting legacy of hatred. It would not be long before from the east the Mongol 'Golden Horde' of China's Genghis Khan would display real cavalry warfare when their mounted bowmen overran and despoiled Eurasia as far west as Poland and Hungary.

Meanwhile, Rome's papacy was preoccupied with establishing its status as supreme head of all Western Christendom, leaving little space for Nestorian feelings of pity for a world lost without Christ. As head of the Catholic (that is, 'all-inclusive') Roman Church, the Pope sent to successive heirs of Genghis in Khanbalik (Beijing) three formal embassies, two by the silk road and a third by ocean junk from the Persian Gulf to Guangzhou. Each embasssy in turn invited him to come to Rome and do him obeisance. 'Not so!' came the Khan's quite reasonable reply. 'It is you who shall come and *ketou* to me!'

There were exceptions. In 1294 a Franciscan friar, John of Monte Corvino, reached Beijing by sea. For the then dominant Tartar race he translated into their tongue the New Testament and Psalms, and in 30 years he baptised some 6,000 persons in the coastal cities. A passing traveller, Friar Odoric, later met some of these in Fujian Province. Thereafter, for a century and a half from 1360 links between China and Europe were totally severed by Muslim domination of the Indian Ocean. Islam's successes had cut the civilised world in two, causing Europe and Asia to develop at different speeds, so enhancing the variance between them.

In 1368 a new Han power drove out the Mongol rulers from the capital, and along with them all stray Westerners. The great Ming dynasty (1368–1644) was in place and it was their high-quality art products that fast won Western interest. Once Portugal had found the seaway round Africa and the tea and spice trades opened, Ming treasures, and later made-to-order articles of chinoiserie, would help fill the Western holds, both of ships making port back in Europe and of the hapless wrecks still lying on the sea bed.

But at last the Roman Church was preparing itself for action. Its Society of Jesus (the Jesuits) was created in 1534. One founder of this was a Basque priest from Spain, Francis Xavier, who, moved by divine compassion, went to coastal south India and, like Jesus in Galilee, toiled for long years with simple fishermen, creating among them many Tamil church groups that still thrive today. Moving east first to Japan, then to China, he waited long for permission to land in Guangzhou. At length, still offshore, he became fatally ill and was laid on an empty island's solid ground to breathe his last. His body, lovingly shipped back to India, still lies there in Goa.

These Jesuits, a scholarly class of priest-scientists, quietly gained landings at some coastal towns and there acquired enough of Chinese speech and manners to win them favour with local mandarins and eventually in Beijing to impress the Ming Emperor himself. Specialising in science, technology and the classics, they made themselves needed and a series of them came for a while to hold high office in the land, with freedom to practise their Christian faith but not to preach it. Such a one was Matteo Ricci, there from 1583 to 1601. When through their witness some even of the imperial family turned to Christ, wider preaching began and in each province there were some ready to respond. The situation was precarious, for any day the Emperor might revise his views, but by 1701 it is said there were very many foreign missionaries in China with some thousands of converts. One wonders how well taught these latter were, for the Jesuit Society made it easy for Chinese to convert while retaining their old gods. Veneration of home shrines they excused as non-religious acts that need not be abandoned. A convert might bow to the kitchen god so long as he or she focused on, perhaps, a tiny token cross hidden somewhere among the flowers garlanding it.[15]

Such concessions began to raise alarm among non-Jesuit Roman Catholics and led to bitter debates between them which soon spread to Rome itself. From there ill-informed instructions came slowly back as, between sincere but differing Catholics in China, the dispute raged on. At length the state grew tired of so factious an alien religion and determined to be rid of it. Guangdong's viceroy ordered all Chinese Christians to renounce their faith, and petitioned the throne to exterminate Christianity empire-wide. An Edict of Expulsion exiled its foreign priests and closed its church buildings and schools, scattering their members and causing much suffering – and many Chinese acts of bravery. In Fuzhou alone three Western priests were strangled and many Christians murdered. By 1726 a single priest remained in the land to care for survivors of 300 congregations. Roman Catholicism went underground, only to recover once more alongside the forthcoming Protestant arrivals. It is this further century, 1726–1842, of absence from China of any Christian mission whatever that saw the new awakenings in Britain and north Europe, from which sprang so much of good that follows in this story. So here we must once more briefly turn west.

For long the Roman Church had ruled the religious life of all Europe. However, many were now becoming disenchanted with the total domination of their faith and even of their domestic affairs by its wealthy and corrupt priestly class, themselves unmarried and thus ill-qualified to grasp and deal with human needs. On payment of massive fees these men decided everything, secular or religious, for their flock and for the smallest of faults exacted heavy fines.

Even access to heaven itself, they hinted, could be bought with money. All services of worship were conducted in Latin, a dead language understood only by scholars. Their own Latin Bible (made as long ago as 405) was locked away and virtually unknown, even to themselves. Read by the laity, they held, it would be injurious; so they backed their rulings by the church's unwritten traditions.

Thus in Britain and north Europe there grew up secretly among scholars a mood of protest (hence 'Protestant') and a desire to return to the Bible itself, first in its original languages and then, they hoped, in their own spoken ones. As early as 1384 one John Wycliffe in England had made a little-known draft translation from Latin to English. But in 1516 the Dutch scholar Erasmus, working from early manuscript sources, published his first edition of the New Testament in its original Greek. Foreseeing where this could lead, he later wrote of Jesus:

> What audience did Christ have? Was it not a mixed crowd who included the blind, lame, beggars, tax-collectors, centurions, workers, women and children? In truth the labourer will read His writings; the artisan, too, the thief, the prostitute and the pimp will read them, and even the Turk [that is, the Muslim]. Christ desires His wisdom to be known as widely as possible. He died for all and He wants to be known by all. This goal will be achieved if his books are translated into every language of every land.[16]

Here at last was the explosion needed to awaken and recall to its origins the West's faith in Jesus.

In Germany the monk Martin Luther (1483–1546) astonished Rome by publishing in 1517 his view that the believer's lifestyle must itself be a prolonged act of repentance towards God. Cash payments to the Roman Church were no substitute for this. Years later in life he explained how this came to him.

I burned with a desire to understand a term used in the first chapter of Paul's letter to the Romans where it is said, 'The justice of God is revealed in the gospel,' for by it until then my dreams were troubled. I hated this word 'the justice of God' . . . which impels Him to punish sinners and those who are guilty. I felt I was a sinner before God and my conscience was extremely disturbed . . . Moreover I did not love this just and vengeful God. I hated Him.

Finally God took pity on me. While I was meditating day and night, examining the implication of those words 'The righteousness of God is revealed in the gospel, as it is written: the righteous one shall live by faith', I began to understand that 'the righteousness of God' here means the righteousness which God gives and by which, having faith in Him, the righteous one lives . . . I felt myself reborn. I seemed to have entered the broad gates of Paradise itself.[17]

Luther had discovered the mercy of God who pardons the sinner, not because of good works or sufficient payment of church fees, but by his grace alone. Luther's proclaiming of justification by faith as God's free gift, his use of German rather than Latin in public worship and his concept of a priesthood of all believers[18] were each reviled as heresies. He was driven into exile, there in hiding to complete and publish in 1522 his German New Testament.

Three years later, also working for safety's sake in Germany, England's William Tyndale (1484–1536) published his classic New Testament in English (1526), 'so that any boy driving the plough might know more of the Scriptures than the average priest'. In England the book was of course banned, and seaports were watched to secure and burn any copies smuggled in. As fit punishment for his insolence the English king had him pursued to Belgium and there publicly strangled and cremated. In parallel with Germany, a move by men of God for a spiritual Reformation had grown up in England; but sadly it was a royal matrimonial affair that provoked conflict between the English and the Pope. King Henry VIII wished to divorce his Spanish wife Catharine who, when he wanted a boy, only conceived girls. The Pope refused to annul the marriage, so Henry broke with Rome and married Anne, who gave him a boy; and then, as secular King, he declared himself also titular Head of the English Church. In his children's succeeding reigns strife between its opposing bishops led to multiple 'burnings of heretics'. Its theology came close to Calvin's, but retained Catholic features such as bishops and saints' days, and its ultimate power remained with the state. It was a sorry compromise. Alongside the Anglican Church others, whether Roman Catholics, Protestant dissidents or anciently Baptists, were for long to have a difficult existence socially in England.

Of the above reformers, Luther's followers became the German and Scandinavian Lutheran churches from among whom many have given so much to China. Another thinker, John Calvin of Geneva (1509–64), having in France converted from Roman Catholic to Reformed ideas, set out to provide the French with a sound system of biblical doctrine and in 1536 published his *Institutes of the Christian Religion*, going eventually to four volumes. His church in Geneva he restructured on a Presbyterian model that spread into Scotland, the Netherlands and Hungary. The Church of England, or Anglican Church, kept its bishops, whereas its dissidents, who despaired of and rejected them, became Congregational churches.

Access to the Scriptures as the Word of God opened a new door for more radical Christian thinkers to study and apply them to personal and church life. These would include H. Zwingli (1484–1531) of Zurich and south

Germany. He dismissed the Roman Church's 'altar' with its resacrifice of elements, bread and wine, transmuted by an ordained priest to become the literal body and blood of Christ (though still resembling mere wine and bread). He replaced it with a simple memorial service at the Lord's Table, with the literal elements unchanged, but symbolising the real presence of the risen Jesus by his Holy Spirit in those partaking. Another such leader was the Dutch Anabaptist Menno Simons (1492–1559), who abandoned the Roman tradition that all infants should be baptised and by that means 'born again'.[19] Baptism they held to be a conscious adult response of self-dedication by grown persons who have had a saving encounter with Jesus. Countless were drawn to this view and this obedience, and Anabaptist and Mennonite church groups came into being, marked by a Christ-centred lifestyle, and (whether by Catholics or by other Protestants) many of them were martyred. Their genuineness is reflected by one such martyr who, on the way to his own execution, escaped across some ice, then saw his heavily armed guards fall through it, so went back and saved their lives, thereby allowing them to fulfil their task.

It would take some years and yet another challenge from God to awaken all the above new Protestant church groups to his call, 'Go and make disciples of all nations.'[20] That, when it eventually came, would bring together three such foreign mission groups in Fuzhou itself – where our story began with the Ni family.

Appendix B
Pinyin Pronunciation

Vowels	Pronunciation
a	As in mama, papa
a (when placed between i and n)	As in cash
e	As in learn
e (when preceded by i or u but not y)	As in wet
i	As in sit
i (when preceded by zh, ch, sh or r)	Pronounced like a vocalised r
i (when preceded by z, c or s)	Pronounced like a buzzing z
o	As in grow
o (when followed by ng)	As in drop
u	Like the oo in book
ai	Like the ie in lie
ao	Like the ow in how
ei	Like the ay in way
ia	As the combination of i and a
ie	As the combination of i and e

Vowels	Pronunciation
iu	As the combination of i and u
ou	Like the ow in low
ua	As the combination of u and a
ui	Pronounced like way
un	As the combination of u and n
uo	As the combination of u and o
iao	Like the eow in meow
uai	As the combination of u and a and i

Consonants	Pronunciation
b	Like p (voiceless) in help
p	Strongly aspirated as in pink
m	As in more
f	As in food
d	Like t (voiceless) in nitwit
t	Strongly aspirated as in top
n	As in nimble
l	As in loud
g	Like k (voiceless) in skill
k	Strongly aspirated as in kid
ng	As in song
h	As in hot
j	Like ch (voiceless) in mischief
q	Like ch (strongly aspirated) as in cheat

Consonants	Pronunciation
x	A sound between the s in see and the sh in she
zh	Like the dg (voiceless) in badge
ch	As in children
sh	As in show
r	As in raw
z	Like the ts in plants (without aspiration)
c	Like the ts in beats, strongly aspirated
s	As in saw
y	As in you
w	As in we

Appendix C
Names of Places

Pinyin	Wade-Giles
Anhui	Anhwei
Baotou	Paotou
Beijing	Peking
Changde	Changteh
Changsha	Changsha
Chengdu	Chengtu
Chongqing	Chungking
Dadu	Tatu
Fenghua	Fenghwa
Fujian	Fukien
Fuqing	Fu-Tsing
Fuzhou	Foochow
Gansu	Kansu
Gaoting	Kutsing
Guangdong	Kwangtung
Guiyang	Kweiyang
Guizhou	Kweichow
Gulangyu	Kulangsu
Guling (in Fujian)	Kuling
Guling (in Jiangxi)	Kuliang
Gushan	Kushan

Pinyin	Wade-Giles
Gutian	Kutien
Hangzhou	Hangchow
Hankou	Hankow
Henan	Honan
Hongkou	Hongkew
Huangpu	Whangpoo
Hubei	Hupei
Hunan	Hunan
Jiangbei	Kiangpei
Jiangsu	Kiangsu
Jiangxi	Kiangsi
Jian-ou	Chien-O
Jinan	Tsinan
Jin-jiang	Tsin Kiang
Jiujiang	Kiukiang
Kunming	Kunming
Lian-Jiang	Lieng Chiang, Lieng Chieng
Luding	Luting
Luo-xing	Lo-hsing
Luo-xing Ta	Lohsingta
Lushan	Lushan
Manzhouli	Manchuria
Ma-shan	Ma-hsien
Mawei	Ma Wei
Ma-zhuang	Ma-chuang
Mei-hua	Mei-hwa
Nanjing	Nanking
Nanping	Yen-ping
Nantai	Nantai
Pudong	Pootung
Qilu	Cheloo

Pinyin	Wade-Giles
Qingdao	Tsingtao
Qishan	Chien Shan
Sangzhi	Sangchih
Shandong	Shantung
Shantou	Swatow
Shanxi	Shansi, Shensi
Shuikou	Shui-kow
Sui-yuan	Sui-yuan
Suzhou	Soochow, Suchow
Taian	Taian
Tai-shan	Tai-Shan
Tianjin	Tientsin
Wenling	Wenling
Wuchang	Wuchang
Wuhan	Wuhan
Wuxi	Wusih
Wuyi Shan	Wu Yi Shan
Xian	Sian
Xinghua	Hinghwa
Xingjiang	Sinkiang
Yamen	Yamen
Yanan	Yenan
Yantai	Chefoo
Yuanling	Yuanling
Yueyang	Yochow
Yunnan	Yunnan
Zhabei	Chapei
Zhejiang	Chekiang
Zhong-zhou	Chung-Chou
Zhoushan	Chuhsien

Appendix D

Chronological Record of Events

Date	Comment
4 Nov. 1903	Watchman Nee born in Shantou.
29 Feb. 1920	Saved in Fuzhou as a result of Dora Yu's ministry.
28 Mar. 1921	Baptised with brother George and his mother Lin He-ping.
1922	Attended Dora Yu's Bible College in Shanghai for a time. Also gave testimony in Christian and Missionary Alliance Auditorium at North Szechuan Road.
Jan. 1923	First issue of *Revival* magazine, 1,400 copies.
Jan. 1923	Ruth Lee came to Fuzhou and held gospel meetings.
Feb. 1923	Rented meeting place in Fuzhou to continue revival meetings.
1924	Graduated from St Mark's College.
1924	Excommunicated from the Fuzhou meeting, moved to Mawei.
1924	Visited Hangzhou, and went on to Nanjing.

Date	Comment
1924	In Nanjing, worked on *Spiritual Light* publication.
Nov. 1924	Visited Sitiawan in Malaysia, and other places in South-East Asia, for about six months.
May 1925	Returned to China from South-East Asia, via Shanghai, where held meetings, and then rented accommodation in Pagoda.
1925	In Zhangzhou, south Fujian, held revival meetings with denominational meetings.
Jan. 1926	Gospel preaching at Mei-hua.
Mar. 1926	Visited Xiamen (Amoy), Gulangyu, Zhangzhou and Tongan, south Fujian, for approximately two months.
Summer 1926	Revival meetings in Anhui.
2nd half 1926	Visited Xiamen (Amoy), Tongan and neighbouring places, south Fujian, established meetings.
Late autumn 1926	In Nanjing. Worked with Ruth Lee translating Schofield's Bible Correspondence Course. Preached in Nanjing University.
Early 1927	In Wuxi, Jiangsu Province, completed the first volume of *The Spiritual Man*, before moving to Shanghai.
Mar. 1927	Visited Shanghai, meetings at Peace Wang's home and later in Keng Ching Lane.

Date	Comment
1927	Moved to Shanghai and also moved Gospel Book Room from Pagoda to Shanghai at the same time.
Jan. 1928	Rented Wen De Li in Shanghai.
Feb. 1928	First Overcomer Conference, in Shanghai.
May 1930	Margaret Barber passed away.
Dec. 1930	Charles Barlow in Shanghai for ten days.
Jan. 1931	Visited Shantou and Chieh-yang, Guangdong Province, and returned to Shanghai at the end of the same month.
1931	Visited Beijing.
Oct. 1931	Second Overcomer Conference, in Shanghai.
End Mar. 1932	Visited Jinan, capital of Shandong Province. Spoke to Qilu University students at a mountain retreat in Tai-shan. Followed with eleven days of meetings at Qilu University.
Jun. 1932	Spoke to denominational believers in the Chinese Independent Church in Yantai for a week, resulting in an assembly being raised up in Yantai.
Jul. 1932	Spoke to Southern Baptist Seminary at Huangxian, a city close to Yantai.
Nov. 1932	Special conference in Shanghai with the Exclusive Brethren contingent.
4 Dec. 1932	Watchman gave a testimony of the work.
1933	Informal training of co-workers in upstairs rooms at Wen De Li in Shanghai.

Date	Comment
Apr. 1933	Visited Jinan in Shandong Province, and from there continued to Yantai.
Jun. 1933	Went via France to London. Visited Brethren assemblies, and went to Honor Oak Road meeting. Went on to Vancouver and New York City and returned to China in August 1933.
Winter 1933	Visited Jinan again.
Jan. 1934	Third Overcomer Conference, in Shanghai.
Spring 1934	Watchman and Shepherd Ma travelled by car through the provinces Zhejiang, Jiangxi, Hunan, Guangxi, Guizhou and Yunnan.
Oct. 1934	Fourth Overcomer Conference, in Hangzhou, Zhejiang Province.
19 Oct. 1934	Married Charity (Zhang Pin-hui) in Hangzhou, Zhejiang Province.
Aug. 1935	Went from Shanghai to Yantai to hold a special conference there on the outpouring of the Spirit.
Sept. 1935	Returned to Shanghai from Yantai and held special conference on the outpouring of the Spirit.
Oct. 1935	Visited Gulangyu in south Fujian to hold a special conference with co-workers, on the same subject as in Yantai.
1936	Began to build a training facility in Zhengru in the suburbs of Shanghai, but just before the building work was

Date	Comment
	completed everything was destroyed when the Sino-Japanese war broke out.
Jan. 1936	Visited Beijing, and went from there to gospel meetings in Tianjin.
May 1936	Spoke in Kaifeng, Henan, and from there returned to Shanghai.
Jan. 1937	Urgent conference for all co-workers from throughout the country, concerning his new vision of the work and the local churches.
Jul. 1937	Held meetings in Manila, Philippines. Held a mountain retreat in Baguio.
Sept. 1937	Travelled from Manila to Singapore, and then on to Sitiawan and Penang in Malaysia.
Nov. 1937	Conference in Hankou for co-workers, on 'Rethinking the Work'. A recrystallisation of the Shanghai conference in January 1937.
Feb. 1938	Went from Shanghai to Hong Kong, Singapore and Penang and held meetings in each of these places.
1938	Travelled through India and arrived in London in July to meet T. Austin-Sparks.
Jul. 1938	Keswick Convention in England.
Oct. 1938	Denmark, then to Norway, Germany and Switzerland. Two months in Paris producing English version of *Rethinking the Work*. Returned to London in January 1939. The book was published

Date	Comment
	in London in May 1939 with the title *Concerning Our Missions.*
May 1939	Left England, returning to China via India and Singapore, arriving back in Shanghai in July 1939.
Aug. 1939	Special conference for eleven days, on the 'Principles of the Body'.
1940	Rented a place in Yu-hua village in the suburbs of Shanghai and conducted training for co-workers. It mostly focused on the Body of Christ. Altogether about 70 or 80 people attended, and the training continued for about two years.
Dec. 1941	Visited Hong Kong following his father's passing on 18 December 1941.
Late 1942	Watchman Nee barred from preaching by the elders at Wen De Li in Shanghai.
1945	At Chongqing, gave messages on Revelation 2 and 3.
Apr. and May 1948	Special conference in Shanghai for local saints and for approx. 80 thirsty souls from throughout the country. This was his first conference on returning to the ministry, and was based on the text, 'Render to Caesar the things that are Caesar's and to God the things that are God's.' At this time he gave the China Biological and Chemical Company to the church.

Date	Comment
1948	First training of workers in Guling Mountain (near Fuzhou) for four months.
1 Oct. 1949	People's Republic of China proclaimed in Beijing.
1949	Second training of workers in Guling Mountain, then in Fuzhou, started in spring, concluded in August.
Late 1949 and early 1950	To Taiwan and then on to Hong Kong where he conducted a series of special meetings, returning to Shanghai in early 1950.
Spring 1950	Went from Shanghai to Hong Kong for a period of two and a half months.
Jun. 1950	Returned to Shanghai.
10 Apr. 1952	Arrested in Manzhouli (Manchuria).
29 Jan. 1956	Tried in Shanghai.
7 Nov. 1971	Charity passed away in Shanghai.
30 May 1972	Watchman Nee passed away in Anhui Province.

APPENDIX E
For Further Reading

*T*he *Normal Christian Life* (incorporating *Sit, Walk, Stand*) is published by Kingsway Publications and is available from any good bookshop or visit our website at www.kingsway.co.uk

For further information and a full list of books by Watchman Nee, please write to:

Christian Fellowship Publishers
11515 Allecingie Parkway
Richmond, VA 23235
United States of America
Email: info@c-f-p.com
Phone: (804) 794–5333
Website: www.c-f-p.com

Notes

Chapter 1

1. 1 Samuel 1:11.

2. 1 Samuel 3; Isaiah 21:6, 11–12; 62:6.

Chapter 2

Background reading: Christopher Hibbert, *The Dragon Wakes: China and the West 1793–1911*, London, 1970; F. Schurmann and O. Schell, eds, *China Readings 1, Imperial China*, London, 1967; J. Doolittle, *Social Life of the Chinese*, London, 1868, written in Fuzhou and an invaluable source of the local background; Eugene Stock, *The Story of the Fuh-Kien Mission of the Church Missionary Society*, London, 1882; and the 4th edition, revised T. McClelland, 1904; D. MacGillivray, *A Century of Foreign Missions in Foochow*, Shanghai, 1907.

1. David Bird, Cmdr RN rtd, in *Country Life*, London, February 1985. The three-masted sailing ship *Cutty Sark* still exists on display to visitors beside London's River Thames at Greenwich.

2. Quoted by E.R. Hughes, *The Invasion of China by the Western World*, London, 1937, p. 65.

3. 'The four pupils were all baptised in 1857,' writes Charles Hartwell. 'They subsequently all became helpers in the work. Pastor Nga, our first ordained native pastor, was one of them. He died in 1890.' Charles Hartwell, *Reminiscences*, Fuzhou, 1904, p. 27. See also D. MacGillivray, *op. cit.*, p. 255. It is probable too that Nga was one of the three young men whose sermons preached one evening in September 1860 are paraphrased in J. Doolittle, *op. cit.*, pp. 599f.

4. Psalm 27:10.

5. Mother Nee's vivid account of her own story is in Ni Lin He-ping, *En Ai Biao Ben* ('An Object of Grace and Love'), Shanghai, 1943, which provides some of the family's history during this period. I owe its translation to the late Hilda Holms.

6. 1 Samuel 1:27–28; and see Ezekiel 3:17.

Chapter 3

Background reading: F. Schurmann and O. Shell, eds, *China Readings 2, Republican China*, London, 1967; E.R. Hughes, *The Invasion of China by the Western World*, London, 1937.

1. Stephen C.T. Chan, *My Uncle, Ni Tuo-sheng*, Eng. trans. by L.T. Lyall (TS), 1968. This son of Watchman's eldest sister Gui-chen (Mrs H.C. Chen) supplies useful details of the following years from his own memories, and from Watchman's 26 'open letters' in the early Shanghai devotional magazine *Revival*.

2. Bernard Martin, *Strange Vigour*, London, 1944, p. 226.

3. See Stephen Chen and Robert Payne, *Sun Yat-sen, A Portrait*, New York, 1946, p. 130. A good short account of China's pioneer reformer is C.R. Hensman, *Sun Yat-sen*, SCM Press, London, 1971.

4. S. Packenham-Walsh, the founder of Trinity College, records its beginnings in *Twenty Years in China*, Cambridge, 1935. Watchman's English teacher at Trinity was Betty M. Williams, wife of the College Principal, David Williams. I am indebted to her for some account of this period.

5. Wing-tsit Chan, *Religious Trends in Modern China*, New York, 1953, pp. 228f.

6. See Chow Tse-tsung, *The May Fourth Movement: Intellectual Revolution in Modern China*, Cambridge, Mass., 1960, pp. 92ff.

Chapter 4

1. Genesis 3:3.

2. Luke 5:11.

3. H.A. Franck, *Roving Through South China*, London, 1925, p. 181.

4. Watchman Nee himself gave a personal account of his conversion and new birth, together with some of its sequels, in talks to an October 1936 conference of fellow workers at Gulangyu (Kulangsu), an island off

the south-eastern coast of Fujian Province. A few extended quotes from these illuminate our narrative. Translations from these appear in Wei Guang-xi (K.H. Weigh), ed., *Watchman Nee's Testimony*, Church Book Room, Kowloon, 1974; Stephen Kaung, 'A Sketch of the Author's Life', in Watchman Nee, *The Finest of the Wheat*, vol. 1, Christian Fellowship Publishers, New York, 1992, pp. 1–33.

    5. Romans 6:13.

    6. Stuart Schram, *Mao Tse-tung*, London, 1966, pp. 56f.

Chapter 5

    1. CMS Report for the year.

    2. Genesis 18:16ff.

    3. Psalm 91:7.

    4. Mark 1:11.

    5. Romans 6:3; 1 Peter 3:21f. See W. Nee, *The Normal Christian Life*, pp. 61ff; *Love Not the World*, pp. 26ff.

Chapter 6

    1. 1 Corinthians 11:23–26.

    2. Is it mere coincidence that in this year 1922 the Chinese Communist Party was created in Shanghai?

    3. Christiana Tsai, *Queen of the Dark Chamber*, Chicago, 1953, ch. 9.

    4. See 'Two Principles of Conduct', in W. Nee, *Twelve Baskets Full*, vol. 2, Hong Kong, 1966, pp. 36ff.

    5. Matthew 17:24–27.

    6. Jessie Penn-Lewis, *The Cross of Calvary and its Message*, Bournemouth, 1903, and *The Logos of the Cross*, 1920 (reprinted as *The Centrality of the Cross*).

Chapter 7

    1. John 15:5. Compare Roland Allen's observation that groups that have learned the gospel from relatively ignorant and untrained Chinese are often found to have learned it both truly and deeply and to be anxious for more. *The Spontaneous Expansion of the Church*, London, 1927, p. 62.

    2. See W. Nee, *Spiritual Knowledge*, New York, 1973, pp. 40ff; *Concerning Our Missions*, London, 1939, pp. 212f.

3. Luke 6:38; 3 John 7. And see his account in W. Nee, *Concerning Our Missions*, 1939, ch. 8.

4. The novelist Pearl Buck echoes this opinion, writing in *My Several Worlds* of 'the beautiful sweet oranges from Fukien, where such oranges grow as I have never seen elsewhere, even in California'.

5. Luke 6:38.

6. John 5:19; 2 Corinthians 12:9.

7. See Joshua 6:12ff, and 1 Samuel 5.

8. Numbers 17.

9. Mark 8:31; John 13:16.

10. It was not yet Watchman's practice by careful editing to compensate for the preacher's licence to overstate.Years later a missionary sympathiser would say of him, 'He was liable to make a telling point by pressing on beyond what was written.'

11. At that time leading thought among Western conservative evangelicals shied away from teaching on the believer's subjective 'fellowship of his sufferings' (Philippians 3:10), seeing it as somehow diminishing the unique substitutionary death of Christ for sinners. Hollington Tong, *Christianity in Taiwan*, 1961, pp. 116f, simplifies the difference to one of moderation or extremism in the matter of a breach with the mission churches, but he is possibly reading back the later history into the situation.

Chapter 8

1. There are six more stanzas. This would become No. 128 in his collection *Xiao-qun Shi-ge* ('Hymns for the Little Flock').

2. Luke 4:42–44.

3. Matthew 5:43–45; Romans 5:3–5; James 1:2.

4. See Luke 17:7–10; and then Matthew 5:41. 'If someone forces you to go a mile, go with him two miles.'

5. A portable form of what elsewhere came to be known as the Persian wheel.

6. W. Nee, *Twelve Baskets Full*, vol. 4, Hong Kong, 1966, pp. 42ff.

Chapter 9

1. See W. Nee, *Full of Grace and Truth*, vol. 1, Richmond, VA, 1980, pp.

14–20; *Sit, Walk, Stand*, Bombay, 1957, London, 1962, p. 26. This account now weaves together the two versions.

2. This would be early January, but rarely do the Chinese and the Gregorian calendars' days exactly coincide.

3. 2 Kings 2:14.

4. On the 'Great King' of Animist villagers in Fujian Province, see Doolittle, *op. cit.*, pp. 85, 124, 380–87. On his procession, see p. 382.

Chapter 10

1. David M. Paton, *Christian Missions and the Judgment of God*, London, 1953, pp. 48f.

2. John 13:35.

3. Genesis 19.

4. 1 Peter 5:6.

5. Isaiah 53:4, 5; 1 Peter 2:24.

6. Romans 6:1–14; 1 Corinthians 1:30; Galatians 2:20. See W. Nee, *Changed into His Likeness*, London, 1967, pp. 78–83.

Chapter 11

1. Zechariah 4:10.

2. W. Nee, *The Spiritual Man*, Eng. trans., 3 vols, New York, 1968. The two prefaces are dated Shanghai, 4 June 1927 and 25 June 1928. At pp. 179ff. of vol. 3 the 1968 editors have added also the transcription of a 1948 address by Nee on the subject of sickness.

3. This appears to have been Nee's fixed view during the 1940s, reaffirmed several times to his co-workers. The 1968 publisher may be right in believing that he would by then have changed his mind, but 'doubtless' is too strong an adverb in the circumstances.

4. 1 Corinthians 10:16ff; 11:23ff; Acts 20:7ff.

5. 1 Corinthians 11:5ff; 14:34; 1 Timothy 2:11ff.

6. *Revival* was first published in January 1923, with a total of 1,400 copies being sent out. *The Christian*, with its different emphasis, replaced *Revival* in January 1925, and after 24 issues was itself replaced by *Revival* again in January 1928. *The Christian* was resumed again in June 1934. Some account of the periodicals edited by Watchman Nee, including extracts from his 1928 editorials, is supplied by his eldest sister's son,

NOTES339

Stephen C.T. Chan, in his excellent memoir, *O-tih Chiu Fu Ni To-sheng* ('My Uncle, Watchman Nee'), Hong Kong, 1970. Chan states that 'his open letters in *Revival* magazine for 1928 reveal the agonies of mind through which his long illness put him'.

   7. 2 Corinthians 1:8; 2:4; 4:8; 6:10.

   8. 2 Corinthians 4:7.

   9. Margaret E. Barber, *Verses of a Pilgrim*, Fuzhou, October 1931, published by her colleague Margaret L. Ballord.

Chapter 12

   1. For details see Stephen C.T. Chan, *op. cit.*, ch. 22.

   2. Officially just *Hymns*, or more fully, *A Few Hymns and some Spiritual Songs, selected 1856, for the Little Flock*, revised by J.N. Darby, London, 1881. The subtitle alludes to Jesus' words in Luke 12:32, 'Fear not, little flock, for it is your Father's good pleasure to give to you the kingdom.'

   3. W. Nee, *The Latent Power of the Soul*. See especially pp. 51, 54ff. This book was first published in 1933 as a postscript to *The Spiritual Man* and owed something to Jessie Penn-Lewis' *Soul and Spirit*.

   4. See L.T. Lyall, *John Sung*, London, 1954, p. 88.

   5. They were: from Britain, Mr C.R. Barlow and Mr and Mrs A. Mayo; from San Francisco, Dr Powell; and from Australia, Mr and Mrs Joyce, Mr Phillips and Mr W.J. House.

   6. Miss Ling had married and would become the mother of nine children, all of them brilliant.

   7. They are popularly known along with some smaller groups as 'Exclusive Brethren' (with reference to their tight principles of Christian fellowship), in distinction from the very much larger and more missionary-minded 'Open Brethren'. Both stem from the same beginnings, and the term 'the Brethren' is thus commonly of wider application than in this present chapter.

   8. Quotes from life in W. Nee, *The Orthodoxy of the Church*, pp. 90f., with Revelation 3:17.

   9. For an account of an exorcism see W. Nee, *What Shall This Man Do?*, p. 152.

   10. On 29 August 1933, Taylor wrote from New York to a colleague, 'He thinks *some* of the saints will not be taken to Himself, by the Lord, at

the rapture, that they will go through the "tribulation" . . . What makes his erroneous prophetic views seem more serious is that the person through whom he was converted, a woman, taught him, as he told me yesterday, something on prophecy, according to what is generally accepted by the saints, so that he has given up truth for error.'

11. For an account of the whole episode from the standpoint of the London Group, see 'Events Relating to China', in A.J. Gardiner, *The Recovery and Maintenance of the Truth*, 2nd ed., Kingston upon Thames, 1963, pp. 272ff. This contains relevant letters of James Taylor, but no replies.

12. In fairness it is necessary to add that so exclusive a view of Christian fellowship is not, by and large, typical of the Brethren movement as a whole.

13. This, one of the most satisfying of Watchman Nee's presentations of Christian truth, is dealt with several times in his recorded preaching; see *Sit, Walk, Stand*, p. 30; *The Normal Christian Life*, pp. 127f; *Changed into His Likeness*, pp. 79ff; *Twelve Baskets Full*, vol. 1, pp. 32ff.

Chapter 13
Background reading: Dick Wilson, *The Long March, 1935*, London, 1971.

1. These talks were published as Ni, *The Meeting Life* (in Chinese), Shanghai, 1934.

2. Outline of the following pages from personal interviews with W. Nee and with M. Ma and his son James.

3. W. Nee, *The Song of Songs*, Fort Washington, 1966.

4. See also his account of the early Brethren writings in *The Orthodoxy of the Church*, Los Angeles, 1970, pp. 69ff. Darby, Bellet, Muller, Mackintosh, Kelly, Anderson and Miller are among those he was familiar with, and he constantly used J.N. Darby's *New Translation of the English Bible*.

5. Hollington Tong, *Christianity in Taiwan*, 1961, p. 117.

6. F.P. Jones, *China Bulletin*, vol. 4, 21 February 1955.

7. The story is told in L.T. Lyall, *John Sung*, London, 1954.

8. Elisha Wu, magazine article (source not traced).

Chapter 14
1. Frank Rawlinson, ed., *The China Christian Year Book*, Shanghai, 1935, pp. 104f.

2. The month, too, of the start of Mao's Long March.

3. James 1:2.

4. Isaiah 54:17. (This sounds like Margaret Barber's friend, Miss Groves, who very early helped him pray for his schoolmates.)

5. See W. Nee, *What Shall this Man Do?*, p. 108.

6. A.J. Gardiner, *op.cit.*, p. 287.

7. The Chinese original of this letter was publicly circulated to believers in the issue of Watchman Nee's *Correspondence* magazine dated July 1935.

8. The Western end of this correspondence is preserved in A.J. Gardiner, *The Recovery and Maintenance of the Truth*, 2nd ed., Kingston upon Thames, 1963, pp. 272ff. The above letter from Shanghai (whose English version for mailing was supplied to the brothers by Miss Elizabeth Fischbacher) is preserved in W. Nee, *Back to the Cross*, New York, 1988.

9. Witness Lee, *The Baptism of the Holy Spirit*, Los Angeles, 1969, p. 12.

10. Compare 1 Corinthians 12:30.

Chapter 15

1. As in Fuzhou where, in the one town, the assembly was already split into two competing groups.

2. Charles E. Notson, 'Individualism Gone Astray: II, The "Little Flock" of Watchman Nee', in *The Alliance Weekly*, 15 November 1952, pp. 729f.

3. *Ibid.*, p. 729.

4. Shaanxi province adjoins the western border of Shanxi, Henan and Hubei provinces. The similarity of the province names Shanxi and Shaanxi can be confusing.

5. George A. Young, *The Living Christ in Modern China*, London, 1947, p. 91.

6. Shanghai, 1938. The book has a Chinese and an English preface.

7. *The Keswick Convention 1938*, London, p. 245.

8. 2 Corinthians 4:7ff; Galatians 2:20.

9. Matthew 7:1f; Luke 6:37f.

10. Genesis 23:4; Psalm 39:12; Colossians 3:1–4; Philippians 3:20f.

11. W. Nee, 'The Normal Christian Life', series first published November 1940 – March 1942, in *A Witness and a Testimony* magazine, ed.,

T. Austin-Sparks, London. And see W. Nee, *The Normal Christian Life*, Bombay, 1957, London and Fort Washington, 1961, edited by conflation of several series of addresses on the same and related themes.

12. 1 John 5:4; Revelation 12:11; 21:7.

13. W. Nee, *Concerning Our Missions*, London and Shanghai, 1939. Abridged and reissued as *The Normal Christian Church Life*, Washington DC, 1962, echoing the title of the above book. But in *The Normal Christian Life* 'normal' is Nee's own calculated understatement for 'victorious' and is a challenge to the subnormal, whereas here 'normal' can only mean 'correct' with the implication that every other pattern of church life or mission is therefore abnormal! Furthermore, *Concerning Our Missions* is not even a book about the 'church' but about the 'work'. And of it he says explicitly, *'The title of the book explains its nature*. It is not a treatise on missionary methods but a review of our past work in the light of God's will as we have discovered it in His word' (p. 11, his italics).

14. G.H. Lang, in a privately communicated review of W. Nee's *Concerning Our Missions*, pp. 92, 94. (Jerusalem's population, too, was of course occasionally swelled by pilgrims.) Lang also points out that in Acts 9:31 Nee strengthens his case by following (p. 95) the plural reading 'churches' where the weight of manuscript authorities is for the singular.

15. As a visitor to Europe's vast cities, Nee saw the problem (*ibid.*, pp. 90f.), but his suggested solution of equating London boroughs or postal districts with New Testament 'localities' subjects the churches to sudden change by secular whim. Did he intend this?

16. W. Nee, Shanghai, 11 June 1940.

17. Mark 2:22.

Chapter 16

1. W. Nee, *Changed into His Likeness*, London, 1968. In its treatment of Jacob this compensated for a somewhat quietist note in his recent teaching from Romans on deliverance.

2. W. Nee, *The Glorious Church*, Los Angeles, 1968. Redemption of mankind has brought man back to the creative purpose of God. As in heaven so on earth, his name is to be hallowed, his will done, by the

risen, exalted second Adam working through his Holy Spirit-filled Body, the church. Here prayer as spiritual warfare finds its real place.

3. The CIM Editorial Secretary, Norman Baker, had kindly shown Nee the current edition of the Mission's *Principles and Practice*, and Nee had had to point out that under the heading of 'Church Government' the document gave little or no room for Chinese opinion as to the pattern of worship to be followed in any case.

4. Especially was this now so in Zhejiang Province. As was noted already in the 1935 *China Christian Year Book* (pp. 104f.), 'in this "the field of the Little Flock", the movement's opposition to a paid ministry was commanding respect in the prevailing economic climate, while its emphasis on the return of Christ aroused a response in the hearts of many discouraged by the worsening political conditions.'

5. Ephesians 4:11, 12; 2 Timothy 4:5. See W. Nee, *What Shall This Man Do?*, ch. 3, 'Catching Men'; also his instructions in *The Good Confession*, New York, 1973, pp. 75ff.

6. With an explicit reference to Acts 20:30.

7. T. Ku, pamphlet entitled *Xiao-qun*, Shanghai, 1940. This, with perhaps others like it, might be seized upon twelve years later as sources for a charge of fantasy 'imperialist' links.

8. 2 Timothy 3:12.

9. Luke 6:36–38; Galatians 6:7.

10. Romans 9:10–12, 16 (NRSV). And see Genesis 45:5; 1 Samuel 1:27, 28; Isaiah 49:5; Jeremiah 1:5; Galatians 1:15.

11. 2 Kings 6:8ff.

Chapter 17

1. Luke 9:62; Psalm 126:6. See W. Nee, *What Shall This Man Do?*, pp. 64f.

2. Luke 16:9–13; Exodus 11:2; 12:36.

3. See W. Nee, *Love Not the World*, ch. 11.

4. Titus 3:8, 14.

5. Acts 18:3; 20:34; 1 Corinthians 4:12; 1 Thessalonians 2:9; 2 Thessalonians 3:8. Compare W. Nee, *Concerning Our Missions*, p. 200.

6. Stephen C.T. Chan, *My Uncle, Ni Tuo-Sheng*, 1968, ch. 24.

7. These talks on Revelation 2 and 3 were published in Chongqing in 1945. See W. Nee, *The Orthodoxy of the Church*, Los Angeles, 1970. Nee

builds on a theory of progressive recovery of Christian truth in our age. Other authors have pursued this line of thought and by placing their own choices of revelation last in the line have sought to give authority to as many different doctrinal emphases.

8. The Wade-Giles spelling for Stephen C.T. Chan's name has been retained in the text, being the name that he currently uses. However, the Mandarin spelling has been used for his mother, Mrs Chen, Watchman Nee's eldest sister.

9. Stephen C.T. Chan, *op. cit.*, ch. 24.

10. *Jia*, 'family', perhaps initially with the concept of a household church as in Romans 16:5, but soon developing, with growing numbers, into congregations requiring large meeting halls (as later in Taiwan) yet still under a single church eldership.

11. Hebrews 13:17.

12. *Pai*, a military term for a row or squad.

13. 1 Corinthians 14:34f; 1 Timothy 2:12. In some city churches women were in fact enlisted to preach and give a lead spiritually.

14. Published in the West as W. Nee, *Basic Lessons on Practical Christian Living*, 6 vols., New York, from 1972. The titles are: *1. A Living Sacrifice*; *2. The Good Confession*; *3. Assembling Together*; *4. Not I, but Christ*; *5. Do All to the Glory of God*; *6. Love One Another*.

15. Regrettably in the light of later events, this system would play into the hands of totalitarian state police.

16. By way of explanation, one brother from the Nanyang Road meeting (who, incidentally, ended up in a prison farm for 23 years) stated that a lesson was learned from this time which was beneficial in the political environment that followed, namely that smaller meetings where everyone is known to one another are a safer arrangement.

17. 'Report of a Fellowship Gathering' by Witness Lee in the first issue of a new magazine, *The Ministry*, ed. W. Nee, June 1948. In later years, when Watchman Nee was in prison, Witness Lee took responsibility in Taiwan and then in Los Angeles. He seemed then to go to extremes in some areas and become more exclusive. This caused problems and, sadly, a major division, particularly in the overseas assemblies, which continues to this day. Lee passed away in Los Angeles in 1997.

Chapter 18

Background reading: F. Schurmann and O. Schell, *China Readings 3; Communist China*, London, 1967; C.P. Fitzgerald, *The Birth of Communist China*, London, Pelican, 1964, a quite excellent account.

1. John 12:24. W. Nee, *The Release of the Spirit*, Mt Vernon MO, 1965.
2. Acts 8:1; 11:19f.
3. Report in *Believers' News*, ed. C.H. Yu, Shanghai, October 1944.
4. This view he elaborated in subsequent instructions, e.g. in an address to workers at Guling in August 1948. See W. Nee, *Further Talks on the Church Life*, Los Angeles, 1969, ch. 6.
5. Witness Lee, 'The Merciful Leading of the Lord', in the first issue of *The Ministry*, ed. W. Nee, Shanghai, May 1948.
6. See W. Nee, *Concerning Our Missions*, p. 104.
7. See Stephen C.T. Chan, *op. cit.*, pp. 51ff.
8. Mark 12:17.
9. All but the last of these are in English translation: *The Normal Christian Worker*, Hong Kong, 1965; *The Ministry of God's Word*, New York, 1971; *Spiritual Authority*, New York, 1972; an appended chapter in *The Spiritual Man*, New York, 1968, vol. 3, pp. 179ff; the *Basic Lessons* series, 6 vols, New York, 1972–4; and chapters 5 and 6 of *Further Talks on the Church Life*, Los Angeles, 1966.

Chapter 19

Background reading: Leslie T. Lyall, *Come Wind, Come Weather*, London, 1961; Edward Hunter, *The Story of Mary Liu*, London, 1956; George N. Patterson, *Christianity in Communist China*, Waco, Texas, 1969; W.C. Merwin and F.P. Jones, *Documents of the Three Self Movement*, New York, 1963; Katherine Hockin, *Servants of God in People's China*, New York, 1962.

1. Allen J. Swanson, *Taiwan: Mainland versus Independent Church Growth. A Study in Contrasts*, Pasadena, 1970, p. 62.
2. With the Shanghai local church's move to new premises on Nanyang Road, a Chinese Christian in another group had circulated a booklet, *Seven Open Letters to Watchman Nee*, attacking him for his 'spiritual arrogance', which compared unfavourably with his self-effacing preaching.
3. Acts 8:1.
4. Psalm 29:10.
5. Ephesians 5:16.

6. The Jesus Family, founded at Ma-Zhuang in 1921 by Jin Dian-ying, applied the communal principles of early Christian practice in Acts 2 and 3 to the Chinese family system, quietly doing on a small scale what the Communists alleged was their own objective. Though erratic in some doctrines and practice, the movement was Bible-loving and warmly evangelical. See D. Vaughan Rees, *The Jesus Family in Communist China*, 1954. The CCP would, however, soon target them for disruption.

7. Writing of this development in *China's Millions*, London, January 1951, L.T. Lyall observed, 'Instead of the lonely pioneer who, by painfully slow and sometimes discouraging processes, sought to establish a witness for Christ among the heathen, a zealous Christian community and a live active church are transplanted into the same heathen area. No imagination is needed to see the possibility of such migrations if they can be undertaken on a wider scale and to even needier unevangelised fields of China.'

8. Hebrews 10:25.

9. Mary Weller, in *China's Millions*, November 1952, p. 103. With this compare the observation of a reviewer two years later: 'It is interesting to note the emergence of the Little Flock, or Christian Meeting House as they prefer to be called, as a major Christian denomination in China.' Francis P. Jones, *China Bulletin*, iii, 7 December 1953.

10. Ostensibly they were offered for discussion and subsequent review, but it was soon found that they had already been accepted as final by the Premier. His kindly official reception of the delegates had veiled other motives and sinister designs.

11. Unlike J.R. Mott who, a generation earlier, had earned Chinese student admiration by declining the same post.

12. Because the idea of doctrinal reform proved offensive to many, the term 'Patriotic' was substituted in the title. Support of the new regime was thus equated with patriotism.

13. Mark 6:35–44; John 6:1–14.

14. Malachi 3:10.

Chapter 20

1. An excellent Canadian account of the ten years in Shanghai from 1949 to 1959 is given by Helen Willis of the Christian Book Room in her *Through Encouragement of the Scriptures*, Hong Kong, 1961.

2. W.C. Merwin and F.P. Jones, *Documents of the Three Self Movement*, New York, 1963, pp. 89ff.

3. *Ibid.*, pp. 22ff.

4. The raid took place at midnight on Friday evening, 27 April 1951, but was not generally known until the next day. The day of the arrests is always cited as 27 April even though they occurred in the early hours of the 28th.

5. *The Story of the Year 1951*, China Inland Mission, London.

6. New China News Agency, 15 May 1951, quoted in Merwin and Jones, *op. cit.*, pp. 49ff.

7. Edward Hunter, *op. cit.*, pp. 190ff.

8. Wing-tsit Chan, *Religious Trends in Modern China*, New York, 1953, p. 262.

9. Many have detected a Christian origin in the very Puritan tone of this phrase, as well as in some of the techniques used. See e.g. C.P. Fitzgerald, *op. cit.*, p. 134. Need one add that ethics is not the whole of Christianity?

10. 2 Corinthians 4:7.

11. Philippians 3:7.

12. *Liberation Daily*, Shanghai, 1 February 1956.

13. *Kang Shang Er-Pao* ('Hong Kong Daily'), 18 February 1956.

14. Robert Ford, *Captured in Tibet*, London, 1957, chs 16ff; Geoffrey T. Bull, *When Iron Gates Yield*, London, 1955, ch. 17; Robert Jay Lifton, *Thought Reform and the Psychology of Totalism*, 1961; Edward Hunter, *Brain-Washing in Red China*, New York, 1951; Suzanne Labin, *The Anthill*, London, 1960.

15. Merwin and Jones, *op. cit.*, pp. 60ff, 89ff.

16. Some 'Little Flock' representatives were present as observers at the National Christian Conference of the Three Self Movement in May 1954, one of them participating on the twelve-member Standing Committee.

17. *Tian Feng*, Shanghai, 1956, nos 4, 7 and 8.

18. A number of editions are extant, produced under Ruth Lee's supervision, with the Shanghai imprint dated as late as 1953 and 1954.

19. See also Mary Wang, *The Chinese Church That Will Not Die*, London, 1971, p. 17.

20. *China Bulletin*, vols 12 and 17–20; Leslie T. Lyall, *Come Wind, Come Weather*, London, 1961, pp. 49ff; *Three of China's Mighty Men*, London, 1973, pp. 97ff; Merwin and Jones, *op. cit.*, pp. 99ff.

Chapter 21

The events and accusations summarised in this chapter were reported in Shanghai in *Liberation Daily*, February 1956; in *Tien Feng*, Shanghai, the official periodical of the Chinese Three Self Patriotic Movement, nos 3–8, 1956; and in *Hsueh Hsi Tung Hsun* ('Studies Reporter'), February 1956, a Shanghai news-sheet of the same movement. Extract translations have appeared in F.P. Jones, *The China Bulletin* of the Far Eastern Joint Office of the Division of Foreign Missions, National Christian Council, New York, vol. 6, 1956, and in Clayton H. Chu, *Religion in Communist China*, US Joint Publications Research Service, New York, 1958, pp. 30ff. I am also indebted to Thomas I. Lee, *China News Release*, no. 11, Minneapolis, 17 July 1956.

1. Others arrested in Shanghai at this time included Lan Ji-yi (co-worker), Zhu Chen (elder) and Du Zhong-chen (elder).

2. Note that this was an inquisition, not in the primary sense of judicial or official inquiry, but in the sense of ecclesiastical tribunal. In those instances where documentation can be checked, the gross misconstruction or exaggeration of the facts suggests that 'evidence' was multiplied by the mindless repetition of question and answer.

3. 1 Timothy 4:1.

4. Dr H.H. Cui's address to the National Conference of the Chinese Church, Beijing, March 1956. W.C. Merwin and F.P. Jones, *Documents of the Three Self Movement*, New York, 1963, p. 141.

5. See W. Nee, *Love Not the World*, London, 1968, the substance of which dates from about 1941.

6. 1 Corinthians 13:13.

7. Merwin and Jones, *op. cit.*, pp. 122f.

8. *Ibid.*, p. 141.

9. *Ibid.*, p. 134.

10. *Ecumenical Press Service*, Geneva, 22 November 1957.

11. *The Millions*, London, July 1958.

12. Fifteen years was the period officially announced and widely

accepted at the time. For some reason, however, in 1963 Merwin and Jones, *op. cit.*, p. xii, gave 'twenty years' as the sentence, and in fact this was the time Nee ultimately served.

Chapter 22

A useful general survey of this period is supplied by Leslie T. Lyall, *Red Sky at Night*, London, 1969. For information on the conditions in the Shanghai First Municipal Prison I am indebted to Leslie Haylen's description in *Chinese Journey*, Sydney, 1959, pp. 73ff., and to the experiences of two Jehovah's Witnesses confined there, Harold G. King, *The Watchtower*, 15 July 1963, pp. 437ff., and Stanley E. Jones, taped report.

1. Mary Wang, *The Chinese Church That Will Not Die*, pp. 90ff.
2. 1 Corinthians 4:9.
3. Isaiah 53:7.
4. Mary Wang, *op. cit.*, pp. 88, 92.
5. Helen Willis, *op. cit.*, pp. 58ff; W.C. Merwin and F.P. Jones, *Documents of the Three Self Movement*, New York, 1963, pp. 180ff.
6. Acts 16:25.
7. A close-up view of this period is provided by two Australian residents, Colin Mackerras and Neale Hunter, in *China Observed*, 1964–67, chs. 12–14.
8. *China Reconstructs*, Beijing, April 1968, p. 2.
9. Hebrews 11:35.
10. Romans 13:1.
11. Matthew 5:11.
12. Genesis 32:24ff; 2 Corinthians 12:10.
13. Matthew 11:25ff.

Chapter 23

1. David M. Paton, *Christian Missions and the Judgement of God*, London, 1953, p. 49. See also Victor E.W. Hayward, *Ears to Hear: Lessons from the China Mission*, London, 1955.
2. Wing-tsit Chan, *Religious Trends in Modern China*, New York, 1953.
3. The Bible's possibly two letters to Roman Christians (Romans and Hebrews) lacking mention of 'the church in Rome' can be seen as a loophole in his argument.

350 AGAINST THE TIDE

4. Genesis 28:10–22; and see 2 Kings 6:13–17; Matthew 26:53.

5. Elisha Wu, Saskatchewan.

6. David Bentley-Taylor, letter to *The Life of Faith*, December 1962.

7. 2 Timothy 2:9.

8. Matthew 10:17ff.

9. F.F. Bruce, *New Testament History*, London, 1969, p. 341.

10. Ephesians 6:18–20; Philippians 1:12–13; Colossians 4:3; 2 Timothy 4:16–18.

11. Revelation 12:11.

12. Mark 13:9ff.

13. Romans 1:16.

14. 2 Corinthians 4:7–12.

15. Revelation 12:1–11. See W. Nee, *The Glorious Church*, Los Angeles, 1968, ch. 4; and see also *The Orthodoxy of the Church*, 1970, pp. 106–7.

16. Quoted by C.P. Fitzgerald, *The Birth of Communist China*, London, 1964, p. 138.

17. Matthew 16:18.

18. Fitzgerald, *op. cit.*, p. 141.

Appendix A

1. The Hebrew plural name Sinim in Isaiah 49:12 is thought by some to mean China, as those turning to Israel's God from an eastern land; but this translation is not confirmed.

2. Acts 8:26–39.

3. Acts 2:9–11, 'Judea'. Since Galilee's and Judea's own dominant state of Syria is not mentioned here among those witnessing the Pentecost event, and the speakers themselves are in Judea, it has been suggested that perhaps a scribe has miscopied a Greek letter, and this name in their otherwise more remotely foreign list could originally have been 'India'. With R. Bentley, quoted by F.F. Bruce, *The Acts of the Apostles*, 1951.

4. John 20:24–29.

5. Matthew 28:19.

6. By AD 318 one extreme view had already needed correcting, namely that of Arius of Alexandria, who taught that Jesus was of a single nature, a mere divine soul in a human body, so not convincingly one of us.

7. See Hebrews 4:14–16.

8. The true dual nature of Jesus is clearly stated in the fifth-century Athanasian creed.

9. See Edward Gibbon, *The Decline and Fall of the Roman Empire*, 1788, vol. II, p. 755.

10. A.J. Broomhall, *Hudson Taylor and China's Open Century*, vol. 1, p. 43, quoting C. Carey-Ewles, *China and the Cross*, p. 24.

11. W.G. de Burgh, *The Legacy of the Ancient World*, II, 1947, pp. 477–8; S. Neill, *A History of Christian Missions*, 1964, pp. 94–6; A.J. Broomhall, *China's Open Century*, vol. 1, pp. 43–53. Also Edward Gibbon, *The Decline and Fall of the Roman Empire*, vol. II, ch. 47, pp. 748–78, has many less relevant details.

12. Seen in 1908 by Aurel Stein, who took samples back to Europe. Much of the documentary material mentioned in this paragraph is still in process of translation.

13. John 18:36.

14. D. Erasmus, *The Plaint of Peace*, 1517.

15. One current Roman Catholic Bible translation in the Chinese language omits the second of Moses' Ten Commandments and completes their number by halving the tenth.

16. D. Erasmus, 'Note to the reader' in his *Paraphrase of St Matthew*, 15:22.

17. M. Luther, *Preface to His Works* (1545). See Romans 4:1–5 (Abraham); 4:6–8 (David).

18. 1 Peter 2:4–6.

19. John 3:1–12; 1 Peter 1:3–5. Rome seems to have inferred its procedure from the mention of a whole household or family baptised at Philippi in Acts 16:30–34.

20. Matthew 28:18–20.

The Normal Christian Life (with Sit, Walk, Stand)

by Watchman Nee

Watchman Nee of Foochow, China, became famous for his liberating teaching on effective Christian living and life in the Spirit. He died in 1972 after twenty years' imprisonment for his faith. His books, based on detailed and often verbatim notes, have influenced millions of readers for many decades.

THE NORMAL CHRISTIAN LIFE
This modern spiritual classic shows
that there is only one way to live a life that is pleasing to God – and it is the work of Jesus on the cross that holds the key.

SIT, WALK, STAND
Based on the book of Ephesians, Nee shows simply and clearly that we must know how to *sit* with Christ in the heavenly places, before we can *walk* worthy of him here on earth, and *stand* before the spiritual enemy of our lives.

 **Kingsway**